The Economics of Health Equity

This book is about equity in health and health care. It explores why, despite being seen as an important goal, health equity has not made more progress within countries and globally, what needs to change for there to be greater success in delivering fairness. An international team of eminent expert from primarily the field of health economics describe how equity in health and health care might develop over the next decade. They examine existing and past barriers to promoting equity, citing case examples and covering issues including access to health services and inequalities between and within countries. The analyses are detailed, but the issues are approached in an accessible fashion, highlighting the factors of common international relevance. This book provides a manifesto for achieving health equity for the future. It will be essential reading for health and social policy makers nationally and internationally.

Di McIntyre is Associate Professor of Health Economics, in the Health Economics Unit at the University of Cape Town, South Africa.

Gavin Mooney is Director of the Social and Public Health Economics Research Group (SPHERe), and Professor of Health Economics at Curtin University in Perth, Australia.

D1569519

The Economics of Health Equity

Edited by

Di McIntyre

Gavin Mooney

CAMBRIDGE
UNIVERSITY PRESS

CAMBRIDGE UNIVERSITY PRESS
Cambridge, New York, Melbourne, Madrid, Cape Town, Singapore, São Paulo

Cambridge University Press
The Edinburgh Building, Cambridge CB2 8RU, UK

Published in the United States of America by Cambridge University Press, New York

www.cambridge.org
Information on this title: www.cambridge.org/9780521705066

First published 2007

Printed in the United Kingdom at the University Press, Cambridge

A catalogue record for this publication is available from the British Library

ISBN 978-0-521-70506-6 paperback

**To all those who suffer from health inequities
and all those who labour to reduce these inequities.**

Contents

Contributors

Patricia Akweongo
Navrongo Health Research Centre
Ministry of Health
PO Box 114
Navrongo, Upper East Region
Ghana

Amiya Kumar Bagchi
Director, Institute of Development Studies
Kolkata
Calcutta University Alipore Campus
1 Reformatory Street, Fifth Floor
Kolkata 700027
India

David Coburn
3161 Henderson Road
Victoria, B. C.
Canada V8P 5A3

Elaine Coburn
17 rue Nicot
59130 Lambersart
France

Lucy Gilson
Centre for Health Policy
University of the Witwatersrand
PO Box 1038
Johannesburg 2000
South Africa

Supon Limwattananon
39/75 Mooban Land and
House Parks
Soi Chollada 2
Thanon Lieng Muang
Amphoe Muang
Khon Kaen, 40000
Thailand

Maureen Mackintosh
Professor of Economics
Faculty of Social Sciences
The Open University
Walton Hall,
Milton Keynes MK7 6AA, UK

Alan Maynard
University of York
Department of Health Sciences
Area 2, First Floor
Seebohm Rowntree Building
York YO10 5DD, UK

Di McIntyre
School of Public Health and Family
Medicine
University of Cape Town
Anzio Road
Observatory 7925
Cape Town
South Africa

Gavin Mooney
Director of Social and Public Health
Economics Research Group
Curtin University
Bentley Campus
Room 436 Bldg 400
Perth WA 6845
Australia

Silvia Marta Porto
Escola Nacional de Saúde Pública, ENSP/
FIOCRUZ
Rua Leopoldo Bulhões, 1480
Rio de Janeiro, RJ – 21041-210
Brazil

Phusit Prakongsai
77/93 Krittikorn Mansion
Lad Phrao Soi 3
Lad Phrao Road
Chatuchak district
Bangkok, 10900
Thailand

Isabela Soares Santos
Agência Nacional de Saúde Suplementar, ANS
Av. General Justo, 26 – Rio de Janeiro
Brazil

Viroj Tangcharoensathien
376 Mooban Panya
Patanakan Road
Suangluang
Bangkok, 10250
Thailand

Michael Thiede
Health Economics Unit
Department of Public Health and Family
Medicine
University of Cape Town
Health Sciences Faculty
Anzio Road
Observatory 7925
Cape Town
South Africa

Claudia Travassos
Fundação Oswaldo Cruz (Oswaldo Cruz
Foundation)
Avenida Brasil 4365
Pavilhão Haity Moussatché
Room 214
Manguinhos 21045-900
Rio de Janeiro
Brazil

Maria Alicia Domínguez Ugá
Escola Nacional de Saúde Pública,
ENSP/FIOCRUZ
Rua Leopoldo Bulhões, 1480
Rio de Janeiro, RJ – 21041-210
Brazil

Biographies

Patricia Akweongo works as a Research Fellow at the Navrongo Health Research Centre/Ghana Health Service in Ghana. Her research focuses on poverty-related diseases and reproductive health. Dr Akweongo has a specific interest in health reform and health equity issues in the context of low- and middle-income countries. She has a Ph.D. in health economics from the University of Cape Town, South Africa.

Amiya Kumar Bagchi is the Director of the Institute of Development Studies, Kolkata. He has taught, researched and guided research in many institutions and universities including Presidency College, Kolkata, University of Cambridge (UK), University of Bristol (UK), Cornell University (USA), Trent University (Canada), Roskilde University (Denmark) and Maison de Sciences de l'Homme, Paris. He was formerly the Reserve Bank of India Professor of Economics and the Director of the Centre for Studies in Social Sciences, Calcutta. He has written several books, the most recent of which include: *Maladies, Preventives and Curatives: Debates in Public Health in India* (Tulika, New Delhi, 2005) and *The Perilous Passage: Mankind and the Global Ascendancy of Capital* (Lanham, Maryland, USA: Rowman and Littlefield, 2005). His research interests include finance, human development issues and other aspects of development and the prospects of democracy in a globalizing world.

David Coburn (Ph.D. Sociology) has carried out extensive research on the changing power dynamics amongst the medical profession – nursing, chiropractic, naturopathy and midwifery – in the context of transformations in the Canadian political economy. Essays on the medical profession are published in the *International Encyclopedia of the Social and Behavioural Sciences* (Elsevier, 2001) and the *Handbook of Social Studies on Health and Medicine* (G. L. Albrecht *et al.*, Sage Publications, 2000). On political economy more broadly see his essay in D. Raphael *et al.* (eds) *Staying Alive* (Canadian Scholars Press, Toronto, 2006) and *Unhealthy Times: Political Economy Perspectives on Health and Care* (Pat Armstrong, Hugh Armstrong and David Coburn (eds) Oxford University Press

2001). His current interests lie in the area of globalization, neo-liberalism and health, particularly how these relate to theories of the links between income inequality and health and amongst economies, societies and health in the context of development.

Elaine Coburn (Ph.D. Sociology) is an Assistant Professor at the American University of Paris and Associate Researcher at the Centre d'analyse et d'intervention sociologiques (CADIS) at the Ecole des Hautes Etudes en Sciences Sociales. Her research focuses on neo-liberal globalization, especially its ideological justifications, as well as global protest against it. Among more recent research interests is a concern with the ontological, epistemological and ethical questions associated with qualitative methodology.

Lucy Gilson has a background in health and development economics and works as a health policy and systems researcher, primarily in Southern and Eastern Africa. She has a particular interest in health and health care equity, and her research has focused on issues of health care financing, organization, management and policy change. Her current research interests include concern for the role of trust in health systems, and in relation to equity. She has published a range of papers and book chapters in these areas, and has also been involved in various capacity building activities. She is currently an Associate Professor in the University of Witwatersrand, South Africa and Professor of Health Policy and Systems in the London School of Hygiene and Tropical Medicine, UK.

Lucy Gilson is part funded by the Consortium for Research on Equitable Health Systems (CREHS), which receives financial support from the UK's Department for International Development. The views expressed here are, however, her own.

Supon Limwattananon (MPHM, Ph.D.), an Associate Professor from Khon Kaen University, earned his Ph.D. in Social and Administrative Pharmacy from the University of Minnesota, USA in 2000. His research areas of interest include pharmaceutical economics and health services research. He joined the International Health Policy Programme (IHPP) in 2005 to participate in two research projects in the health equity area. The EU-funded EQUITAP (Equity in Asia-Pacific) Project demonstrated the equity achievements of universal health care coverage and the World Bank/ASEM Trust Fund's Monitoring and Evaluation of Health Equity Project explored the readiness of the health information system for equity monitoring and evaluation.

Maureen Mackintosh is Professor of Economics at the Open University, UK. Her research interests are in the economics of markets for 'social' goods including health care. She is currently collaborating with Tanzanian, Indian and Finnish colleagues on research on improving access by the poor to good-quality low-cost medicines. Recent publications include: Mackintosh, M. and Koivusalo, M. (eds.) *Commercialisation of Health Care: Global and Local Dynamics and Policy Responses*

(Palgrave, 2005); and Tibandebage P and Mackintosh M. 'The market shaping of charges, trust and abuse: health care transactions in Tanzania' (*Social Science and Medicine* **61**: 2005).

Alan Maynard is Professor of Health Economics at the University of York, England. He is also Adjunct Professor in the Centre for Health Economics and Research Evaluation (CHERE), Technology University of Sydney, Australia. He was Founding Director of the Graduate Health Economics Programme at York (1977–83) and subsequently Founding Director of the Centre for Health Economics at York (1983–95). He is a Founding Editor of *Health Economics*, a journal now in its 15th year. He has worked as a consultant for national and international agencies in over 20 countries including Bolivia, China, Kyrgystan and Malawi. He has been involved in NHS management since 1983 and has been chairman of a NHS hospital, with 700 beds and an annual turnover of £170mn, since 1997. He has published extensively in journals, written and edited a dozen books and remains fascinated by health policy processes and the reluctance of decision-makers to translate evidence into practice.

Di McIntyre (Ph.D.) is an Associate Professor at the University of Cape Town, South Africa. She founded the Health Economics Unit in 1990, and was Director of this Unit for 13 years. She has served on numerous policy committees and has extensive research, technical support and capacity development experience, both within South Africa and other parts of the African region. Her particular research and technical support experience relates to health care financing (especially user fees and social health insurance); health equity issues; resource allocation (including needs-based formulae and fiscal federalism issues); public–private mix issues and pharmaceutical regulation.

Gavin Mooney is Director of the Social and Public Health Economics Research Group (SPHERe), Professor of Health Economics at Curtin University in Perth, Australia, Visiting Professor at the Centre for Health and Humanity at Aarhus University (Denmark) and Honorary Professor at the Health Economics Unit at the University of Cape Town. He was the Founding Director of the Health Economics Research Unit at the University of Aberdeen in Scotland. Gavin has well over 200 publications in health economics, including 20 books, and has lectured in nearly 30 countries. He has a strong interest in equity in health care, particularly with respect to Aboriginal health, and in the economics of the social determinants of health. In recent years he has become particularly interested in communitarianism and using this philosophy in the economics of health, especially with respect to equity.

Silvia Marta Porto (M.Sc. Public Administration, Ph.D. Public Health) is a Senior Researcher at the Brazilian National School of Public Health (Escola Nacional de Saúde Pública, ENSP/FIOCRUZ). She teaches and undertakes research in health economics, mainly related to health care financing. She has served as the President of the Brazilian Association on Health Economics since 2002.

Phusit Prakongsai (M.D. Mahidol University, Certificate in Preventive Medicine Thai Medical Council) has ten years of field experience in public health and health service management at three district hospitals in rural areas of Thailand. He was the principal investigator of several research projects on health policy, health insurance and health care finance at the International Health Policy Program, Thailand. Currently, he is doing a Ph.D. in Public Health and Policy at the London School of Hygiene and Tropical Medicine with the thesis topic of 'Equity in health care finance and benefit incidence analysis before and after universal health care coverage in Thailand'.

Isabela Soares Santos is a technician at the National Agency of Private Health Insurance (ANS/MOH) in Brazil. She is currently undertaking her doctorate in Health Economics and Public Health at the National School of Public Health/ Oswaldo Cruz Foundation (MOH/Brazil), where she obtained her master's degree (dissertation entitled 'Health insurance for employees'). She has been working on issues relating to the public–private mix in the Brazilian health system and on the analysis of the equity of Brazilian health sector financing. She teaches Administration, Planning and Health Politics on Private Insurance at Getulio Varga's Foundation's M.B.A.

Viroj Tangcharoensathien (M.D., Ph.D.) is Director of the International Health Policy Program in the Ministry of Public Health, Thailand. He received the 1991 Woodruff Medal Award for an outstanding Ph.D. thesis of the London School of Hygiene and Tropical Medicine (entitled 'Community financing: the urban health card in Chiangmai, Thailand'). Upon his return, he focused on research into health care financing, health insurance development and equity in health. He initiated and updates the National Health Accounts and National AIDS Accounts. He works closely with decision-makers in the Ministry of Public Health and other government departments, while maintaining his independence as a policy researcher, and undertakes consultancies and capacity building activities as well as technical support for countries in the region.

Michael Thiede is an Associate Professor and the Director of the Health Economics Unit at the University of Cape Town, South Africa. He is conducting research on health care inequities, pro-poor strategies in health reform and the economics of pharmaceutical markets. His teaching focus is on microeconomics for the health sector. As a health economist, Dr Thiede has been involved in research-to-policy transfer in both Germany and South Africa, where he has served as a member of different committees providing support to the national Department of Health. His work experience as a consultant for public and private sector clients includes projects in pharmaceutical pricing strategies, hospital management and issues relating to the public–private mix. He received his Ph.D. in economics from the University of Kiel, Germany.

Claudia Travassos (M.D., M.P.H., Ph.D. in Public Administration) is a Senior Researcher at the Center of Scientific and Technological Information (Centro de Informação Científica e Tecnológica, CICT/FIOCRUZ). She teaches and undertakes research in Health Care Service Research. She is currently a member of the Executive Board of the International Society of Equity on Health (ISEqH).

Maria Alicia Domínguez Ugá (M.Sc. Economics, Ph.D. in Public Health) is a Senior Researcher at the Brazilian National School of Public Health (Escola Nacional de Saúde Pública, ENSP/FIOCRUZ). She teaches and undertakes research in health economics, mainly in relation to health care financing. She was previously the President of the Brazilian Association on Health Economics. She currently leads the Department on Health Planning and Administration of ENSP/FIOCRUZ.

Acknowledgements

We are grateful to all our contributors not only for their contributions but for sticking so well to the deadlines we set and for accepting so willingly our suggestions on their drafts. What a delightful bunch to work with!

Di thanks the staff of HEU for all their support; Gavin thanks Val Reid for her assistance.

Our thanks to Betty Fulford and Dawn Preston at CUP for their help.

Finally, we are, most of all, grateful to our partners, Louise and Del, for their encouragement, patience and love.

Di McIntyre, Cape Town December 2006
Gavin Mooney, Perth December 2006

All royalties from this book will go towards scholarships to provide some financial assistance for students undertaking the Online Postgraduate Diploma in Health Economics, initially developed by Gavin Mooney at Curtin University and now being run by the Health Economics Unit at the University of Cape Town.

Section 1

Introduction

Why this book?

Gavin Mooney and Di McIntyre

Equity in health and equity in health care have been ill-served in recent years. While for many health care systems equity is stated to be an important goal, in several of these equity in policy terms has been paid little more than lip-service. While it is also the case that there has been an increasing research interest in the social determinants of health, the extent to which the recognition of the impact of these on health has led to action at a policy level has been limited. Poverty and inequality are now well recognized in the academic literature, especially in social epidemiology but in public health more generally, as contributing to population ill health. National and global policy makers, however, have been all too little concerned to address poverty and inequality and, inevitably, even less concerned to do so for reasons purely of improving health.

Health economists have contributed considerably to debates about the construct of equity in health care, be this seen in terms of health, access or use and whether horizontal or vertical equity. Beyond considerable success in the 1970s and 1980s in assisting methodologically to improving equity in health care through needs-based, RAWP-type resource allocation formulae (DHSS 1976), policy on equity in health care has been a field where health economists have made relatively little impact.

Considerations of 'need' were initially very useful in RAWP-type resource allocation formulae and indeed the scene of most policy success by economists on equity in health care. Quite why this was the area of success is not clear. Certainly in the UK, where such efforts began in the mid-1970s, the then Labour government was concerned that some of the equity ideals of the NHS had not been realized. It was further recognized that, crudely, fewer of the health problems but more of the health care facilities and, hence, resources were in the south of England, the latter largely because of the geographical inheritance of facilities by the National Health Service (NHS) when it was founded in 1947. There was also an appearance of objectivity in the formulaic approach to equity. The 'science' of numbers and the dependence on a mathematical formula seems to have been politically appealing.

The Economics of Health Equity, ed. Di McIntyre and Gavin Mooney. Published by Cambridge University Press. © Cambridge University Press 2007.

There are a number of reasons why the health economics of equity has struggled in recent years. In part it is because we have had an obsession with the measurable. Too great a concern with quantification has resulted in a gap emerging between health economists' conceptual thinking and their empirical work. As Sen (1992 p. 49) has argued in the context of equity: '"Waiting for toto" may not be a cunning strategy in a practical exercise.'

The unfortunate result of the concern with the measurable is that while most health care systems that do have a stated equity objective (and this in turn means most health care systems) define it in terms of access, what health economists have been measuring is use. This focus on use (which is measurable) has then distracted the subdiscipline from seeking to grapple, other than in principle, with access.

Sadly then, measuring has got in the way of defining equity. The prime candidates for the construct of equity in health care have been equal health; equal access for equal need; and equal use for equal need. There has been more or less agreement that the difference between the last two is that equal access means equal opportunity to use as opposed to actual use being equal. Most formulations of the 'for equal need' component have been in terms of seeking to ensure that access or use is the same for groups of people with equal health problems. More recently, prompted by the work of Culyer (1991), there have been efforts to consider need in terms of capacity to benefit. This notion highlights that for a need to exist, health care must be effective; ineffective care cannot be 'needed' as there is no capacity to benefit from such care. It also suggests that need should not simply be equated with ill health, as is too often the case; there is capacity to benefit from preventive interventions.

The distinction between horizontal and vertical equity is potentially important. Horizontal equity is about the equal treatment of equals; vertical equity about the unequal but equitable treatment of unequals. Equal access (and equal use) for equal need in itself is about horizontal equity. It is patently unfair that people with the same problems be treated differently. That is what has driven most polices on equity in health care at least on the delivery side. At the same time, treating people who are unequal equally is also unfair but more, as it were, complicatedly unfair!

For horizontal equity it is relatively easy to argue who is equal or the terms of such equality, e.g., people who have equally great health needs, essentially people who are equally sick. What is more problematic is that when we move to considerations of vertical equity, there is then a need to determine first how great any inequalities are, e.g., in health need, and then to decide how great any differences in policy response should be to these inequalities in need. Such judgments are clearly subjective and, as such, much more difficult to fit into some seemingly (even if falsely) objective, scientific, RAWP-style formula. Nevertheless, health economists should be tackling issues of vertical equity more directly than they currently do, given the massive disparities in health and socio-economic status that exist in many countries and between countries.

As editors, we have been tempted to set out a definition of health equity in this introduction. We have however chosen not to. First, we subscribe to the view that however equity is defined it will not be the same in all countries, cultures or societies. There is unlikely to be a universally valid definition. Second, if pressed, while we might be tempted to argue for a definition that is along the lines of equal access for equal need, that opens up three cans of worms. What is access? What is need? And what about vertical equity, which risks being excluded by an 'equal access to equal need' type of definition? The book does discuss some potentially helpful ideas for defining equity but that is as far as we believe it is justified to go.

It remains the case that we are simply not seeing the breakthroughs in improved equity in the delivery of health care that were hoped for in the halcyon days of concerns for equity in health care in the immediate post second world war years. The prime example here is the British National Health Service introduced in 1947 and seen, accurately, by its founder Nye Bevan as being primarily about equity (Foot 1973).

Health economists have been active on the financing side in examining how different funding arrangements affect different income groups. In particular, they have analyzed tax-based systems, mandatory and voluntary insurance premiums and out-of-pocket payments to see how progressive or regressive each of these is. Important work has also been done by health economists at a comparative level internationally. The extent to which governments have picked up on this work in efforts to promote greater progressivity in financing has been limited. Sadly, this is especially so in the developing world.

There have been many advances in research in the social determinants of health, particularly relevant here being the work of social epidemiologists such as Wilkinson and Marmot (2003). They have provided good evidence that poverty and inequality can adversely affect health. Even they, however, have done too little to try to explain why poverty and inequality continue to exist to the extent that they do and indeed in some countries and across the globe, according to some indicators, are seen to have increased. Health economists have been largely absent from these endeavours. Of the little economic work here that has been undertaken, Navarro (2002), Coburn (2000) and Deaton (2003) have led the way; the first is not a regular member of the health economists' community, the second is a sociologist (but a contributor to this book) and the third is a mainstream economist.

Globally, attempts to reduce poverty and inequality and, in turn, improve health equity have not engaged the world community as one might have wanted. At a nation state level many governments have sought actively to control public spending and relied more and more on the market to provide all sorts of services that were previously in the public domain and seen even as public and social institutions. Private sector involvement in the provision of health care has increased; the ethos of the market in health service thinking has increased yet more. The commodification of health care is much more prevalent today than it was 20 or even 10 years ago.

It is also the case that, politically, making the case for vertical equity, in essence a form of positive discrimination, is difficult. It involves more explicitly, and to a greater extent, a redistribution of resources from the well to the sick and almost certainly from the rich to the poor. Few governments in recent years, especially with the spread of neo-liberalism and its endorsement of small government, have been willing to use the tax system to bring about such redistribution. Private sector growth has exacerbated the problems.

Equity in health as opposed to in health care is much less debated and much less researched by health economists. It is not immediately clear just why. In general, it seems that so much of health economics has been in effect health *care* economics. This is odd, since within health care economics the emphasis has been very much on health. This is especially true with respect to economic evaluation, where cost utility analysis (CUA) with its concerns restricted to health has dominated and cost benefit analysis, which at least has the capacity to include wider dimensions of benefit, has very much taken a back seat. Yet that emphasis on health has not translated into much of a concern among health economists for the production of health at a broader social level, i.e., through the social determinants of health.

The dominance of CUA in economic evaluation may be a partial explanation for some of the neglect of the social determinants of health since, strictly, CUA is only applicable in the context of resource use that has health as the only output. Cost benefit analysis, which is what is needed for economic evaluation in the social determinants of health, is harder to apply, much more data intensive and methodologically more complex.

A yet simpler explanation may be that there has been less funding available for economic analyses to be conducted on the social determinants of health. Funding for health economics research has tended to follow funding for medical research, so that pharmaceuticals, clinical trials more generally and health services research, especially on funding issues, have been seen as the more fertile and in fact have been the more fundable areas of health economics research.

There is need for care here. It is not that the wider social, non–health care issues around health equity have been totally neglected by health economists. But the balance has been much more at the microscopic end of the scale than the macroscopic.

Switching to a yet wider or higher level, there has been little consideration by health economists of equity in health globally. The North-South divide in terms of income is stark. It is as well in terms of health. How the policies of the World Bank, the International Monetary Fund (IMF) and the World Trade Organization (WTO) affect global equity in health have been little examined by health economists. Certainly WHO's Commission on Macroeconomics and Health had health economist representation but in general health economists have been missing from the global scene. For example we have been unable to find any health economics assessment of the likely impact of the Doha agreement (Hertel and Winters 2006) which, as it is firmly aimed at poverty reduction, if successful, will, in turn, have an effect on the distribution of ill health and hence equity in health globally.

More specifically, with the exception of the likes of Vicente Navarro (2002), there is little by way of a health economics critique or even assessment of neo-liberalism, the hegemony of neo-liberalism and their impact on health and its distribution. This almost certainly relates in turn to the lack of health economists' research on the social determinants of health. This is because neo-liberalism, together with the individualistic market thinking it breeds and the small government posturing it promotes, is not conducive to building the social capital and social cohesiveness treasured by advocates of the social determinants of health.

It is not just that health economics has largely failed to make an impact on equity; health and economic policies have largely failed to make an impact on equity in general at a macroscopic level. More recently, there has been less concern with social justice not just in health but in western societies more generally with, for example, public expenditure as a proportion of national income in general falling and taxation in many countries losing some of its progressive edge.

On equity there have, however, been some successes in a range of areas in the world such as Cuba, the state of Kerala in India, Sri Lanka and Costa Rica. It can be argued, too, that Scandinavia has long been a region where equity in both income and health has been a major part of public policy – and with some considerable success. We need more health economics analyses to tell policy makers what they can learn from these countries and regions.

The contributions to this volume critically consider some of the health and health system equity challenges facing us. After this introductory chapter, David and Elaine Coburn lead off in a theme on equity in general, providing an overview of health inequity issues from a global perspective. This is followed by a chapter from Amiya Bagchi, which takes both an historical and global look at equity in health and health care in the context of social, economic and cultural issues. Then Gavin Mooney reflects on the importance of focusing on community and culture, particularly indigenous culture, in pursuing both health and health system equity. The section ends with a chapter by Alan Maynard, who compares and contrasts libertarian and egalitarian approaches and what they mean for health systems, particularly drawing on the experience of the British National Health Service.

Chapters 6 and 7 examine the conceptualization and application of health service access. Michael Thiede, Patricia Akweongo and Di McIntyre explore the different dimensions of access and illustrate how each dimension can be evaluated using data from Ghana. Lucy Gilson explores in some detail, through the lens of trust, one specific dimension of access, namely cultural access (or acceptability). This is the dimension of access that too often receives least attention yet it is critical to address if we are to promote health system equity.

The next section focuses more directly on equity and health systems. Maureen Mackintosh examines the delivery side and picks up on the particularly important element of health care delivery of the availability of human resources and the need for their redistribution at a global level. Di McIntyre focuses more on the financing side and considers the role of alternative health care financing approaches in addressing health system inequities, particularly in the context of the substantial private health sectors that exist in many African countries. By pursuing financing mechanisms that strongly promote health system cross-subsidies in this public-private mix context, income redistribution can be promoted simultaneously.

Chapters 10 and 11 discuss equity at an individual country level, examining Brazil and Thailand. Silvia Marta Porto, Claudia Travassos, Maria Alicia Domínguez Ugá and Isabela Soares Santos analyze how equity in Brazilian health care has improved, explaining why but also how it can be improved yet more. Viroj Tangcharoensathien, Supon Limwattananon and Phusit Prakongsai consider both the delivery and financing sides of health systems through reviewing progress towards equity in Thailand. These two chapters also serve as a useful end point for the country, regional and global perspective chapters by providing insights into how to monitor progress towards equity.

All of the authors offer positive suggestions as to how health equity might see a more positive future. There is hope.

The final chapter, by Di McIntyre and Gavin Mooney, provides not so much a conclusion to the book but rather a reflection on where we might be going on equity in health and health care, and the contributions that are needed from health economists to further this.

REFERENCES

Coburn, D. (2000) Income inequality, social cohesion and the health status of populations: the role of neoliberalism. *Social Science & Medicine.* **51**: 135–146.

Culyer, A. J. (1991) *Equity in health care policy.* Paper prepared for the Ontario Premier's Council on Health, Well-Being and Social Justice. Toronto: University of Toronto.

Deaton, A. (2003) Health inequality and economic development. *Journal of Economic Literature.* **41**(1): 113–158.

Department of Health and Social Security (1976). *Sharing Resources for Health in England. Report of the Resource Allocation Working Party*. London: HMSO.

Foot, M. (1973) *Aneurin Bevan*. London: MacGibbon and Kee.

Hertel, T. W. and Winters, L. A. (2006) *Poverty and the WTO: Impacts of the Doha Development Agenda*. New York: Palgrave Macmillan and the World Bank.

Navarro, V. (2002) (ed.) *The Political Economy of Social Inequalities*. New York: Baywood.

Sen A. (1992) *Inequality Re-examined*. Oxford: Clarendon Press.

Wilkinson, R. and Marmot, M. (2003) *Social Determinants of Health: The Solid Facts*. Copenhagen: WHO Regional Office for Europe.

Section 2

Equity in general

2

Health and health inequalities in a neo-liberal global world

David Coburn and Elaine S. Coburn

Summary

Health inequalities are central to current health policy internationally and in many nations. As health improvements have slowed, the extent and depth of health inequalities in the developed world have become too obvious to ignore. At the same time the profound differences in health between the developed and under-developed world, between obesity for some and starvation for others, has created a moral crisis. Yet, the often proclaimed solution to human problems, neo-liberal free trade producing economic growth and improved human wellbeing, i.e., market fundamentalism, has proven a failure. The dogmatic application of neo-liberal doctrines perversely increases those social inequalities that are among the basic causes of health inequities. The issue then becomes one of creating conditions that would permit more variegated approaches to improving human wellbeing and reducing inequalities. Ironically, the dynamics of globalization, broadly defined as a view of human beings sharing the same planet and the same fate, has produced opposition to the untrammelled dominance of multinational corporations and the states they influence or control. If we know something about who and what the enemy is, we do not as yet know solutions other than doing something differently and more humanely. There are examples of countries and areas that do better than others at translating economic growth into improvements in human welfare. We can learn from them. Yet the onus remains on us to do whatever is within our capabilities to develop a more just and equal world.

Introduction

The rich live longer, healthier lives than do the poor. In US metropolitan areas, the health differences between high and low socio-economic status areas equal '[t]he combined loss of life from lung cancer, diabetes, motor vehicle crashes, HIV infections, suicide and homicide' (Lynch *et al.* 1998). In the USA, people in the

The Economics of Health Equity, ed. Di McIntyre and Gavin Mooney. Published by Cambridge University Press. © Cambridge University Press 2007.

very poorest households are four to five times more likely to die in the next ten years than are those in the richest (Kaplan 2000). The differences in longevity between the highest socio-economic status group and the lowest (of five groups) in Britain in 1996 were 9.5 years for men and 6.4 years for women.

Amongst nations there are wide inequalities in health status with the richest and healthiest nations showing almost double the life expectancy of the very poorest. Some nations have mortality rates for children under five that are 30 times higher than that of other nations. Yet it is *not* true that richer countries always show better average health than do poor countries.

The contrast of inequalities within and between countries, and the explanations for these, are a major concern of this chapter.

Health disparities within and between nations are referred to as health *inequalities* and, by many, as health inequities. Generally, health inequities are those differences or inequalities that are considered unjust or that reflect or are the consequences of an underprivileged position.

To understand health inequalities within and between nations best, we need to take a step back from the proximate determinants of health to examine the social structures within which inequalities of all kinds, and not just health inequalities, are produced. Doing so indicates that the class structure of capitalism and in particular a specific version of capitalism, neo-liberalism, produces and exacerbates social and health inequalities within and between nations. But there have been different historical *phases* of capitalism (Ross and Trachte 1990) as well as different contemporaneously existing *types*. Health inequalities, and the broader social and income inequalities with which they are associated, are embedded in different societal forms. Because health cannot be divorced from other aspects of social life, health inequalities are inextricably involved with conflicts over national and international political, social and economic policies and such contentious issues as globalization, economic growth and discussions about 'the good society'.

The modern interest in health inequalities dates from Engels, in 1845 (Engels 1987) but, more recently, from the Black report (1980) and the Acheson report (1998). These reports are part of a continuing British interest in the relationships between socio-economic status (SES) and health (for example, Shaw *et al.* 1999). Health inequalities are now at the centre of attention of regional (EU) and international organizations. During the UK Presidency of the EU, for example, a number of reports on health inequalities were commissioned (*Health Inequalities: Europe in Profile*, Mackenbach 2005; *Health Inequalities: A Challenge for Europe*, Judge *et al.* 2005). In 2005, the WHO established a special Commission on Social Determinants of Health, headed by Sir Michael Marmot. In the same year, the EU founded an Expert Group on Social Determinants and Health Inequalities.

Why this burgeoning interest?

A major impetus to the increasing concern with inequalities arose because of better documentation of major inequalities in health between socio-economic groups. Even more troubling, the data indicated that, though average levels of health were generally increasing, health inequalities between groups have been getting bigger, not smaller. Health inequalities are not 'going away' but are getting worse. Inequalities are also more noticeable now when improvements in longevity or infant mortality are slowing down than when they were rapidly improving. Even within the less developed nations health inequalities are ubiquitous and the poor in these nations are thus doubly at risk, by nation, and by socio-economic status.

Health inequalities; national and international

Any assessment of inequalities depends on what we compare. Do we contrast absolute or relative inequalities? Some nations, groups or areas within nations may show twice the relative infant mortality (IM) of other nations (or socio-economic groups or areas), but the meaning of such inequalities differs depending on the absolute levels of infant mortality involved. An infant mortality rate of 6 deaths per 1000 live births is twice that of 3 deaths/1000 but a rate of 80/1000 is twice that of 40 per thousand. Assuming an ethical stance that one life at birth is worth the same as another, it would seem that the inequalities revealed above, similar to many differences within high and low health nations, imply that world inter-nation differences and the inequalities within the less developed nations are currently the most significant. The great attention paid to inequalities within the developed world is laudable and necessary. We have to act where we can. However, in doing so we must not lose sight of massive global health inequalities and millions of potentially relatively easily preventable deaths in the less-developed world.

The analysis of health inequalities, and the determinants of these, are fraught with explanatory and measurement issues. Many social factors have a lifelong and cumulative influence rather than immediate effects resulting in issues of time lag effects. Some measures, infant mortality, for example, *are* more highly related to current conditions than, for example, factors associated with cardiovascular disease. And what seems to be important is what can be measured. Mortality statistics are relatively widespread and routinely collected. The same cannot be said for data on morbidity or illnesses which do not necessarily lead to immediate death (HIV/AIDS is an exception). Few analyses even touch on the topic of mental illness. Yet it is estimated that 480 million people suffer some form of mental or behavioural problem and there are nearly 900 000 suicides per year. Nevertheless, it is in this situation, with all of these deficiencies, in which decisions have to be made.

At one time it was thought that health inequalities were simply the consequence of unequal access to health care. The assumption was that health would improve and health inequalities would disappear with the advent of universal access to care. Now we know differently. In 1990, Evans and Stoddart equated the provision of medical care with turning up the furnace (or air conditioning) in a house without regard to the adequacy of the insulation. Medical care today is regarded as important in the amelioration of disease and injury, and in easing the burden of disease. However, the onset of disease and injury are now viewed mainly as being due to social causes. Thus, the emphasis is on 'the social determinants of health' and on the social determinants of health inequalities. Nevertheless, health care is one of the determinants of health inequalities although it can be claimed that equitable health care systems are themselves the product of some of the same social and class struggles which are associated with lessening social and health inequalities (Korpi 1989; Korpi and Palme 1998). As social products, both health inequalities and unequal access to health care are subject to amelioration by social action and social policies.

The fact that, within nations, the rich live longer and healthier lives than do the poor is not simply due to the fact that unhealthy people, families, or groups 'drift down' from higher to lower socio-economic positions. Most of the evidence indicates that the declining social position of those in poor health does not explain health inequalities or inequities. Moreover, there may be great inter-nation variation in the degree to which ill health actually does produce lowered socio-economic status. Lowered SES may be more closely tied to poorer health in more marketized nations lacking social welfare buffers to such crises as illness.

On the national level, poor average levels of health negatively influence national wealth – the international equivalent of the 'drift down' hypothesis. Much attention is now being directed to the potentially positive economic effects of human capital, particularly better health and education, and reduced levels of poverty, on economic growth. Whereas earlier it had simply been assumed that improved economies would lead to increased human wellbeing, now at least some attention is being paid to the opposite causal pathway, that of health and other human assets on economic growth. We are by now all familiar, via the Russian example, with the opposite situation, that of the effect of economic downturn and social upheaval on life expectancy. Since 1989, for example, the life expectancy of Russian men has declined 13 years, to approximately 60 years, about the same as India (United Nations Human Development Report 2005).

Ranking individuals according to their health status would produce a national (or worldwide) distribution of health. Much of this health ranking would not be considered as inequitable because some part of individual health differences might be viewed as arising from genetic or related characteristics about which we currently cannot do very much, since they are the 'luck of the draw'. Yet, there would also be differences by sex, by race or ethnicity, or by socio-economic status reflective of socially patterned health inequalities. Within nations we know that blacks in the United States and native peoples in Canada, Australia and elsewhere in white settler nations, live much shorter lives, by as much as 20 years, than do the white population (Marmot 2005 p. 1100).

Combining various social characteristics, such as race, ethnicity, income, or area, can produce much larger differences in life expectancy or infant mortality than any one of these alone. Much of the literature on health inequalities, however, focuses on socio-economic differences in health. Though some social differences may have additive health effects, many types of group health disparities are a result of social exclusion or the lower socio-economic status of those with particular race, sex or ethnic characteristics – hence the centrality of socio-economic status in many studies of health inequalities. Socio-economic status seems to be a central cause because socio-economic position is related to many different forms of social exclusion or discrimination and to many different types of disease or disability (Phelan *et al.* 2004). Hundreds of studies have examined the SES–health relationship; however, with few exceptions (Muntaner and Lynch 1999; Navarro 1999), there has been an overwhelming tendency to focus on the possible mechanisms through which social factors might be tied to health rather than on the causes of inequality itself. The lack of attention to the possible determinants of social inequalities is doubly interesting given international and national political and economic trends, which one would assume to have implications for our understanding of health inequalities. These trends include the 'globalization' of the world economy as well as the rise of New Right political regimes and the 'decline of the welfare state'.

In fact, any discussion of health inequalities needs to confront the currently prevalent, almost hegemonic, doctrine regarding the relationships between social and economic factors and health. This doctrine, neo-liberalism, or in some versions, neo-conservatism (economic neo-liberalism plus social conservatism) is the dominant paradigm of the day pushed by pre-eminent nations such as the United States and Britain (the Anglo-American countries seem to be the world fountains of neo-liberalism), and by the international organizations which they heavily influence and staff, such as the World Bank, the International Monetary Fund and the World Trade Organization (Dasgupta 1998; Petras and Veltmeyer 2001). There has been recent reconsideration of the pure version of this doctrine due to obvious failures when these policies have been applied internationally. Compare, for example, the World Bank's recent focus on global poverty and on the economically positive influence of improvements in human capital when juxtaposed to its previous unilateral doctrine of 'free trade improves human well being'. Nevertheless the major argument is still made that economic growth is dependent on the dismantling of barriers to the flow of investment, goods and services, or 'economic globalization'. In turn, economic growth produces increasing wealth which may then be used to underwrite social benefits, including access to health-positive resources and to improved and more equal health care. Thus – no problem – all we have to do is to promote free trade between nations and privatization within nations. In this view, health inequalities are not considered terribly problematic since either everyone's health will eventually improve, 'a high tide will lift all boats', or it is considered that any inequalities are either temporary, or perhaps unavoidable. In its starkest form this doctrine has a chilling message – that there is a trade-off between economic development eventually benefitting all, and current inequalities: to obtain the former we are unavoidably stuck with the latter.

Though less blatantly advanced now than previously, IMF policies still coerce nations, in exchange for badly needed loans, to 'open up' their economies, reduce government supports and subsidies, favour privatization of government programmes, eliminate subsidies for basic nutrition and health care, etc. These 'structural adjustment policies' may have been renamed but the substance remains (Labonte *et al.* 2005),

We cannot understand health inequalities or health trends without analysis of the social factors that produce and accompany health differences and that determine health status (Graham 2004). How can one have greater equality in health matters in fundamentally unequal societies? In turn we cannot do something about social inequalities without consideration of the prevailing structures of power. Power structures on the national and the international level influence the prevalence of ideas, the development of policy, and the implementation or non-implementation of policy. The idea that some have more power than others implies conflict – and it is in a situation of conflict of ideas, of structures, of policy, that debates about what to do about health inequalities are taking place.

A neo-liberal 'Washington Consensus' (Finnegan 2003; Teunissen and Akkerman 2004) has generated increasing resistance. Anti-globalization social movements have made it much more difficult for neo-liberals to pursue their aims when faced with opposition by the very groups or nations that neo-liberals say are supposed to benefit from neo-liberal policies. In both the developed and less-developed world have risen non-government organizations struggling against the blindly ideological prescriptions of the true believers in market fundamentalism.

'Anti-globalization' is, however, too crude a term. Most protestors are not 'anti-globalization', simply against the imposition, through 'free trade' of corporate rights over the rights of citizens or nations. Much media discussion of globalization by default actually refers to economic globalization, and to a particular version of economic globalization, that of neo-liberalism. Yet globalization in its broader meaning defines those interactions that indicate that we are all part of a single world, ecologically, socially, politically and economically. The problem with much current usage of the concept is that influential corporations, international agencies and key national governments have collapsed the meaning of globalization onto neo-liberal economic policy. This perspective assumes that there is really only one aspect of globalization and one way to globalize – societies must adjust to markets rather than the reverse. This is a fundamental misappropriation of the concept of globalization.

Paradoxically, globalization broadly defined can produce positive orientations towards a 'world community', the fact that we are all members of 'spaceship Earth' – the antithesis of the individualistic competitive world which is at the heart of marketized political and economic prescriptions. Globalization in wider perspective can promote collective human effort to solve mutual problems.

Both global and national processes are important. International forces directly and indirectly shape national policies. However, countries react differently to international pressures depending upon the place of a nation in the international economy and division of labour, and historically developed national institutions, economies, political cultures and class structures. Moreover, nations are not necessarily autonomous actors but are partly defined by their place in the world capitalist system (Moore 2006).

Neo-liberalism: a brief critique

We contend that the neo-liberal or economic globalization orthodoxy is factually incorrect and produces perverse (health) outcomes. The central tenet of neo-liberalism, that free trade uniquely produces economic growth, is simply not true. There are, and have been, many avenues to economic growth and not just one. Moreover there are three additional issues with this paradigm, a policy firmly, almost religiously, held. The first is that the paradigm produces unidimensional thinking in which all problems benefit from the same solution. In Canada, the Fraser Institute, a corporate sponsored right-wing think tank, always knows what the solution is regardless of the problem considered: poverty, racial discrimination, improved health or education – more markets or privatization. In the development field, orthodox thinking seldom strays far from the 'free trade/free enterprise produces prosperity and improves human life' mantra. No thought or analysis is required, since the solution is always the same.

The second issue with the economic orthodoxy is that it neglects the relationships between the economic, the political, the social and health. It ignores the fact that in order to have a particular kind of economy, we also need particular kinds of political and social arrangements. Types of economy have social foundations, moreover they also have social consequences (Korpi and Palme 1998; Esping-Andersen 1999). Thus, neo-liberal economies need neo-liberal forms of societies and neo-liberal social economies cannot translate economic improvements into improvements in wellbeing, without reinforcing social and health inequalities. When it comes to human wellbeing, the political, social and ideological arrangements that underpin neo-liberalism also produce and exacerbate the social conditions which underlie health inequalities within and amongst nations. For example, economic growth reduces poverty more effectively in nations with high income equality as opposed to nations high in inequality because in the more equal countries a greater share of economic growth accrues to those lower in income than it does in the high inequality countries. Yet neo-liberalism leads to striking income inequalities.

Neo-liberal doctrines are either unconcerned with, or positively endorse, inequalities (as encouraging work motivation, participation in markets, etc.), or, at a minimum, consider it inevitable, necessary or temporary (Coburn 2000). Neo-liberals only reluctantly acceded to welfare state measures and quickly came to oppose these in an era of corporate global power. Any area subject to being taken out of the market during the welfare state era came under unrelenting pressure towards 'recommodification'. Neo-liberal political regimes focus on means testing regarding various income support measures, on reducing entitlements and on undermining the power of unions or progressive groups opposing the strict application of market mechanisms. Nevertheless, various 'types' of welfare state differentially resisted the pressures of economic globalization. As Esping-Andersen (1990; 1999) has indicated, the Social Democratic welfare states, underlain by differing class formations in which working class and progressive movements were more powerful than in other states, were more resistant to neo-liberal pressures than were the Liberal welfare states or even the Familist or Conservative welfare states.

Moreover, neo-liberals are particularly 'individualist' in attacking various forms of collective or state action – insisting that we face markets only as individuals or families – that we 'provide for ourselves'. Neo-liberal doctrines are antithetical to social cohesion or to social 'trust' (now much emphasized by the World Bank (see social capital website at www1.worldbank.org/prem/poverty/scapital/home.htm) and others (Kawachi *et al.* 1999)). The most appropriate relationship is that embodied in contracts reflecting material self-interests. Privatization in fact means the individual ownership of what were once possessions or functions of the state as representative of society, or of those things which were previously the possession of everyone (including natural products, land, fish, etc.). Privatization and the lack of non-contractual connections amongst citizens, imply a generalized increase in scepticism or distrust towards one's fellows. Furthermore, since markets are efficient and just allocators of rewards, then economic or 'social' problems are attributed to individual failings. Recipients of social welfare measures are 'welfare bums'. It is utterly perverse that much is now being made of the notion of social cohesion or social capital as one avenue through which improved health status might be produced, given the fact that neo-liberal belief systems are postulated almost entirely on an individualist anti-collectivist ethos.

The third problem with the neo-liberal paradigm is related to the second issue, that is, the tendency to confound economic development with improvements in human wellbeing. Discussions about 'standards of living' are not at all focused on human wellbeing but only on macroeconomic indicators. David Coburn lives in Canada, and frequently in Canada's history the Canadian 'standard of living' has been compared unfavourably with that of the United States, particularly by those right-wing groups wishing to emulate US economic and social policies. It is pointed out that the US GNP/capita is higher than the Canadian GNP/capita. The suggestion is, therefore, that Canada should more closely imitate US economic and social policy. Yet, in fact, the United States shows greater income inequality, higher crime and incarceration rates, longer working hours and poorer health and greater health inequalities, than does Canada or almost any other of the OECD nations for that matter. Moreover, comparing income distributions, as opposed to GNP/capita averages, most Canadians are economically better-off than most Americans. The average GNP/capita in the US is brought up by the fact that the United States shows a much higher percentage of extremely wealthy people than does Canada.

We all currently live under various versions of a capitalist mode of production. The capitalism of today, however, is different from the capitalism of Britain in the seventeenth and eighteenth centuries. The capitalism of today in the developed nations is also different from the 'welfare state' capitalism of 1945–1970. We are now in a new *phase* of capitalism, global capitalism, in which business and corporate power has been reasserted in an overwhelming manner.

There are also different *forms* of capitalism in the contemporary world. Within the developed world, that is, countries in Europe, North America and the English-speaking world generally, nations have been categorized as having different types of capitalism according to the way they organize the provision of care for their citizens, that is, their different types of welfare state regime. We show that the onset of global neo-liberalism and the existence of different welfare regime types are important factors – first, regarding social and health inequalities within nations, and second, with respect to health differences amongst the developed nations.

A note on class versus socio-economic status

As used here, class refers to a structural and relational rather than an SES approach. In fact, class is seen as determining and shaping SES and income inequalities. To oversimplify a complex literature, classes are conceived in relation to one another and in relationship to the means of production (concerning class and health, see

Muntaner and Lynch 1999; Scambler and Higgs 1999 or Navarro 1998; Navarro and Shi 2001). Thus, there are business classes (capital) and working or oppositional classes and social movements. In general, the interests of one of these are inversely related to the interests of the other. On the other hand, socio-economic status simply refers to individuals or families who score higher or lower on various characteristics without any real social relationships between these and without any necessary antagonism between those lower or higher.

Health and inequalities in a global world

Throughout the second half of the twentieth century there were general improvements in life expectancy and infant mortality. Since 1960, life expectancy has increased by about 16 years in developing countries and six in the developed nations and infant mortality has dropped dramatically – there was some convergence. Yet, since 1990 regarding life expectancy 'the convergence has ground to a halt.' (United Nations Human Development Report 2005, p. 25) In Russia and sub-Saharan Africa, life expectancy has actually declined. Similarly, there has been a slowdown in the rate of improvement in child deaths and the divergence between rich and poor nations has been increasing. Most recently, a report on food insecurity reports that 820 000 000 people in the developing world were hungry in 2001–2003, only three million less than a decade earlier, despite lofty goals to eliminate world hunger (UN Food and Agricultural Organization 2006).

The health improvements that did occur are not due to economic growth. There is little, if any, correlation between rates of economic growth and health improvements (Deaton 2003; 2004; Milanovic 2003). Even regarding economic growth, Milanovic argues that growth rates were much higher between 1960 and 1980, presumably before the full impact of global neo-liberalism, than between 1980 and 2000, during a time of economic globalization. Problems with the doctrine that neo-liberalism produces economic growth are also indicated by Navarro's (1998) findings that, in the developed world, the Social Democratic nations showed generally higher growth rates in the post World War II period than did the Liberal (neo-liberal) welfare states.

Examining social or income inequalities, while there have been reductions in the percentage of the world's population living on less than US $1 per day, inequalities do not show the same trend. The United Nations reports clear movement towards increased income inequality within countries in the past two decades. Of 73 nations with available data, 53 (with 80% of the world's population) showed increases in within-nation inequality (United Nations Human Development Report 2005 ch. 2). The result is massive inequality on a world scale. The world Gini index, a measure of equality in which 100 is complete inequality and 0 is complete equality, is 67, compared with Gini indices in the high income OECD nations of 37 and Sweden's 33. Sub-Saharan Africa, Latin America and the Caribbean and East Asia and the Pacific Areas all show Gini indices above 50. When countries are used as the unit, global income distributions have also widened. If the latter data are weighted by the populations involved, however, the data show somewhat less income inequality than in previous decades, simply because of the huge populations of India and China, both of which saw increased average income.

On the global level, the cross-sectional relationships between levels of national wealth and health (not the same as the correlation between rates of growth in income and health) show a strong but far from universal relationship for nations under about $5000 US GDP/capita (at purchasing power parity or PPP). Above that level, particularly for the 30 or so nations of the OECD, the correlation between GDP/capita and average health is weak or non-existent. This finding drove some analysts to argue that, in the developed nations, income inequality was more important for health than was the national level of income itself.

This division, of poor from wealthy nations, and the notion of the 'epidemiological transition', the change from communicable diseases (in the poor nations) as the chief causes of death to the non-communicable or chronic disease pattern in the wealthier nations, has led many analysts simply to divide the world up into rich and poor countries. Alternatively, official international agencies tend to view the world geographically – Europe, Latin America, etc. A few analysts have tried to come up with more theoretically meaningful divisions. For example, Gough *et al.* (2004) applied Esping-Andersen's (1990; 1999) division of the developed world into the three welfare state types to the less-developed world. Gough *et al.* concluded that there were three meta-types, consisting of welfare state regimes, informal security regimes and insecurity regimes. A major point of these authors was that these regional regimes differed radically on such important matters as state capacities and historically developed policy paths. Finally, 'World System' theorists believe that nations and the global system interact so that nations are shaped not only by their own pre-existing historically developed assets, institutions and class structures but also by their role in the world economy, with consequences for the health and health inequalities in these nations (Moore 2006). World System theorists see the world in terms of core, semi-periphery and periphery based on the structural position of a nation in the world system. China may have only a moderate GNP/capita but in other respects it is powerfully located in the world economy.

Because most data are collected in terms of rich/poor or global 'regions' we simply follow this convention without implying that it is the right analytical approach.

The developed nations

Why is there so much inequality within and between nations in the developed world? The most prominent, but still contentious, hypothesis focuses on income inequality (Wilkinson 1996; Kawachi *et al.* 1999; Clarke and Smith 2000). It is argued that the major determinant of the health of the developed nations (hence, of inequalities between nations) is not GNP/capita but rather the degree of income inequality itself, and its correlate or consequence, lowered social cohesion or trust (which itself contributes to poorer health). Thus, countries, regions or areas showing higher degrees of income inequality also have lowered social cohesion and lower average levels of health. This is because hierarchy (e.g., socio-economic status) is related, through biopsychosocial mechanisms, to lowered self-esteem. This would help to explain SES/GDP– health relationships both within and between nations.

Opponents of the income inequality thesis contend that the relationships found by Wilkinson are artefactual (Ellison 2002)or that income inequality does not have the causal significance that income inequality advocates contend it has (Muntaner and Lynch 1999; Deaton 2003). If the health of the poor is improved more per dollar or euro, etc., than is the health of the rich per dollar or euro, then the postulated relationship between income inequality and health may be purely a function of the shape of the curve relating income to health (Gravelle 1998). This hypothesis would also suggest a focus on the health of the poor. In fact income inequality may have an influence but it does not have the *causal* significance given to it by Wilkinson. Income inequality is really a proxy for many other forms of social inequality that all influence health (Navarro 1998; Muntaner and Lynch 1999; Coburn 2004). Income distributions are simply a measure of the degree to which an area, city or nation takes care of its citizens (Ross *et al.* 2000). Thus, we are not simply talking about national differences in income inequality but different national (welfare) 'types'.

Income equality forms an important part of welfare states because one of the aims of welfare states is to correct or ameliorate market-produced income inequalities, either by providing universally available services (not adequately measured by income) or by compensating citizens during times of individual or social crisis. Hence, income inequality may be more highly correlated with health within more market-oriented societies than within less market-oriented societies. As used here, income inequality is taken to be a proxy for a whole set of measures with which it is correlated and causally related and this would also encompass any emphasis on the relationships between poverty and health.

Finally, a third hypothesis focuses on medical knowledge. A prominent economist, Angus Deaton (2003; 2004) and others (Cutler *et al.* 2006) contend that national differences in health are simply a result of the differential rate of spread of health and medically relevant knowledge. Certainly, within nations those higher in status and education seem quicker to adopt healthy lifestyles, and have access to more health-promoting resources, than do those lower in status and education. The exact cause of this quicker adoption by those higher in socio-economic status is not known. Nor does Deaton explicate the social mechanisms through which some nations spread knowledge or practices more quickly and extensively than do others, although the importance of education, public health measures, and government actions regarding these are mentioned as important. Thus the latter again seems to overlap with the 'welfare state' model.

We illustrate the welfare state model through an examination of income inequality (a fairly readily available measure of welfare state 'results') and infant mortality (a health measure with the least 'lag' effect) amongst different types of welfare state, specifically comparing the 'liberal' and 'social democratic' types.

Neo-liberalism, income inequalities and health inequalities within nations: some examples

Prior to the 1970s, the USA and the UK showed declining inequalities. Beginning about 1968 in the USA and 1977/78 in the UK, income inequality, for example, began a steep and rapid rise (Gottschalk and Smeeding 2000). In the USA, the lowest 60% of households actually experienced a *decrease* in after-tax income between 1977 and 1999. During the same period, incomes of the top 5% of households increased by 56% and those of the top 1% mushroomed by 93% (Bernstein *et al.* 2000). Data also indicate that welfare regimes actually did what they were supposed to do: lessen poverty and inequality. In fact, despite being one of the richest nations on Earth, in 1991 the United States had one of the highest rates of *absolute* (as well as relative) poverty amongst the developed nations – of 15 countries only Italy, Ireland, Australia and the UK had higher rates – the latter three all having neo-liberal policies (Kenworthy 1999 p. 1125). And, in general, within the OECD nations the neo-liberal nations showed higher inequality than did the Social Democratic nations.

Infant mortality is an often-used measure of health, and even of social conditions, because unlike some other measures such as longevity, infant mortality rates tend to reflect current social conditions. Moreover, (comparing the Liberal with the Social Democratic nations) amongst the more-developed nations, the neo-liberal nations showed poorer average levels of infant mortality for all decades from the 1960s through to the year 2000. Moreover, the liberal welfare regime states, including the USA, the UK and Canada showed worsening relative rankings regarding infant mortality rates relative to 18 OECD nations between 1960 and 2000 than did the Social Democratic nations (Coburn 2004).

Most relevant for this analysis, different welfare regimes and rising inequalities of various kinds have important implications for health inequalities within nations, since social inequalities of many kinds are related to health status differences. Thus, despite 'expanding economies', health inequalities have increased. A recent study showed inequalities in mortality for all causes between low and high socio-economic status areas to have increased amongst adults in the USA by 50% and 58% (for males and females respectively) from 1969 to 1998 (Singh and Siahpush 2002). A commentator on Britain, a nation that experienced a prolonged period of neo-liberal politics, noted that: 'The inequalities in health between social classes are now the greatest yet recorded in British history,'(Yamey 1999; see also Dorling 1997). Another British study shows an increasing ratio 'between social classes I (high) and V (low) (which) widened from 2.1 in 1970–72 ... to 3.3 in 1991–3,' (Blane and Drever 1998).

More neo-liberal states show greater inequality, greater poverty and poorer overall health status. Yet some tentative data seem to indicate that the level of health inequalities between manual and non-manual workers at least, may be as high in Sweden, for example, as it is in England. It might be that Sweden has more vulnerable disadvantaged populations generally, because it simply keeps more people alive to productive ages (see Coburn 2004), or that some health inequalities in the developed nations reflect differences in education or information flows, as Deaton contends. Other evidence shows that during a time of severe Nordic economic crisis and recession in Finland and Sweden, inequalities in health remained largely unchanged (Lahelma *et al.* 2002). The argument was that the institutions of the welfare state buffered against widening health inequalities in that period. In any event, because Sweden has much better overall health levels than England, the absolute differences in Sweden between socio-economic classes are much smaller than they are in England.

It does seem that there can be a 'virtuous circle' in which economic growth is actually translated, through social policy, into lowered inequalities of many kinds, and (perhaps partially because of lowered inequalities), higher average levels of health.

The less-developed world

The main health problems in the world today lie in the underdeveloped nations and stark global health inequalities. In some nations, obesity is a major health issue, while in other parts of the world millions die or are stunted by starvation and hundreds of millions more have little opportunity to develop their human capacities. We are not living in a world of scarcity but in a world in which resources are radically maldistributed relative to need. This international picture directly contradicts the claim of neo-liberals that free markets can best meet human needs (Labonte *et al.* 2005; Labonte and Torgerson 2005) – in fact, within such a system on the global level the wants of the wealthy supersede the needs of the poor.

The case of health care research, and pharmaceutical research specifically, is instructive. The development of drugs and pharmaceuticals is characterized by the term 90/10. That is, 90% of the research and resources is focused on the issues affecting the 10% of world health problems in the affluent nations. Why? Because in the developed nations there is a 'market' for such products as blood pressure or cholesterol-lowering medications while there is little market for much more acute serious conditions in the less-developed world (Labonte *et al.* 2005). It is no accident that the World Health Report (2003) notes that: 'Of the 4.1 million people in sub-Saharan Africa in urgent need of antiretroviral drugs, fewer than 2% have access to them.'

The distribution of health in the world in the early twenty-first century is shocking. While the healthiest nations have overall longevity rates ranging around 80 years, the unhealthiest nations show rates of half that – around 40–45 years. Life expectancy at birth in 2002 ranged from 78 years for women in developed countries to less than 46 years for men in sub-Saharan Africa. The WHO uses a measure of longevity that indicates the equivalent number of years in full health (health adjusted life expectancy or HALE) that a newborn can expect, based on current mortality rates. Japan has the highest HALE longevity in the world at 73.6 years (with Sweden close behind). Angola showed 28.7 years. And this is comparing averages, not contrasting, for example, the poorest health levels in Angola with the highest health levels in Japan or Sweden, which would show even greater disparities (United Nations Human Development Report 2005 chs 1 and 2).

Regarding child mortality, a child in Swaziland is 30 times more likely to die before the age of 5 than a child born in Sweden; a child in Cambodia is 17 times more likely to die than a child in Canada. Some of these differences are increasing, particularly in sub-Saharan Africa. In 1980, child death rates in sub-Saharan Africa were 13 times higher than in rich countries; 25 years later they were 29 times higher (United Nations Human Development Report 2005 ch. 1).

Average national health levels also ignore inequalities within countries. Within a group of 22 low or middle income nations over a three to six year period in the late 1990s, 13 showed an (not necessarily statistically significant) increase in inequality by income for survival rates under age five, while nine showed improvement (Wagstaff 2000). Moreover, this study showed no relationship between overall national levels of improvement in health and health inequalities, suggesting that policies to reduce inequalities need to be aimed specifically at the poor (Gwatkin 2000; Moser *et al.* 2005).

There are similar inequalities in almost every nation. Within India the death rates for children under five in Kerala (a state often mentioned as a jurisdiction having much better health than its wealth would suggest) was 19, as opposed to 123 in Uttar Pradesh. Kerala also showed other positive health data, such as 80% of children receiving vaccination compared with 11% in Behar (United Nations Human Development Report 2005 p. 30). China has shown rapidly increasing economic growth in the past two decades yet a slowing of improvement in average health and rapidly increasing health inequalities. The death rate for children under five is 8 per 1000 in Shanghai and Beijing compared with 60 in Guizhou, the poorest province.

As noted, amongst nations below about US $5–6000 GNP/capita national wealth is highly correlated with national health. The important point about the correlation between GNP/capita and health status for the poorer nations, however, is that there are still wide disparities in health for nations at similar levels of GNP/capita: 'Life expectancy at birth is about a year longer in Sri Lanka than in Malaysia, even though the latter is more than twice as wealthy as the former. Similarly, life expectancy in Costa Rica is 25 years longer than in Gabon, although both are at a similar economic level.' (McKee 2001). For nations at any particular level of GNP/capita, a range of health outcomes is possible. Cuba and Mexico both have around $1000 GNP/capita but 70 more children per 1000 survive to age five in Cuba than in Mexico. Similarly the GNP per capita of Sri Lanka and Indonesia are similar but 60 more children per thousand survive to age five in the former nation than in the latter. There are sometimes startling comparisons even between the developed and the less-developed world. The US white infant mortality rate is worse than Malaysia's. The lesson is that, even for the less-developed world, high GNP/capita is neither a sufficient nor a necessary condition for a good average level of health.

And, clearly, it is nations retaining some control over their role in the world economy that seem both able to profit from processes of globalization in terms of economic growth and are better able to translate growth into improved health. One study compared the policies and outcomes of Indonesia, Thailand and Malaysia during the economic crises of the late 1990s. The former two nations followed World Bank prescriptions for adjustment including cutbacks in government spending. Malaysia, on the other hand, pursued its own independent policy. Whereas Indonesia and Thailand had negative health outcomes, the crisis had little impact on Malaysia. The author of this study (Hopkins 2006) noted the: 'importance of social safety nets and the maintenance of government expenditures in minimising the impact of economic shocks on health.'

The major issue is that the current forms of 'development' are based on a neo-liberalism that has impaired health improvements and raised inequalities rather than lessened these. The emphasis simply on economic growth as a cure-all is also misplaced. Deaton (2003) indicates that: 'the cross-country data show almost no relationship between changes in life expectancy and economic growth over 10, 20, or 40 year periods between 1960 and 2000.'

The conclusion to be drawn is that the translation of economic growth into improved health requires appropriate national institutions and public action.

In the absence of public action, simple market mechanisms tend to produce adverse rather than positive results for health and for health inequalities. There is also a relationship between inequality within nations and the degree to which growth can reduce these. High income inequality, for example, simply means that the poor profit relatively less from economic growth or improvements than the rich, exacerbating inequality. Regarding overall health levels, one crucial factor seems to be high literacy rates and especially women's education. Perhaps because traditionally women are the family caregivers, women's education seems to be the vehicle for direct improvements in health levels. Some types of economic growth, of 'development' are better than others.

What can be done?

Many prescriptions for health policy are simply utopian in that they ignore current regimes of power. Yet, action is already being taken. Viewing health inequalities as part of the product of neo-liberal economic globalization and health and health inequalities as being caused by, and covarying with other forms of inequality, connects health with much broader struggles. Ever since corporations escaped from national controls to become more or less unfettered internationally, there has been opposition to corporate power. Some of this opposition has come from differences in policies amongst states, but most has arisen from social movements in both the North and the South, in the developed and in the less-developed world. Every meeting of the World Trade Organization has been a target for civil action but has also been accompanied by meetings of citizen groups from dozens of different nations with a more progressive agenda than that put forward by official international organizations. Events like the World Social Forum seek to take the initiative away from the neo-liberals who dominate official policy-making institutions such as the annual World Economic Forum held in Davos, Switzerland. Pointedly taking place in the developing world – thus far, India or Brazil – the World Social Forum explicitly aims to challenge 'neo-liberalism and . . . domination of the world by capital and any form of imperialism' by democratically debating alternative forms of organization 'centred on the human person' (see: www.wsfindia.org). Globalization has thus shown contradictory trends, towards corporate dominance but also towards the organization of international opposition to such dominance.

A huge variety of groups with disparate specific goals have taken steps to co-operate. As Carroll and Ratner (2005) have noted, in today's global world there is one Goliath – global capital – but there are many Davids. All of these are mobilized against unfettered global capitalism. This organization is visible on many levels. Within the context of North America alone, there are many examples of the different forms this opposition may take. In the free-trade zone maquiladoras located along the US-Mexico border, workers protest against unsafe conditions on the shop floor. At other times, protest against conditions linked with neo-liberal economic policies is less ambiguous and more overtly political. This was spectacularly true with the uprising of the Zapatista Army of National Liberation on January 1, 1994, when Mexican peasants rose up in arms to protest against neo-liberal policies on the same day that the North American Free Trade Agreement was implemented. Farther north, in Ontario, Canada, public and private sector unions mobilized in eleven one-day strikes from 1995 to 1998. During these 'Days of Action' against the policies of the then-Conservative provincial government, unions and social movement participants voiced their protest against neo-liberal policies, such as the freezing of the minimum wage, the relaxation of health, safety and environmental legislation and attacks on the poor, including the stigmatization and criminalization of welfare recipients. At the national level, the Council of Canadians, the Canadian Centre for Policy Alternatives and others have created a coalition against the threatened privatization of water, linking with similar movements in Britain, Ecuador and elsewhere.

Like the World Social Forum, the European Social Forum, opposed to neo-liberalism and a world dominated by capital, meets under the slogan 'Another World is Possible'. Many of these meetings emphasize health and health inequalities. Often, such movements of opposition to neo-liberalism speak in the language of human rights. These rights are reconceptualized to challenge neo-liberal models that imagine human rights only in the context of private individuals. Instead, 'alterglobalist' NGOs insist that human beings are embedded in communities, with mutual responsibilities towards one another. The 'rights of the human person' as a social being are juxtaposed against the rights of capital.

One aspect of many of these movements has been a focus on health, on the health effects of environmental degradation and on equal access to health care. For example, the World Social Forum, held in Delhi, India in November 2006, proposed sessions on women, sustainable development and social services that explicitly addressed the links between these broader topics and the issue of health and health inequalities. (see www.wsfindia.org/isfconsultation.doc). In this way, non-government organizations emphasize the extent to which health inequalities can be understood only within a broader political economy concerned with – among other issues – wealth and poverty, the privatization of the global commons and public services, and the everyday experiences of women.

The struggle against the privatization of water is emblematic of the ways in which advocacy and mobilization around health and health inequalities are explicitly linked to broader challenges against neo-liberal economic policy. Privatization brings unequal access to a fundamental human resource. Around the world, a wide range of non-government organizations are united in their calls to maintain access to water as a publicly provided good, a basic human right, and a necessity for good health, against neo-liberal privatization schemes. This includes the American-based group 'Water for All' operating through the NGO Public Citizen, the Council of Canadians and the 'Anti-Privatisation Forum' based in Johannesburg, South Africa, which links its struggle against the privatization of water to broader struggles against neo-liberal macroeconomic policies that deny basic human needs essential for health (see www.apf.org.za/). Likewise, the Ghana National Coalition Against the Privatization of Water, which successfully mobilized in 2001 against a World Bank conditionality proposing the privatization of the urban water supply, seeks to uphold access to water as 'a human right against corporate exploitation' (see www.ghanacap.org/page.aspx). For these groups, access to safe potable water is explicitly conceptualized as part of a broader international struggle emphasizing 'need versus profit' and stressing that basic goods and services are rights rather than commodities. International mobilization around health is organically linked to broader struggles over neo-liberal economic policy and the states and international institutions, like the World Bank, that support them.

Health, including but not confined to health inequalities, has become a focus of progressive forces. Health and health equity provide potent weapons against global neo-liberalism – it is difficult to argue against health and health equity as positive goods. Involved in these battles have been quasi-professional organizations such as those involved in public health, in health and health care ethics, and those involved in the rights of the poor, including their rights to resources that would permit health improvements. Health is enmeshed with human rights, the environment, and anti-economic globalization social movements generally. It is through and by these groups, connected with political movements, or simply as movements in civil society, that health inequalities have become part of national and international agendas. Health connects with and resonates with broader struggles to tame an international capitalism reflecting the interests of the few.

Struggles over health and health inequalities are not simply matters of scientific 'fact'. Health struggles are political struggles. Scientists play a part in these on one side or another. One way in which some scientists can contribute is to document existing health and health inequality issues. Often these are hidden through the absence of relevant data. Revealing so-far obscured inequalities is a first step in leading to action to reduce them.

Action can be taken in many ways and at many levels, one form being participation in collective organizations. National political activities are obviously significant. Collections of ordinary citizens have proven crucially important in documenting what some ignore. We cannot, however, escape our own individual responsibility to take whatever actions our capabilities and environments direct us to. There is no one way to improve the human condition but many ways.

We are faced internationally with degradation of the planet and a vision of the Earth's resources as finite. Are these to be sold to the highest bidder in the market or can they be employed in a more just and equitable manner? These are the fundamental questions with which we are faced and about which we have to make our own individual commitments.

Discussion

Health inequalities are the central focus of health policy in the European Union. Internationally, the WHO and the UN both emphasize health inequalities and the links between poverty and health (as now does the World Bank). The failure of IMF doctrines has had an effect. 'Free' trade is never free and does not inevitably lead to economic growth. Economic growth is only conditionally related to improvements in wellbeing – better health and lower health inequalities. And, perversely, neo-liberalism produces increased social and income inequalities and lowered social cohesion, which are themselves related, through various avenues, to health inequalities.

On the one hand have come attempts to document how health inequalities are linked to their proximate determinants. More recently have arisen efforts to show how economic and political policies produce or ameliorate within and between nation inequities. The latter are by far the most stark. Paradoxically, corporate attempts to escape national controls have given rise to a truer version of globalization, which implies and makes overt the fact that we cannot ignore what happens in other regions, areas or nations.

One cannot have 'any' kind of economy with 'any' kind of society. Neo-liberal economies are part of neo-liberal societies, which have the detrimental effects noted. What we should be talking about practically and theoretically are different types of societies and economies and different types of economic growth rather than the unicausal and monolithic image presented by neo-liberal orthodoxy. The problem is not necessarily with the nature of developing societies, although that is indeed an issue, but with the dominant, unilingual, Anglo-American version of what is good for everyone.

Influential Americans assert 'the end of history'. Rather, globalization writ large has led us to the beginning of history. It is a beginning because, perhaps for the first time, we cannot divorce the fate of others entirely from our own. We are being forced to realize that we are not simply the subject of economic laws; we are not going to be ruled by them. We created our world. We can change it.

REFERENCES

Acheson, D. (1998) *Independent Inquiry into Inequalities and Health.* London: The Stationery Office.

Bernstein, J., Mishel, L. and Brocht, C. (2000) *Anyway You Cut It: Income Inequality on the Rise Regardless of How It's Measured.* Economic Policy Institute. briefing paper no. 99. www.epinet.org/content.cfm/briefingpapers_inequality_inequality

Black, D., Morris, J., Smith, C. and Townsend, P. (1980) *Inequalities in Health: Report of a Research Working Group.* London: Department of Health and Social Security. (the Black report).

Blane, D. and Drever F. (1998) Inequality among men in standardised years of potential life lost 1970–93. *British Medical Journal.* **317**: 255–256.

Carroll, W. K. and Ratner, R. S. (eds) (2005) *Challenges and Perils: Social Democracy in Neo-Liberal Times.* Halifax: Fernwood Publishing.

Clarke, P. and Smith, L. (2000) More or less equal? Comparing Australian income-related inequality in self-reported health with other industrialised countries. *Australian and New Zealand Journal of Public Health.* **4** (August 24): 370–372.

Coburn, D. (2000) Income inequality, social cohesion and the health status of populations: the role of neoliberalism. *Social Science and Medicine.* **51**: 135–146.

Coburn, D. (2004) Beyond the income inequality hypothesis: globalization, neo-liberalism and health inequalities. *Social Science and Medicine.* **58**(1): 41–56.

Cutler, D. M., Deaton, A. S. and Lleras-Muney, A. (2006) *The Determinants of Mortality.* National Bureau of Economic Research. NBER working paper no 11963. www.nber.org/papers/w11963

Dasgupta, B. (1998) *Structural Adjustment, Global Trade and the New Political Economy of Development.* London: Zed Book.

Deaton, A. (2003) Health, inequality and economic development. *Journal of Economic Literature.* **41**(1): 113–158.

Deaton, A. (2004) *Health in an Age of Globalization.* National Bureau of Economic Research. NBER working paper no 10669. www.nber.org/papers/w10669

Dorling, D. (1997) *Changing Mortality Ratios in Local Areas of Britain 1950s to 1990s.* York: Joseph Rowntree Foundation. www.jrf.org.uk/knowledge/findings/socialpolicy/pdf/sp126.pdf.

Ellison, G. T. H. (2002) Letting the Gini out of the bottle? Challenges facing the relative income hypothesis. *Social Science and Medicine.* **54**(4): 561–576.

Engels, F. (1987) *The Condition of the Working Class in England.* London: Penguin Classic.

Esping-Andersen, G. (1990) *The Three Worlds of Welfare Capitalism.* Princeton, NJ: Princeton University Press.

Esping-Andersen, G. (1999) *Social Foundations of Postindustrial Economies.* Oxford: Oxford University Press.

The European Health Report 2005: Public Health Action for Healthier Children and Populations.

Evans, R. G. and Stoddart, G. L. (1990) Producing health, consuming health care. *Social Science and Medicine.* **31**(12): 1347–1363.

Finnegan, W. (2003) The economics of empire: notes on the Washington consensus. *Harper's Magazine.* (May): 41–54.

Gottschalk, P. and Smeeding, T. M. (2000) Empirical evidence of income inequality in indus-
trialized countries. In Atkinson A. B. and Bourguignon F., eds, *The Handbook of Income
Distribution*, Vol. 1. Amsterdam: Elsevier. pp. 261–307.

Gough, I., Wood, G., Barrientos, A. *et al.* (2004) *Insecurity and Welfare Regimes in Asia, Africa
and Latin America*. Cambridge: Cambridge University Press.

Graham, H. (2004) Social determinants and their unequal distribution: clarifying policy understandings. *The Milbank Quarterly*. **82**(1): 101–124.

Gravelle, H. (1998) How much of the relation between population mortality and unequal
distribution of income is a statistical artefact? *British Medical Journal*. **316** (23 May):
382–385 and responses.

Gwatkin, D. R. (2000) Health inequalities and the health of the poor: what do we know? What
can we do? *Bulletin of the World Health Organization*. **78**(1): 3–18.

Hopkins, S. (2006) Economic stability and health status: evidence from East Asia before and
after the 1990s economic crisis. *Health Policy*. **75**(3): 347–357.

Judge, K., Platt, S., Costongs, C. and Jurczak, K. (2005) *Health Inequalities: A Challenge for
Europe*. Expert report commissioned by the UK Presidency of the EU.

Kaplan, G. A. (2000) Economic policy is health policy: conclusions from the study of income
inequality, socioeconomic status, and health. Paper presented at the Income Inequality,
Socio-economic Status and Health Conference, Washington, DC.

Kawachi, I., Kennedy, B. and Wilkinson, R. G., eds. (1999) *The Society and Population Health
Reader: Income Inequality and Health*. New York: The New Press.

Kenworthy, L. (1999) Do social-welfare policies reduce poverty? A cross-national assessment.
Social Forces. **77**(3): 1119–1139.

Korpi, W. (1989) Power politics and state autonomy in the development of social citizenship –
social rights during sickness in eighteen OECD countries since 1930. *American Sociological
Review*. **54**: 309–328.

Korpi, W. and Palme, J. (1998) The paradox of redistribution and strategies of equality: welfare
state institutions, inequality and poverty in the Western countries. *American Sociological
Review*. **63**(5): 661–687.

Labonte, R. and Torgerson, R. (2005) Interrogating globalization, health and development:
towards a comprehensive framework for research, policy and political action. *Critical Public
Health*. **15**(2): 157–179.

Labonte, R., Schrecker, T. and Sen Gupta, A. (2005) *Health for Some: Death, Disease and Disparity
in a Globalizing World*: Toronto: Centre for Social Justice.

Lahelma, E., Kivelä, K., Roos, E. *et al.* (2002) Analysing changes of health inequalities in the
Nordic welfare states. *Social Science and Medicine*. **55**: 609–625.

Lynch, J. W., Kaplan, G. A., Pamuk, E. R. *et al.* (1998) Income inequality and mortality in
metropolitan areas of the United States. *American Journal of Public Health*. **88**(7):
1074–1080.

Mackenbach, J. P. (2005) *Health Inequalities: Europe in Profile*. Expert report to the UK
Presidency of the EU.

Marmot, M. (2005) Social determinants of health inequalities. *Lancet*. **365** (19 March): 1099–1104.

McKee, M. (2001) The scale of inequality. *NSW Public Health Bulletin*. **12**(5): 130–133.

Milanovic, B. (2003) The two faces of globalization: against globalization as we know it. *World Development.* **31**(4): 667–683.

Moore, S. (2006) Peripherality, income inequality, and life expectancy: revisiting the income inequality hypothesis. *International Journal of Epidemiology.* **35**(3): 623–632.

Moser, K. A., Leon, D. A. and Gwatkin, D. R. (2005) How does progress towards the child mortality millenium development goal affect inequalities between the poorest and the least poor? Analysis of demographic and health survey data. *British Medical Journal.* **331**(19 November): 1180–1182.

Muntaner, C. and Lynch, J. (1999) Income inequality, social cohesion and class relations: a critique of Wilkinson's neo-Durkheimian research program. *International Journal of Health Services.* **19**(1): 59–81.

Navarro, V. (1998) Neoliberalism, globalization, unemployment, inequalities, and the welfare state. *International Journal of Health Services.* **28**(4): 607–682.

Navarro, V. (1999) The political economy of the welfare state in developed capitalist countries. *International Journal of Health Services.* **29**(1): 1–50.

Navarro, V. and Shi, L. (2001) The political context of social inequalities and health. *Social Science and Medicine.* **52**: 481–491.

Petras, J. and Veltmeyer, H. (2001) *Globalization Unmasked: Imperialism in the 21st Century.* Halifax: Fernwood Publishing.

Phelan, J. C., Link, B. G., Diez-Roux, A., Kawachi, I. and Levin, B. (2004) Preventability of death and SES gradients in mortality: a fundamental cause perspective. *Journal of Health and Social Behavior.* **45**: 265–285.

Ross, N. A., Wolfson, M. C., Dunn, J. R. *et al.* (2000) Relations between income inequality and mortality in Canada and in the United States. *British Medical Journal.* **320**(1): 898–902.

Ross, R. J. S. and Trachte, K. C. (1990) *Global Capitalism – The New Leviathan.* Albany, NY: University of New York.

Scambler, G. and Higgs, P. (1999) Stratification, class and health: class relations and health inequalities in high modernity. *Sociology.* **33**(2): 275–296.

Shaw, M., Dorling, D., Gordon, D. and Davey Smith, G. (1999) *The Widening Gap: Health Inequalities and Policy in Britain.* Bristol: The Policy Press.

Singh, G. K. and Siahpush, M. (2002) Increasing inequalities in all-cause and cardiovascular mortality among US adults aged 25–64 years by area socioeconomic status, 1969–1998. *International Journal of Epidemiology.* **31**(3): 600–613.

Teunissen, J. J. and Akkerman, A, eds. (2004) *Diversity in Development: Reconsidering the Washington Consensus.* The Hague: FONDAD.

United Nations Food and Agriculture Organization (2006) *The State of Food Insecurity in the World.* Rome: Food and Agricultural Organization of the UN.

United Nations (2005) *Human Development Report 2005*, Oxford: Oxford University Press.

Wagstaff, A. (2000) Socioeconomic inequalities in child mortality: comparisons across nine developing countries. *Bulletin of the World Health Organization.* **78**(1): 19–29.

Wilkinson, R. G. (1996) *Unhealthy Societies: The Afflictions of Inequality.* London: Routledge.

WHO (2003) *World Health Report 2003.* Geneva: WHO.

Yamey, G. (1999) Study shows growing inequalities in health in Britain. *British Medical Journal.* **319**: 1453.

3

Governing the market in health care: the social and political requirements

Amiya Kumar Bagchi

Summary

The chapter opens with a brief overview of progress in advancing longevity and reducing ill health since the nineteenth century. The contributions of public measures for prophylaxis, sanitation, women and childcare, and improving the built environment, along with those of medication, are discussed briefly. The very recent incursion of big private drug companies and their associate providers of health, and their contribution in slowing down improvements in the period of neo-liberal reforms, especially in developing countries, are analyzed. The inter-relationship of state failure and market failure in societies ruled by landlords and speculative capital in alliance with international corporate capital is brought out. The ironical situation of poor states training doctors who then serve badly financed health care systems of developed countries is scrutinized. The pollution of traditional knowledge through the agency of mercenary practitioners in an atmosphere of mass illiteracy, mass poverty and exclusion from their legitimate claims on the public sector is discussed. The social and political requirements for substantially abating the state failures and enabling the state to govern the market in the interest of the poor are discussed.

The axial ages of survival chances

For most of the history of humankind, the basic determinants of human health had little to do with any separable health care sector. Those determinants included the standards of nutrition, the environment of work and daily living, and the prevalence of pathogens in the environment and their rise or sudden eruption. They were then supplemented by remedies for disease obtained through local knowledge and experimentation. In most societies, specialists, whom we call medicine men, shamans, physicians, etc., arose to supplement the remedies known to mothers and grandmothers. In commercialized societies, these specialists

The Economics of Health Equity, ed. Di McIntyre and Gavin Mooney. Published by Cambridge University Press. © Cambridge University Press 2007.

charged fees, or the society made a collective provision for their upkeep. A separable health care sector arose only during the last two or three centuries.

In most of the poor developing countries of the world, the basic determinants of health still lie outside a specialized, formally certified health sector. Many of their inhabitants are born as underweight babies, grow up malnourished, imbibe polluted water and air, and are subject to pathogens causing endemic or sudden infection. When ill, their only recourse may be remedies given by quacks with doubtful skills in any system of medicine. The irruption of a highly commercialized modern health care sector in these countries poses some really tricky problems for their politicians and administrators to design policies that would deliver a minimally adequate level of health care to the poor. The mixture of the private and the public poses very difficult problems even in advanced countries – the most scandalous case being that of the USA, which, with the most advanced drugs and pharmaceuticals industry and the best medical technology in the world, is unable to provide any health care worth speaking of to 18% of its people (KFF 2005).

Borrowing a phrase from Janet Hunter (2000), we can distinguish four axial ages of health transition of mankind since the English industrial revolution of the eighteenth century, meaning the ages in which the world turned on its axis as far as chances of human survival were concerned (Bagchi 2004, 2005), At the outset of the industrial revolution, with uncontrolled urbanization, and growth of highly polluting industries, the longevity or expectation of life at birth (denoted from now on as e_0) and the heights of ordinary people declined in most of the North Atlantic seaboard countries. During the second axial age, starting in the 1870s, the situation changed with the creation of a more healthy infrastructure, provision of clean water and adoption of prophylactic measures in the advanced industrializing countries and their overseas offshoots. Infant mortality rates (that is, the number of infants per thousand dying within a year of their birth) fell first in Scandinavian countries and then in most other countries of north-western Europe. Aided by some measures of social security such as a basic health insurance, accident insurance and old age pensions, e_0 increased from 25–30 years in the developed capitalist countries around 1870 to about 60 years on the eve of World War II. But in the colonial countries, with majority non-white populations, this period witnessed some of the biggest famines in history and little improvement in e_0 (Bagchi 2005 chs 7, 13–18).

The third axial age began after World War II when decolonization swept over Asia and Africa, and the Soviet Union and Communist China posed a challenge to the global capitalist order. With the institution of the welfare state in practically all countries with a majority of white people, the adoption of some measures of public health care by most developing countries and socialized medicines in countries of the socialist bloc, infant mortality rates declined and e_0 increased everywhere. The wide gap between the life chances of persons born in affluent countries and others began to narrow. This period was also characterized by low income inequality in the developed capitalist countries and, of course, in the socialist bloc.

Since about 1980, we have entered a fourth axial age in which improvements in terms of decline in infant mortality rate and increase in e_0 have slowed down everywhere and have gone into reverse in a wide swathe of countries (Cornia and Menchini 2005; WHO 2006). During 2000–05, longevity ranged from 81.9 years in Japan to 36.6 years in Botswana (Table 3.1). In sub-Saharan Africa (SSA), longevity may decline further because of a raging AIDS epidemic, combined with other infectious diseases, most of which have been rooted out from affluent countries. Inequality between and within countries has increased to unprecedented levels. The WHO, under the pressure of the World Bank and other watchdogs of transnational capital continually seeking new areas to hunt in, has diluted its objective of health for all, as enshrined in the Alma Ata declaration of 1978 (Navarro 2004), but recognizes that high income inequality has damaging effects on health (WHO 2006). The factors that led to the enormous increase in the life chances of people of affluent countries in little more than a century are well known (Bagchi 2004, 2005 chs 1, 7). The challenge is to see what socio-economic measures can be suggested to get out of the fourth axial age and provide proper health care to every human being. Economists who are not otherwise opposed to the so-called market system recognize that private health care cannot deliver universal health care even to people of affluent countries (see, for example, Krugman and Wells 2006).

In this chapter, I will try to indicate some of the ways in which countries have tried to tackle the issues of health care, both utilizing the market and regulating it in the interest of the public good. I will also briefly indicate the damage done to the health care systems of many countries by an inadequate recognition of these problems and the lack of policy measures to tackle them. I will use India, China, France, Cuba and the USA as examples of failure and success in these areas.

The entry into the fourth axial age

After World War II, liberation of major non-white colonies, and competition between the Western capitalist bloc and the Soviet bloc created space for most of the developing countries of Latin America, Africa and Asia to adopt various measures of public action to accelerate both economic and human development. From the late 1970s, however, many of these countries were caught up in economic crises that were largely caused by the advance of neo-liberal policies in the G7 countries led by the USA. In the 1980s, stretching into the 1990s and beyond, many developing countries had to undertake structural adjustment programmes that

Table 3.1. Human survival 1975–2003

Country	Life expectancy at birth (data refer to estimates for the period specified)		Infant mortality rate (per thousand live births)		Probability at birth of surviving to age 65 (% of cohort), 2000–05. (data refer to the probability at birth of surviving to age 65, multiplied by 100)		Annual population growth rate (%) (data refer to medium variant projections)	
	1970–75	2000–05	1970	2003	Female	Male	1975–2003	2003–2015
Norway	74.4	79.3	13	3	90.6	84.7	0.5	0.5
Australia	71.7	80.2	17	6	91.5	85.7	1.3	1
Canada	73.2	79.9	19	5	90.7	85	1.1	0.9
United States	71.5	77.3	20	7	86.7	79.1	1	0.9
Japan	73.3	81.9	14	3	93.3	85.7	0.5	Less than half the unit shown
United Kingdom	72	78.3	18	5	89.4	83.6	0.2	0.3
France	72.4	79.4	18	4	91.2	80.9	0.5	0.3
Germany	71	78.7	22	4	90.5	82.3	0.2	Less than half the unit shown
Russian Federation	69.7	65.4	29	16	76.3	44.7	0.3	−0.5
Ukraine	70.1	66.1	22	15	76.4	46.6	−0.1	−1.1
Kazakhstan	63.2	63.2	Data not available	63	71.9	48	0.2	Less than half the unit shown
Estonia	70.5	71.2	21	8	83.9	57.2	−0.2	−0.3
Belarus	71.5	68.1	22	13	79.3	50.6	0.2	−0.6
Republic of Korea	62.6	76.9	43	5	90.2	76.9	1.1	0.3
China	63.2	71.5	85	30	81.3	74.2	1.2	0.6
Sri Lanka	63.1	73.9	65	13	85.6	76.1	1.3	0.7
South Africa	53.7	49	Data not available	53	38.1	28.9	2.1	0.2

Table 3.1. (cont.)

Country	Life expectancy at birth (data refer to estimates for the period specified)		Infant mortality rate (per thousand live births)		Probability at birth of surviving to age 65 (% of cohort), 2000–05. (data refer to the probability at birth of surviving to age 65, multiplied by 100)		Annual population growth rate (%) (data refer to medium variant projections)	
	1970–75	2000–05	1970	2003	Female	Male	1975–2003	2003–2015
India	50.3	63.1	127	63	67.4	59.2	1.9	1.4
Botswana	56.1	36.6	99	82	16.5	13.1	2.5	−0.4
Ghana	49.9	56.7	111	59	52.9	50.4	2.6	1.9
Uganda	51.1	46.8	100	81	34.4	32.9	3.3	3.7
Nigeria	42.8	43.3	140	98	33.2	31.6	2.7	2
Malawi	41.8	39.6	189	112	24.5	23.2	3.1	2.2
Burkina Faso	43.8	47.4	163	107	41.7	37.9	2.6	2.9
Burundi	44.1	43.5	138	114	33.1	29.7	2.3	3.4
Chad	40.6	43.6	Data not available	117	35.1	31.2	2.8	2.8
Côte d'Ivoire	49.8	46	158	117	38.5	34.8	3.5	1.7
Ethiopia	43.5	47.6	160	112	40.7	36.6	2.3	2.3
Cameroon	45.7	45.8	127	95	36.1	33.1	2.6	1.6
Kenya	53.6	47	96	79	31.8	35	3.2	2.5
Senegal	40.1	55.6	164	78	54.6	49.4	2.7	2.2

Source: UN 2005b

often led to an actual decline in their per capita incomes (Bagchi 2005 chs 22–23; Weisbrot *et al.* 2005). Contrary to propaganda of neo-liberal publicists, the rates of growth of most developing countries, except for a few in east and south-east Asia, were higher during their period (1960–80) of import-substituting, government-supported industrialization than in the period when they were coerced into opening up their economies under adverse conditions.

During 1960–80, the infant mortality rate declined and e_0 improved as the result of better sanitation, prophylaxis and public health care, and better nutritional standards, supported by economic growth. These effects have considerably slowed down and in the case of sub-Saharan Africa (and ex-Soviet countries) have gone into reverse, especially since the 1990s. Structural adjustment policies effectively shrunk their economies, and made them pay huge amounts in settlement of debts, often contracted by dictators and their cronies. In addition, there was massive capital flight from those countries to tax havens and developed market economies, where flight capital paid no tax (Baker *et al.* 2003). Most areas of the developing world have been net exporters of capital, with damaging consequences for their wellbeing. Over the period 1970–96, even sub-Saharan Africa, collectively the poorest region in the world, is estimated to have exported more as debt service and flight capital than it received as aid and other foreign remittances (Boyce and Ndikumana 2000). The inability to stall the spread of the HIV/AIDS and tuber-culosis epidemic of sub-Saharan governments can be directly linked to this economic stagnation, combined with the disabling of the state under the neo-liberal dispensation.

After discounting for the effects of World War II, in the USSR we find a steady improvement in longevity and other demographic indicators until the 1960s (Allen, 2003 chs 6 and 10). The end of the Soviet regime had an immediate impact effect on e_0, especially of men in the Russian Federation and several other countries of the erstwhile Soviet bloc. Drastic declines in income, the end of universal social security, including health care, and shrinking job opportunities leading to a rise in alcoholism, a steep rise in mental illnesses and inability to treat diseases, adversely affected most demographic variables (Bagchi 2004, 2005 ch. 23). Between 1988 and 1994, e_0 fell from around 65 years to 57.3 years for Russian men and from 74.4 years to 71.3 years for Russian women (Andreev *et al.* 1998). Russia has not recovered from the health crisis in subsequent years. While the average e_0 was 69.7 years over 1970–75, it had gone down to 65.4 years in 2003 (UN 2005b, table 10). Even more disastrously, total population had begun shrinking: over the period 2003–2015, the population was expected to contract by 0.5% per year, if the current trends continued (UN, 2005b, table 5).

The UN Development Project's *Human Development Report 2005* (UN 2005b, box 1.2) refers to 'missing males' in Russia, because of the abnormally high male mortality compared with women, reflected in an e_0 for males of 59 years as against 72 years for females. It also mentions the high degree of incidence of cardiovascular disease as a 'First World' factor. But a high incidence of cardiovascular diseases can be caused by poor nutrition and nurture during childhood and the birth of low-weight babies to malnourished mothers (Barker 1995; Osmani and Sen 2003). Negative rates of demographic growth are expected in several other ex-Soviet countries, such as Hungary, Estonia, Latvia, Belarus and Ukraine (UN 2005b). In all these cases, the probability of surviving to age 65 is far lower for males than for females. In the case of the North Atlantic seaboard countries and for Australia or New Zealand, with e_0 of 78 years and above in 2003, in respect of the probability of surviving to age 65 the corresponding male–female difference is rarely above 0.10, whereas in the case of the ex-Soviet countries, the difference extends up to 0.267, 0.298 and 0.313 in the cases of Estonia, Ukraine and the Russian Federation, respectively (Table 3.1). In some of these countries, such as the Russian Federation and Estonia, the maternal mortality is also high; higher than, for example, in Malaysia and Mauritius, which have lower levels of per capita income (UN 2005b, table 10). The insecurity of a working population, deprived of public provision of employment, health care and basic necessities of life, and faced with much higher levels of unemployment and physical violence, seems to be a major factor in these developments.

In Table 3.1, I have reproduced some selected demographic variables from the *United Nations Human Development Report* (UN 2005b), for a representative sample of advanced market economies, ex-Soviet countries and developing countries, especially those belonging to sub-Saharan Africa. The countries in which health indicators have gone into reverse include Botswana, which had been praised by Drèze and Sen (1989 pp. 69–71, 152–8) for its effective famine prevention and entitlement protection systems, leading not only to very few deaths caused by drought in 1982–87 but also to a steep decline in the proportion of underweight children between 1983 and 1986. Table 3.1 indicates, however, that e_0 in Botswana has fallen by almost 20 years over the quarter century since 1970–75. That drastic fall has also resulted in an expected decline of population between 2003 and 2015. In Uganda, a country that had been lauded earlier by the World Health Organization (WHO 1999), for its efficient AIDS control programme, e_0 has fallen by almost five years over the last quarter of the twentieth century. Moreover, a person born there in 2003 had a less than one-third chance of surviving to age 65, as against a probability of 80 to 90% or above of a child born to parents in the affluent countries.

The infant mortality rates in ex-Soviet countries continue to be relatively low compared with many developing countries, and the infant mortality rates in many sub-Saharan countries, high as they are, have declined since 1970. But both these groups of countries have far higher adult mortality rates (that is, mortality rates per thousand persons aged between 15 and 60 years) than in the affluent countries or the high-performing countries of East Asia. For example, in 2004, in the Russian Federation, this rate was 485 for males and 180 for females as against corresponding rates of 91 for males and 57 for females respectively in Canada, and 158 for males and 99 for females in China. The adult mortality rates for males and females were 667 and 598 respectively in South Africa and 525 and 446 for males and females respectively in Uganda (WHO 2006 annex table 1). In sub-Saharan Africa, the major killers are AIDS and tuberculosis. In 2003, the percentages of adults aged from 15 to 49 infected with HIV in South Africa and Zimbabwe, two of the most HIV-infected countries in the world, were 21.5% and 24.6% respectively, and the numbers of tuberculosis-affected persons per 100 000 in the two countries were 341 and 621 respectively. By contrast, in Cuba, a relatively low-income, beleaguered country but having an effective public health care system, the percentage of HIV-infected adults was 0.1 and the number of tuberculosis patients per 100 000 was only 13.

There is a strong connection between the prevalence of HIV infection and tuberculosis (Reid *et al.* 2006). Governments and international organizations had promoted a number of flagship programmes for controlling tuberculosis in developing countries, but (Reid *et al.* 2006 p. 483):

the HIV epidemic exacerbated by chronic underfunding of health systems, particularly in Africa, has caused a reversal of the gains in tuberculosis control achieved in the early 1980s ... Between 1990 and 2005, tuberculosis incidence increased 7.0% per year in countries with high adult HIV prevalence (>5%) but only 1.1% per year in countries with lower HIV prevalence ... In Zimbabwe, before the advent of HIV, tuberculosis rates were among the lowest in the region, at about 60 cases per 100 000 population annually. As HIV began to spread in the late 1980s, tuberculosis incidence began to rise, but with a delay of 4–5 years. By 2004, tuberculosis notification rates had increased almost sevenfold to over 400 cases per 100 000 per year.

This sketch gives a rough picture of how, despite major scientific advances in the fields of preventive and curative measures and the recognition of the importance of clean drinkable water and breathable air, large areas of the world are experiencing reversal of the kind of advances that have increased longevity to more than double their historical levels, added anywhere up to 30 cm to the statures of males and considerably brought down the morbidity of people in affluent countries and a few islands with socialized public health systems such as Cuba. But even in many affluent countries, such as the USA, with the fragmentation and inadequate coverage produced by a market-governed health system, many people are suffering and often dying prematurely without being able to access the benefits of advances in science and technology. A principal contention of this essay is that the increasingly lax governance of markets in trade, finance and production, especially in the sectors producing agricultural products and drugs and pharmaceuticals, has led to this unappealing outcome.

India typifies the chaos that prevails in the health sector of the poorer developing countries, as indicated below (Rao 2005 p. 43):

> The health system in India consists of a public sector, a private sector and an informal network of providers of care operating within an unregulated environment, with no controls on what services can be provided by whom, in what manner, and at what cost, and no standardized protocols to help measure the quality of care. There are wide disparities in access, further worsened by the poor functioning of the public health system.

An already grim situation deteriorated further in many countries, including India, after neo-liberal policies, which drastically pared, and augmented the role of the state and the private sector, respectively in health care (Navarro 2004; Duggal *et al.* 2005; Rao *et al.* 2005a). Not only were public health care institutions deprived of the resources needed for their upkeep but many of them were handed over to the private sector, thus allowing the accrual of more private gain at public cost, including the suffering of patients. The whole health care system became more geared towards serving the rich. Contrary to the expectation of neo-liberal economists, the greater degree of privatization of hospitals, health care systems (and schools) did not lead to a smaller degree of absenteeism of health care specialists (or teachers) in public or private institutions (Banerjee and Duflo 2006; Chaudhury *et al.* 2006).

Why ungoverned markets cannot deliver health for all

There are a number of compelling reasons why health care and expenditure on it cannot be treated as just a result of private choice, and part of normal consumer expenditure in any economy, affluent or poor, and these reasons are well recognized in the literature. First, an infectious disease can affect others besides the person first affected, and its treatment and measures against its spread are needed to protect everybody likely to be affected by the infection. Secondly, the converse is also true: the physical and biological environment in which a person lives affects his ability to resist diseases or to benefit from the nutrition that he can procure. The absorptive capacity of a person suffering from gastroenteric diseases or malaria or hookworm infection generally goes down (Bagchi 2005 ch. 1 and references cited there).

Third, health care is pervaded by what economists call asymmetric information: the patient does not know the nature of the disease, how to go about diagnosing it, what treatment to undergo, which doctor, surgeon or health care unit to go to, what post-treatment care to observe, which of a number of brands of the same generic medicine to purchase, and so on. One implication of this is that insurers of health, as of accidents or life chances, would find it profitable to exclude many applicants who are more likely to suffer from ill health than others. However, the latter are precisely the group who require more health care. This is designated as the phenomenon of adverse selection. In this situation, public intervention, making it compulsory, for example, for everybody to be insured, can be unambiguously welfare-enhancing (Arrow 1963; Wilson 1977). Fourth, much of the expenditure cannot be determined beforehand: with real and illusory advances in medicines, surgery, and procedures associated with them, there can be many expenditures for which the bills have to be met later.[1] With competition between different hospitals in the USA for the custom of fee-paying patients, for example, there is a kind of 'medical arms race', with hospitals buying more and more expensive equipment than their nearest competitors (Glied 2003 p. 127). For all these reasons, competition in the health care sector does not ensure the best treatment at the same cost.

In addition to these problems, the emergence of drug companies as some of the biggest corporations in the world, and their deliberate manipulation of the market and the blocking of least-cost solutions that might hurt their profits, has added a huge dimension of system-driven immorality in the provision of medicines and health care. The world's biggest drug corporation, Pfizer, played a leadership role in the series of negotiations that led to the final signing of the agreement creating the World Trade Organization (WTO), that among other things, outlawed the innovative process patent route to the discovery of old products and extended the life of product patents to twenty years (Drahos and Braithwaite 2003). Later, big drug firms resisted attempts by developing-country governments, such as Brazil and South Africa, to use even the provisions embodied in the TRIPS clauses of the WTO to procure cheaper generic varieties of anti-retroviral and other drugs needed to fight infectious diseases, such as AIDS, in those countries (Goozner 2002; Chaudhuri 2005 ch. 3). For all practical purposes, the US government acted as the client state of the drug transnational companies. This clientelist relation became glaringly obvious when Bayer, the producer of the anti-anthrax drug, ciproflaxin, tried to block the sale of much cheaper generic versions to the US government. It eventually agreed to sell ciproflaxin to the US government at a price lower than was originally quoted for it, but still much higher than that of the generic versions (Goozner 2002).

---

[1] Angus Deaton, a top-flight economist specializing in consumer expenditure, poverty analysis and the economics of education and health, underwent a hip replacement operation in 2005; he could not find out how to locate the best surgeons, the best hospitals and, even with a cover of private health insurance, how much of the bill he himself would have to pay: all these were regarded as secrets by doctors, hospitals and insurance companies (Deaton 2006).

For most of the 1990s and beyond, drug companies have remained among the most profitable business corporations in the USA. The enormous profitability of the companies is supposed to be justified by their large expenditures on research. The cost of research and drug discovery has been held to be one of the principal factors behind the rising cost of health care in affluent countries (Weisbrod 1991; Krugman and Wells 2006). However, as Marcia Angell (2004 p. 55) pointed out, research and development expenditures for the top ten companies, 'amounted to only 11% of sales in 1990, rising slightly to 14% in 2000. The biggest single item in the budget is ... something usually called "marketing and administration" ... In 1990, a staggering 36% of sales went into this category and that proportion remained about the same for over a decade.' Especially since the 1980s, big drug companies have devoted their energies primarily to erecting barriers against profit-threatening competition, entering into collusive agreements with potential competitors (such as the producers of generic drugs, postponing the introduction of generics even beyond the expiry date of patents or arriving at price-fixing formulae and keeping prices high for every producer), fighting expensive legal battles to stop (often, imagined) patent infringements, and unethically influencing the publication of research findings of collaborative research and development with universities or other research institutions (Krimsky 2003; Angell 2004, 2006; Horton 2004). They have produced few really new drugs for treating any disease, most of them being variations on old drugs. Moreover, they have produced practically no new drugs for treating the infectious diseases still killing the world's poor, especially in the developing countries. According to a report by Doctors without Frontiers (cited by Goozner 2002), of the 1393 putatively new drugs introduced by the world's eleven largest drug companies in the last quarter of the twentieth century, 'only 13 were aimed at tropical diseases.' Only four of the thirteen were developed by commercial pharmaceutical companies (Chaudhuri 2005 p. 154). In developing as well as affluent countries, pharmaceutical companies target primarily what are called lifestyle diseases, meaning mainly the diseases of the rich. Infectious diseases such as malaria, tuberculosis and leishmaniasis, which are still the major causes of morbidity and mortality of the poor in developing countries, attract little research and development effort of commercial firms. Many of the germs responsible for these diseases have become resistant to the old medicines and in many cases bacteria and viruses have mutated so that they cannot be tackled by old curatives (Goozner 2002; Wellems and Miller 2003; Chaudhuri 2005 ch. 5).

The inefficacy of most so-called aid programmes of the World Bank and agencies of G7 countries in combating HIV/AIDS or malaria in sub-Saharan Africa is pretty obvious from the data cited in Table 3.1. According to recent estimates, 800 000 young children in Africa die of malaria every year (Dugger 2006):

In Uganda, population 28 million, not one of the 1.8 million [mosquito] nets approved more than two years ago by the Global Fund to Fight AIDS, Tuberculosis and Malaria [had yet arrived by the end of June 2006.] The World Bank, after pledging to halve malaria deaths in Africa six years ago, had let its staff working on the disease fall to zero. And the United States Agency for International Development admitted to outraged senators last year that it spent more on high-priced consultants than on life-saving commodities, like mosquito nets that cost $5.75 apiece and last up to five years.

The influence of the market is highly damaging to the poor in the world's richest economy, namely, the USA. According to an estimate of the Henry J. Kaiser Family Foundation (KFF 2005), 18% of US residents in 2004 were without any insurance cover, which means that they had to pay for any health care they needed or suffer without it. Tragically, of those who were below the federal poverty level (FPL) of $19 307 for a family of four, 37% were without Medicaid or any employer-provided health insurance. The percentages of uninsured US residents declined as incomes moved progressively above the FPL. In other words, health insurance was unavailable to the people who needed it most.

Contrary to some popular perceptions, although the uninsured formed 40% of the immigrant population, this was not the group primarily responsible for the increase in the uninsured population. The increase has to be laid at the door of decline in employer-provided insurance, increase in unemployment rates and more niggardly provision for Medicaid (Holahan and Cook 2005).

Commodification of health care and its career under financial liberalization can perhaps be illustrated by the case of HCA, Inc., which was founded in 1990 by the family of (Republican) Senator Bill Frist. On 31 December 2004, it operated a total of 189 hospitals, and employed 191 400 persons. It also owned the fourth largest medical malpractice insurer of the United States. In April 2005, the Foundation for Taxpayer and Consumer Rights (FTCR) filed a complaint to the ethics committee of the US Senate asking for investigation of conflict of interest in Senator Frist's advocacy of limiting the damage for medical malpractice. Further, in June 2005, Senator Frist sold off his holdings in HCA stock just when its price peaked, and the price fell drastically in July when HCA reported disappointing profits. The FTCR wanted the sale to be investigated by the Securities and Exchange Commission (SEC) (www.consumerwatchdog.org accessed on 21 November 2006). Here we see how the health care of millions of people can be subjected to vagaries in the stock market and can be the subject of lobbying for limiting the scope of patient rights by powerful politicians.

In a further twist to this tale, on 24 July 2006, three private-equity funds, namely, Bain, Kohlberg Kravis, Merrill Lynch, and the family of Bill Frist, the US Senate majority leader and son of the founder, acquired HCA for $31.6 billion. But their actual stake was only $5.5 billion. The rest of the money would be raised as debt (Sorkin 2006). This means that whatever oversight the Securities and Exchange Commission could have exercised over the operations of the company will now vanish. The patients will now be at the mercy of a non-transparent firm, and could get any redress against malpractice only through expensive litigation. This case also starkly demonstrates the close political connection of the US administration with big business.

The search for profits by drug companies leads them effectively to subvert the ethics of research and drug recommendation. Three cases will suffice to illustrate these problems: (a) Dr Nancy Olivieri of the University of Toronto was dismissed because she wanted to publicize the negative results of a drug the university was developing for a drug company and was reinstated only after judicial enquiry confirmed her suspicion (Horton 2004); (b) Dr Peter Gleason received more than $100 000 from Jazz Pharmaceuticals in 2005 alone, for promoting Xyren, for treating depression and pain relief, while suppressing publication of its dangerous side effects (Berenson 2006) and (c) Vioxx, an anti-arthritis drug produced by Merck, had severely adverse side effects, which were known to Merck, but Vioxx was still marketed by it. Furthermore, the Federal Drug Administration, the US official watchdog whose approval is necessary before marketing a drug, had approved it without exercising due diligence (Angell 2006).

Alternative models: governing the market versus being governed by it

I will turn now to Cuba, a country with a per capita (purchasing power parity) income of $3900, as estimated by the CIA in 2006 (www.cia.gov/cia/publications/factbook/geos/cu.html), which outranked all countries of Latin and Central America and the Caribbean, except Argentina, Chile, Costa Rica and Uruguay in terms of human development index (HDI) compiled by the UNDP and had, in 2003, an e_0 of 77.3 years, an infant mortality rate of 6 (the US rate was 7) (UN 2005b) and had, in 2005, an adult HIV prevalence rate of 0.1% as against 1.5% in Jamaica (UN 2006) and even higher in most other countries of the Caribbean. Cuba's positive difference between its human development index rank and its gross domestic product per capita rank in 2005 was an astonishing 40, and its physician density as measured by the number of physicians was 591 per 100 000, higher than in any other country (UN 2005b). Cuba's accomplishments include:

... low-technology and organisational innovations such as neighbourhood-based family medicine as the focus of primary care; regionalized systems of hospital services and professional training; innovative public health initiatives and epidemiologic surveillance; universal access to services without substantial barriers related to race, social class, gender, and age; and active programmes in alternative or traditional treatments such as 'green medicine' and 'thermalism'. High-technology accomplishments include innovations in pharmacology and biotechnology, surgical procedures, and care of patients infected by human immunodeficiency virus (HIV). (Waitzkin *et al.* 1997).

Cuba has put human development ahead of economic development; it has been able to use its remarkable advances in education, nutrition and health care, and outcomes of research and training in health care, to overcome the disaster of the withdrawal of support from the Soviet bloc after its collapse in 1989 and withstand the illegal economic embargo imposed on Cuba by the USA and its allies.

The foundation of Cuba's health care system is its network of family physicians. Along with voluntary associations, they keep surveillance over all persons who might contract an infectious disease and take preventive, and where necessary, curative measures. 'Each family practitioner is required to see every patient in his or her catchment area at least twice a year . . . Family physicians are supported by a system of laboratories, referral centres, and consultation resources, based in local polyclinics and municipal hospitals,' (Watzkin *et al.* 1997). Education about nutrition and sexual behaviour is provided in schools and consultation chambers or polyclinics. The effectiveness of this system was brilliantly demonstrated in Cuba's successful fight against the spread of HIV infection (Krales 2004). Already by 2003, Cuba's rate of adult HIV infection was only 0.7%. This has since been brought down further to 0.1%. A major instrument for fighting AIDS has been testing of pregnant women on a regular basis and providing adequate nutrition to HIV patients so as to prevent the spread of opportunistic infections, principally tuberculosis (Reid *et al.* 2006).

Laying primary stress on preventive measures, Cuba developed domestic production of childhood vaccines and led the world in the production of vaccines against meningitis B and hepatitis B. In the 1990s, Cuba established a Scientific Pole at an estimated cost of $100 million. It was run like a corporate research and development hub, but the results expected were social outcomes rather than profits (Giles 2005). Apart from meningitis B vaccine, it has also produced an anti-cancer 'vaccine that, despite considerable opposition from anti-Castro politicians, has been licensed for use in the United States' (Giles 2005). Since 2001, Cuba has developed its own cocktail of anti-retroviral drugs, at a much lower cost than the big drug companies (Krales 2004). Among other high-technology achievements of Cuba is its production of policasonol, an oral medication derived from sugar cane 'that lowers cholesterol and atherogenic lipoproteins', and of 'interferons, monoclonal antibodies, interleukins, and thrombolytic agents, for both export and internal use,' (Waitzkin *et al.* 1997). By the end of the 1990s, Cuba was earning more than $100 million from its pharmaceutical exports (Waitzkin *et al.* 1997).

Cuba not only gives intensive training to its own doctors, but also trains doctors for other countries and sends its own doctors to them. 'The Latin American School of Medical Sciences (LASMS) . . . stands ready to educate a minimum of 500 doctors each year – for free. The only requirement is that after they graduate, they must come back to the United States and practise medicine among the poor,'

(Muhammad 2004). Not only poor countries but the poor, especially African-Americans in the USA, can take advantage of the Cuban system since many of them do not have access to doctors and health care: the infant mortality rate among US blacks continues to be much higher and the e_0 much lower than among US whites. By 2004, 17 654 foreign students from 113 countries had graduated from Cuban medical schools and 17% of them were from Africa. Since they are expected to go back to their home countries, they are helping to reverse the brain drain that has become one of the worst aspects of the health crisis in sub-Saharan Africa (WHO 2006). Cuban doctors have also helped provide health care to the poor of countries such as Venezuela, which have sought Cuba's friendship and help, defying the US embargo (Malapanis and Catalán 2003; Guillermoprieto 2005). Following the typical incentive structure of capitalist countries without public health care, Venezuelan doctors catered mainly to the rich, and as part of the elite, bitterly opposed President Chavez and his pro-poor policies. Chavez introduced a family-based and community-based system, staffed by Cuban doctors for the inhabitants of the barrios of Caracas, and other poor people, with enormous success.

Can the Cuban system be replicated in other developing countries? Before answering that question, we will take a brief look at the health care system in India, the second most populous country in the world. In India, private financing of health came to as much as 87% of total health expenditure around 2002 (Misra *et al.* 2003 p. 143). In the poorer states such as Bihar and Uttar Pradesh, the average patient personally met 90% of his or her out-of-pocket expenditures (Rao *et al.* 2005b, p. 241). Public health centres are inadequate in number, and badly supplied with staff, medical supplies and equipment, and diagnostic facilities (Rao 2005). As in other countries in which rural areas are still plagued by landlord and dominant lineage power, illiteracy and poverty, absenteeism of professionals is a major problem in public health care and in most cases, even in private health care facilities (Banerjee and Duflo 2006; Chaudhury *et al.* 2006). Private health care facilities proliferate. Those for the rich are expensive and out of reach for 90% of the population. The latter resort to quacks practising allopathy or some indigenous system of medicine, obtaining poor or perverse treatment in their hands (Banerjee *et al.* 2004; Rao *et al.* 2005). Rural areas fare much worse than urban areas under this dispensation.

China, the world's most populous country, and staunchly socialist since 1949, had built up a low-technology but socialized health care system in the period up to 1978. It expanded that health care system in the rural areas down to the end of the 1980s; however, from the 1990s, the Chinese state has virtually ceased providing socialized health care, except for a small, mainly urban population. It has introduced user charges for health care. Except for the shrinking group of employees of state-owned enterprises, the cost has to be defrayed by the patient and his family. As a result, many people, especially in the interior provinces and rural areas, are going without any effective medical treatment, though compared with India, China has a much lower degree of malnutrition, and so people have a far higher degree of resistance to disease. According to the *Economist* (2004), while in Mao Zedong's time, 'nine out of ten country people had access to subsidised health clinics run by the much celebrated "barefoot doctors",' by 2004, '90% of the population [had] no health insurance' and 'in the cities, nearly 60% [were] uncovered.'

According to the *China Human Development Report* (UN Development Report 2005a), in rural China the maternal mortality rate was 61.9 per 1 000 000 and, barring a small section of urban residents, 'most Chinese labourers – rural migrant workers, employees of township enterprises, and farmers – are virtually excluded from the social security system', including public health care. It is no wonder that China, which had a higher e_0 in 1970–75 than South Korea and Sri Lanka, had slipped below those countries in 2004–05.

The Chinese authorities have recently recognized these problems. In his report to the fourth session of the tenth National People's Congress, the Chinese Prime Minster, Wen Jiabao mentioned that 'there was an 18.3% increase in spending on education, health, science and technology, and "culture" in 2005 . . . . a trial co-operative health care system was extended to 671 rural counties, to the benefit of 177 million peasants,' (China Quarterly 2006 p. 519). For the future, China would work towards a comprehensive social security system both for urban residents and for rural areas (China Quarterly 2006 p. 524).

Finally, we turn to France, the country that in 2000 the WHO rated as the top performer in health care. A part of the health care expenses was borne by the employers and the employees, but everybody in France was covered. The state would reimburse the costs of treatment and the patients could choose among the doctors and hospitals. The patients did not have to go through a gatekeeper. But with a growing fiscal burden caused by advancing technology and an ageing population, from 2006, France has decided to move over to what has been termed as a state-led managed care system – as contrasted with the market-led managed care system prevailing in the United States (Rodwin and Le Pen 2004; Owen 2007). Under the new system, everybody has to register with a médecin traitant (MT). A fee has to be paid for visiting a médecin traitant, of which the state will reimburse 70%. If somebody visits a doctor with whom he or she is not registered, the state will reimburse only 60% of the fee. Visits to a specialist will also be channelled through the médecin traitant of the patient. Patients will get a lesser percentage of reimbursement from the state if they go to a specialist independently. Patients will have to pay more for their medicines under this system. Obviously, France is also being pulled in the direction of less public health care and more out-of-pocket expenses than before. But this state-managed semi-public health care is still a lot better than the almost entirely market-guided US system. In order to cover all the inhabitants of affluent countries, obviously the state will have to rein in marketization of hospitals, restrain competition among pharmaceutical companies through marketing and advertizing campaigns, and promote genuine research and development, prevent them from appropriating and unethically manipulating the results of research in universities and other research facilities and disallow the market for health care corporations. Thus a serious attempt has to be made to revive essential elements of the welfare state, with a commanding state presence in social sectors. That will involve a reversal of most of the changes brought about by financial liberalization, privatization and the stimulation of the financial sector at the cost of the real economy.

In poor countries such as India, basic requirements are the abolition of landlord power, ensuring access of the poor to proper nutrition, education and publicly funded public health care down to the level of the village, and preventing the mushrooming of fee-charging private hospitals and medical colleges. Land reforms are instruments for freeing the peasants of the non-market power of landlords, augmenting their incentives for work and investment, and providing access to private markets (through the route of income growth) and public facilities (through the route of enabling the peasants' voices to be heard). Land reforms are also constitutive elements in their human development, because it gives them a sense of autonomy in decision making (Bagchi 2002).

The poorer countries must also get together to get rid of the TRIPS provisions of the WTO: that step will also benefit the poorer people of affluent countries by bringing down the prices of medicines. The breakdown of the recent ministerial-level talks on WTO provides a golden opportunity for pushing for this step. Public sector research into drugs and other health-related areas should also cover the indigenous systems of medicine. Following the example of Cuba, a pharmacology must be created for herbal medicines recommended, for example, by Ayurveda, the ancient Indian medicine system, after proper testing and clinical trials. The same procedures should be followed in the cases of other systems such as Unani, acupuncture, naturopathy, and so on. Such testing is conspicuous by its absence in India and most other developing countries (Vaidya 2005; Varma 2006; for contrasting views on 'alternative medicine', see Iwu and Gbodossou 2000 and Knipschild 2000). With these changes, doctors' training must be firmly linked to their apprenticeship in community health clinics and their fidelity to the Hippocratic oath should be tested. Their training should be upgraded by periodic refresher courses and practice in health care institutions other than their normal base.

I have earlier referred to the Cuban health care system, which in many ways is the best system operating anywhere. However, it may be thought that in societies in which there are active markets for health care and training of doctors, the purely state-guided Cuban system cannot be replicated. However, the experience of Kerala, a constituent state of the Indian Republic, demonstrates that with adequate measures for freeing peasants from landlord power, providing the poor, and especially children, with cheap nutrition, and continually expanding the literacy base, remarkable results can be attained even within a market society (the following analysis is based on UN 1975; Panikar and Soman 1984; Kannan 2000; Narayana 2007). Even before independence, the 'native state' of Travancore, which along with the other native state of Cochin and British-ruled Malabar, became the new state of Kerala, was spending a larger proportion of its budget on health and education than the British Indian government for the other parts of India. Kerala was already the most literate state of India at the time of independence. Allied with earlier social movements, a strong left-wing movement emerged and the first communist-led government came to power in 1957. Under this government, strong moves were made towards land reforms by redistributing land away from landlords to their insecure tenants, and expenditures on education and health were further increased. Although the first communist-led government was dismissed by the central government, the succeeding non-left governments could not reverse the changes initiated by the communists. Kerala saw almost a regular alternation of left-wing and right-wing governments. But new initiatives were adopted for instituting a comprehensive food rationing system, and providing meals to children attending primary school. Land reforms led to crop diversification and increase in peasant incomes, and unionization of labour in most sectors raised real wages. Kerala's high levels of education provided employment opportunities to the educated workers outside the state, and increasingly in the oil-producing states of West Asia. Neo-liberal reforms of the 1990s greatly curtailed the power of the local government to maintain an adequate public distribution of food grains or spend money on public education and health care on earlier scales. But an educated population, with increasing incomes, now took over the major part of the expenditures on health care upon themselves, incurring high costs in the process. A grassroots planning system continued to use community iniatives in health and education and stemmed some of the damage caused by neo-liberal policies. The outcome has been that in the beginning of the twenty-first century, health care and literacy indicators of Kerala were far higher than those of richer states of India, and higher even than those of China, whose per capita income was several times that of Kerala (Drèze and Sen 2002 table 4.1).

In conclusion, the following propositions may be laid out. First, under neo-liberalism, the power of large corporations has increased all over the world; the role of the state has contracted in almost every country and, with that, public health care has diminished in relative terms, and often in absolute terms as well;

the countries most affected by these developments are the ones that most need public health care and social security in general; the problems have been aggravated by the huge amount of capital flowing from developing countries to the affluent; in practically every country, inequality between persons, regions and classes increased and with that the life chances of the poor deteriorated.

Cuba remains the only poor country that has achieved wonderful results both in health care, medical education and advances in vaccines and drugs with its socialized medicine. All countries, but especially the poor developing countries, can learn from Cuba. I have sketched some of the social and political changes needed by developing countries to move towards socialized health care. This would be a difficult task, but is achievable, as I have argued with the example of Kerala. The survival of hundreds of millions of human beings is at stake, not only in sub-Saharan Africa, but even in a country like India, which has the dubious distinction of being home to the largest numbers of HIV-positive and tuberculosis patients in the world (UN 2006). It is utterly urgent to establish public health care, education and nutrition centres with continual monitoring by trained medical and nutrition experts in every village to arrest the spread of HIV and tuberculosis. India's network of Panchayati Raj institutions can be utilized for the purpose. The Indian constitution provides for the election of a three-tier system of local bodies, on the basis of adult suffrage, from the village up to a group of villages (called a block) and then up to the district or zilla. For urban areas there are elected municipal bodies. These bodies operate within particular constituent states but are politically independent. They receive funds from the state governments and the central government to look after health care and nutrition, education, local roads and irrigation channels, and so on. If the system works well, it should be continuously attentive to local needs, which are voiced by the elected representatives but have also to be validated by regularly convened village assemblies. (Of course, the system is still working very imperfectly in most parts of India, otherwise the health outcomes in every part of India would be of the same standard as those of Kerala.) Similar institutions, with effective mobilization of people at every level and delivery of health service by professionals of diverse sorts can be developed in other countries also.

REFERENCES

Allen, R. C. (2003) *Farm to Factory: a Reinterpretation of the Soviet Industrial Revolution.* Princeton: Princeton University Press.

Andreev, E., Scherbov S. and Willekens, F. (1998) Population of Russia: what can we expect in the future? *World Development.* **26**(11): 1939–1956.

Angell, M. (2004) The truth about the drug companies. *New York Review of Books*, **51**(12, 15 July) 52–58.

Angell, M. (2006) Your dangerous drugstore. *New York Review of Books*. **53**(10, 8 June): 38–40.

Arrow, K. J. (1963) Uncertainty and the welfare economics of medical care. *American Economic Review*. **53** (December): 941–973.

Bagchi, A. K. (2002) Agrarian transformation and human development. In Ramachandran, V. K. and Swaminathan M., eds, *Agrarian Studies: Essays on Agrarian Relations in Less-Developed Countries*. New Delhi: Tulika. pp. 153–165.

Bagchi, A. K. (2004) The axial ages of the capitalist world-system. *Review*. **XVII**(2): 93–134.

Bagchi, A. K. (2005) *Perilous Passage: Mankind and the Global Ascendancy of Capital*. Lanham, Maryland: Rowman & Littlefield.

Baker, R. W., Dawson, B., Shulman, I. and Brewer, C. (2003) *Dirty Money and Its Global Effects*. Washington, DC: Centre for International Policy.

Banerjee, A., Deaton, A. and Duflo, E. (2004) Wealth, health, and health services in rural Rajasthan. *Economic and Political Weekly*. **39**(9): 944–949.

Banerjee, A. and Duflo, E. (2006) Addressing absence. *Journal of Economic Perspectives*. **20**(1): 117–132.

Barker, D. J. P. (1995) Foetal origins of coronary heart disease. *British Medical Journal*. **311**(6998): 171–174.

Berenson, A. (2006) Indictment of doctor tests drug marketing rules. *New York Times*. (22 July).

Boyce, J. K. and Ndikumana, L. (2000) *Is Africa a Net Creditor? New Estimates of Capital Flight From Severely Indebted Sub-Saharan African Countries, 1970–1996*. Department of Economics and Political Economy Research Institute, University of Massachusetts, Amherst.

Chaudhuri, S. (2005) *The WTO and India's Pharmaceutical Industry: Patent Protection, TRIPS, and Developing Countries*. Oxford: Oxford University Press.

Chaudhury, N., Hammer J., Kremer, M., Muralidharan, K. and Rogers F. H. (2006) Missing in action: teacher and health worker absence in developing countries. *Journal of Economic Perspectives*. **20**(1): 91–116.

China Quarterly (2006) Quarterly chronicle and documentation (January–March 2006). *China Quarterly*. (June): 517–569.

Cornia, G. A. and Menchini, L. (2005) *The Pace and Distribution of Health Improvements during the Last 40 Years: Some Preliminary Results*. Paper presented at the UNDP-French government sponsored 'Forum on Human Development', Paris, 17–19 January. www.networkideas.org/featart/feb2005/Cornia_Menchini_Paris_Paper.pdf.

Deaton, A. (2006) Letter from America: trying to be a good hip op consumer. *Royal Economic Society Newsletter*. (113): 3–4.

Drahos, P. and Braithwaite, J. (2003) *Information Feudalism: Who Owns the Knowledge Economy?* Oxford: Oxford University Press.

Drèze, J. and Sen, A. (1989) *Hunger and Public Action*. Oxford: Oxford University Press.

Drèze, J. and Sen, A. (2002). *India: Development and Participation*. Oxford: Oxford University Press.

Duggal, R., Dilip, T. R. and Raymus, P. (2005) *Health and Healthcare: a Status Report in Maharashtra*. Mumbai: Centre for Enquiry into Health and Allied Themes.

Dugger, C. W. (2006) Push for new tactics as war on malaria falters. *New York Times.* (28 June). www.nytimes.com.

Economist (2004) China's health care: where are the patients? *Economist,* (19 August): 20–22.

Giles, J. (2005) Vive la revolución? *Nature.* **436**(21 July): 322–324.

Glied, S. (2003) Health care costs: on the rise again. *Journal of Economic Perspectives.* **17**(2): 125–148.

Goozner, M. (2002) Medicine as a luxury, *The American Prospect,* **13**(1). www.prospect.org/print/V13/1/goozner-m.html.

Guillermoprieto, A. (2005) The gambler, the Cuban connection. *New York Review of Books.* **52**(10): 24–34.

Holahan, J. and Cook, A. (2005) *Are Immigrants Responsible for Most of the Growth of the Uninsured?* Washington, D.C., Kaiser Commission on Medicaid and the Uninsured, The Henry J. Kaiser Family Foundation. www.kff.org.

Horton, R. (2004) The dawn of McScience. *New York Review of Books.* **51**(4): 7–9.

Hunter, J. (2000) The roots of divergence? Some comments on Japan in the 'axial age' 1750–1850. *Itenarario.* **24**(3/4): 75–88.

Iwu, M. M. and Gbodossou, E. (2000) The role of traditional medicine. *The Lancet Perspectives.* **356**(December): s3.

Kannan, K. P. (2000) *Food Security in a Regional Perspective: a View From 'Food Deficit' Kerala.* Thiruvananthapuram (India), Centre for Development Studies Working Paper no 304.

KFF (2005) *The Uninsured and Their Access to Health Care.* Washington, D.C., Kaiser Commission on Medicaid and the Uninsured, The Henry J. Kaiser Family Foundation. www.kff.org.

Knipschild, P. (2000) Alternative treatments: do they work? *The Lancet Perspectives.* **356** (December): s5.

Krales, E. (2004) Cuba's response to AIDS: a model for the developing world. *Counterpunch.* (11 November). www.counterpunch.org/krales11112004.html.

Krimsky, S. (2003) *Science in the Private Interest: How the Lure of Profits Corrupted Biomedical Research.* Oxford: Rowman & Littlefield.

Krugman, P. and Wells, R. (2006) The health care crisis and what to do about it. *New York Review of Books.* **53**(5): 38–43.

Malapanis, A. and Catalán, C. (2003) Cuban doctors in Venezuela operate free neighborhood clinics. *Venezuelanalysis.com.* www.venezuelanalysis.com/print.php?artno=1041.

Misra, R., Chatterjee, R. and Rao, S. eds (2003) *India Health Report.* New Delhi: Oxford University Press.

Muhammad, N. I. (2004) The compassion of Cuba's health care. *FinalCall.com News.* www.finalcall.com/artman/publish/printer_1469.shtml.

Narayana, D. (2007) High health achievements and good access to health care at great cost: the emerging Kerala situation. In Haddad, S., Baris, E. and Narayana, D., eds, *Safeguarding the Health Sector in Times of Macroeconomic Instability: Policy Lessons for Low-and Middle-Income Countries.* Lawrenceville, NJ: Africa World Press.

Navarro, V. (2004) The world situation and WHO. *Lancet.* **63**(9417): 1321–23.

Osmani, S. and Sen, A. (2003) The hidden penalties of gender inequality: fetal origins of ill-health. *Economics and Human Biology.* **1**(1): 105–121.

Owen, P. (2007) *Healthcare in France: a Guide for the Expatriate*. Figanieres, France: Expat Health Direct.

Panikar, P. G. K. and Soman, C. R. (1984) *Health Status of Kerala: Paradox of Economic Backwardness and Health Development*. Trivandrum (India): Centre for Development Studies.

Rao, K. S. (2005) Delivery of health services in the public sector. In *NCMH Background Papers, Financing and Delivery of Health Care Services in India*. New Delhi: National Commission on Macroeconomics and Health, Ministry of Health & Family Welfare, Government of India. (August) pp. 43–64.

Rao, K. S., Nundy, M. and Dua, A. S.(2005a) Delivery of health services in the private sector. In *NCMH Background Papers, Financing and Delivery of Health Care Services in India*. New Delhi: National Commission on Macroeconomics and Health, Ministry of Health & Family Welfare, Government of India. (August) pp. 89–124.

Rao, K. S., Selvaraju, S. Nagpal, S. and Sakthivel, S. (2005b) Financing of health in India. In *NCMH Background Papers, Financing and Delivery of Health Care Services in India*. New Delhi: National Commission on Macroeconomics and Health, Ministry of Health & Family Welfare, Government of India. (August) pp. 239–255.

Reid, A., Scano, F., Getahuri, H. *et al.* (2006) Towards universal access to HIV prevention, treatment, care, and support: the role of tuberculosis/ HIV collaboration. *Lancet Infectious Diseases*. **6**: 483–95.

Rodwin, V. G. and Le Pen, C. (2004) Health care reform in France – the birth of state-led managed care. *New England Journal of Medicine*. **351**: 2259–2262.

Sorkin, A. R. (2006) HCA buyout highlights era of going private. *New York Times*. (25 July).

UN (1975) *Poverty, Unemployment and Development Policy: a Case Study of Selected Issues with Reference to Kerala*. New York: United Nations Department of Economic and Social Affairs (ST/ESA/29).

UN Development Programme (2005a) *China Human Development Report 2005*. Oxford: Oxford University Press. www.undp.org.cn/.

UN (2005b) *Human Development Report 2005*, Oxford: Oxford University Press.

UN (2006) *Report on the Global AIDS Epidemic*. www.unaids.org.

Vaidya, A. D. B. (2005) Effective integration of Indian systems of medicine in health care delivery: people's participation, access and choice in a pluralistic democracy. In *NCMH Background Papers, Financing and Delivery of Health Care Services in India*. New Delhi: National Commission on Macroeconomics and Health, Ministry of Health & Family Welfare, Government of India. (August) pp. 77–87.

Varma, D. R. (2006) From witchcraft to allopathy: uninterrupted journey of medical science. *Economic and Political Weekly*. **XLI**(33 19 August). 3605–3611.

Waitzkin, H., Wald, K., Kee, R., Danielson R. and Robinson, L. (1997) *Primary Care in Cuba: Low-and High-Technology Developments Pertinent to Family Medicine*. (www.cubasolidarity.-net/waitzkin.html).

Weisbrod, B. A. (1991) The health care quadrilemma: an essay on technological change, insurance, quality of care, and cost containment. *Journal of Economic Literature*. **29**(2): 523–552.

Weisbrot, M., Baker, D. and Rosnick, D. (2005) *The Scorecard of Development: 25 years of Diminished Progress*. Washington, D.C.: Centre for Economic and Policy Research. www.cepr.net.

Wellems, T. E. and Miller, L. H. (2003) Two worlds of malaria. *The New England Journal of Medicine*. **349**(16): 1496–98.

WHO (1999) *Health a Key to Prosperity: Success Stories in Developing Countries*. www.who.int/inf-new/aids2.htm.

WHO (2006) *World Health Report 2006*. Geneva: World Health Organization.

Wilson, C. (1977) A model of insurance markets with incomplete information. *Journal of Economic Theory*. **16**: 167–202.

4

Equity in the context of diversity of culture and diversity of economic systems

Gavin Mooney

Summary

This chapter argues that the construct of health and the nature of health care systems and, in turn, of equity in health and health care are in significant part cultural phenomena. This is in distinction to the universalism with respect to these issues that is usually the case in health economics assessments of both health and equity.

Acknowledgement that these are cultural phenomena, and that the literature on the social determinants of health indicates that being comfortable in one's culture is good for our health, means that globally there is a need to protect the diversity of societies and of cultures. Further, the nature of a society and its culture are heavily influenced by the economic system in which they exist. This chapter, therefore, argues that an important way of protecting the diversity of societies and of cultures is through the preservation of the diversity of economic systems.

Such preservation of diversity can be undermined by the impact of neo-liberalism's individualism and its adverse effects on the development of a sense of community. This can result in reducing social capital, which in turn can adversely affect population health and its distribution.

In the light of these observations, a new paradigm for the economics of health equity is proposed, based not on the values of individuals qua individuals, but more on the values of communities. Adopting a communitarian stance provides a new and potentially more useful approach to the economic analysis of equity in health and health care. This paradigm requires that the importance of community and of its social institutions is recognized and questions of culture and cultural values brought into play.

The last part of the chapter provides one example of the practical use of this paradigm.

The Economics of Health Equity, ed. Di McIntyre and Gavin Mooney. Published by Cambridge University Press. © Cambridge University Press 2007.

Introduction and background

Across the globe it is clear that policies on equity in health and in health care have by and large failed. The contribution of the work of health economists in promoting equity has been small. This chapter argues that a part of the reason for this is that the economic analysis of equity in health and health care has been operating with a deficient paradigm and that a new approach to analyzing equity is needed.

Given the disparities in most countries in health and health-related disadvantage and in access to health care between different groups, for example rich and poor, urban and rural populations, indigenous and non-indigenous, the notion of equity has a role to play in health policy. This equity imperative can be read into many health policy statements in many countries. The issue thereafter is to decide what is to be meant by equity.

Equity can be seen as synonymous with the notion of justice or fairness. It is generally defined as equality in the distribution of some phenomenon or phenomena (e.g., goods, welfare or rights). Equality per se is, however, seldom able to be equated with equity; there is usually some caveat or qualification accompanying the equality statement (such as 'for equal need').

It is important to draw a distinction between horizontal and vertical equity. The former is the equal treatment of equals; vertical equity is the unequal but equitable treatment of unequals.

In horizontal equity, it is assumed *inter alia* that a health gain is a health gain is a health gain (or that a QALY – 'quality-adjusted life year' – is a QALY is a QALY), no matter who gets it. For vertical equity (such as for, say, addressing inequities faced by poor people), one approach would be to give added importance to benefits to the poor by giving weights above 1 to benefits which accrue to groups deemed to be disadvantaged. These equity weights would be determined socially (Mooney 2001). Most health care policy on equity settles for horizontal equity, the equal treatment of equals, which is a thinner version than that of vertical equity.

Beyond that, in the literature, there has been much discussion over the appropriate principle for equity policy in health care. Some of the principles proposed are equal expenditure per capita, equal resources per capita, equal resources for equal need, equal access for equal need, equal use for equal need, equal marginal unmet need and equal health. To a large extent the debate over what might be deemed an appropriate equity principle mirrors a wider debate over what the appropriate criteria are for social justice or fairness. This is not surprising given that the issue of equity is driven by values – essentially social values.

The failure of equity in health and health care is, in part, a reflection of the failure of policies on social justice more generally to gain a place at national and international policy forums. For example, the gap in income between rich and poor, both across the globe and within countries, has been increasing. In 1960, the average per capita gross domestic product in the richest 20 countries in the world was 15 times that of the poorest 20. That is now 30 times. 'By the late 1990s, the richest 20% of the world's population had 86% of world gross domestic product; the poorest 20% had 1%' (UNDP 1999 p. 3).

There are many reasons why equity in health and health care has not made more advances, just as there are many reasons for the poor contribution of health economics to equity policies. First and foremost in this chapter it is stressed that there has been inadequate attention paid by health economists to the links between health and culture and in turn between equity and culture. Health is a cultural construct; yet few of the analyses of health economists have recognized this. Instead they have assumed that, for example, quality-adjusted life years might have universal validity, sometimes going further and arguing that quality-adjusted-life-year measurements might be transferable from one society to another and one culture to another.

It is also the case that the nature of the economic system can have a major impact on the nature of a society or culture, for example on the extent of poverty and of inequality that exist. More neo-liberal societies emphasize more the merits of individualism; more socially 'solidaristic' societies focus more on a sense of community and the building of social capital. Also the nature of the construct of health can vary across different cultures, very notably between indigenous and non-indigenous cultures, with, for example, health being seen as a more holistic concept in indigenous societies. Further, but still related, the extent to which the economic system and culture support more or less individualism or less or more social capital and social cohesiveness can affect equity in general in the society but also equity in health and equity in health care. It is not happenstance that the more egalitarian, more communitarian societies of Scandinavia place a high weight on equity in general, with large public sectors, high and progressive taxation and greater equity in health and health care. Health economists have been slow to acknowledge these kinds of relationships with the result that most of their analyses of equity have assumed that both health and equity are universal phenomena. There has then been a neglect of the need to defend and protect both diversity of culture and diversity of economic systems, which underpin different cultures.

There are, however, other reasons for the relative failure of health economics to have much impact on equity policies in health and health care. First, at a theoretical level in health economics, the emphasis on welfarism and extra-welfarism and the fact that both are driven by individual preferences is problematical for equity, which in essence is better seen as a social rather than individualistic construct. Second, most equity analyses have focused on health care and not health and largely failed to examine the equity implications of the social determinants of health and of many macroscopic issues. Third, the health care system has tended to be valued only for its outputs and not as a social institution per se.

Taking the universalist stances of health economists with respect to both health and health equity together with these three points means that health economists have tended not to look to the nature of economic systems, in particular the increasing hegemony of neo-liberalism, to help to explain equities and inequities in health and health care.

This chapter seeks to grapple with these issues. In the next section it is shown how placing the value system underlying equity into the hands of the community rather than individuals, in fact adopting a communitarian stance, provides the beginnings of a new and what is claimed to be a more useful paradigm for the economic analysis of equity in health and health care.

As the following section indicates, the proposed paradigm requires that questions of culture and cultural values come into play. It is also especially recognized there that the construct of health varies culturally. This discussion allows consideration of the need to preserve the diversity of cultures which can be assisted by the preservation of the diversity of economic systems. The increasing economic hegemony of neo-liberalism is tending to destroy rather than maintain different cultures.

An example is then presented of the use of the proposed paradigm. This is in the context of Australian Aboriginal health. This also includes a discussion of how citizens can be allowed and in turn encouraged to influence policy on equity. Finally, there is a brief conclusion.

Welfarism, extra-welfarism and communitarianism

I have proposed elsewhere (Mooney 1998) that a more communitarian-based approach would allow greater scope for health economists to contribute better to equity in health and health care. The theories of welfarism and extra-welfarism which currently underpin the thinking on equity of most health economists are both driven by the values of individuals as individuals. They are also consequentialist in that only outcomes or ends (rather than processes or means) are valued. Both welfarism and extra-welfarism tend also to make claims to be, and are usually interpreted as being, universalist. These problems with welfarism and extra-welfarism represent impediments to progress with equity as a more social, community or culturally based phenomenon. It is proposed that a new paradigm based on communitarianism can provide a better way for health economists to embrace equity. In particular, in the specific context of this chapter, such an approach accommodates the fact that health, health care systems and health equity are not universal in their construct or organization but are often very much culturally determined or at least influenced.

Welfarism can take different guises. It is normally argued, however, that, first, any welfare is derived by individuals as individuals and, second, such welfare is obtained only from goods or commodities. Value is obtained from welfare, which in turn is seen as involving pleasure, happiness or desire (Sen 1992). Welfarism is the basis of market economics (and neo-liberalism more specifically), where the individual consumer is seen to be sovereign and his or her willingness to pay is interpreted as a measure of the strength of preference for goods and services. Welfarism, certainly as it plays out in markets, is little, if at all, concerned with equity. This is best seen in the market's lack of concern with ability to pay and reliance only on willingness to pay as a measure of preferences.

Sen (1992) is critical of welfarism on two fronts, recognizing, first, that individuals are different in terms of their abilities to convert commodities into ways of providing themselves with wellbeing and, second, that not all have an ability to 'manage to desire' adequately. The source of valuing that Sen uses, however, remains, as with welfarism, with the individual.

The question then arises: if health economists are not to rely on what people 'manage to desire', then how are they to find out what people would desire if they were able to desire better? The fundamental issue here that Sen identifies is that welfarism is dependent on individuals' values coinciding with individuals' desires. When they do not, welfarism is left with a rather serious valuation problem.

This is an important issue. It is central to the question of equity in health care. For example, if some people do not manage to desire good health, should that position be respected by health care policy makers or should it somehow be adjusted to 'compensate' for the 'inadequate' values that emerge from such individuals? If other people do not manage to desire good health enough or if yet others are prepared to settle for a rather lower level of health than some do, or that others would if they were in the same circumstances, then what?

Culyer (1990) argued against welfarism in health care on the basis that it was only goods based. His 'extra-welfarism' opens the door to any and all *non-goods* based utility, but is still based on the values of individuals as individuals. Particularly important to Culyer's position, however, is that there is scope in extra-welfarism for some external judgment being applied as to what is to count as being able to be valued and what is not. This directly contradicts the welfarist view that it is *only* individual preferences that are to count. Culyer went on to argue that health is identified by extra-welfarists as the principal output of health care services. It turns out, in most extra-welfarist analyses, that health is considered to be the only output.

In contrast to both welfarism and extra-welfarism, communitarians place the community at the centre of their analyses and of their value system (Avineri and De-Shalit 1992). Community involves a group of people with some common life through reciprocal relationships, mutual obligations and responsibilities. Communitarianism emphasizes the social and community aspects of life, arguing in essence that life and relationships are all communally based. Identity is first and foremost a social, community-based concept. This is very different from the atomism of modern liberalism and the idea there of a disembodied self, which is echoed certainly in welfarism and to some extent also in extra-welfarism. Communitarians believe there is value in being a part of – being embodied in – the community. The philosophy allows for, indeed encourages, altruism and caring between individuals and also between different groups within a community.

Previously, I have developed the idea of 'communitarian claims' as a way of trying to address some of the problems of the individualism and universalism of both welfarism and extra-welfarism. Broome (1991) proposed that a 'claim' to a good involves a duty that a candidate for that good should in fact have it. I previously extended this idea and suggested (Mooney 1998) that the concept of communitarian claims might be helpful in deciding how best to allocate society's scarce resources in health care. Such communitarian claims 'recognise first that the duty is owed by the community of which the candidate [citizens of countries, geographic regions, health professionals, philanthropists, other funders of health care, etc.] is a member and secondly that the carrying out of this duty is not just instrumental but is good in itself', (Mooney 1998 p. 1176).

With respect to communitarian claims, it is the community as a whole that determines what constitutes a claim and what the strengths (or weights) are of different claims. The community can determine, for example, whether poor health is the sole basis for a claim on health care resources or whether the need for health maintenance could also represent a claim, as might a desire, say, for compassion for the dying and grieving through palliative care. There might be a view that building respect for autonomy in decision-making or for being informed or reassured also constitute claims over health care resources. Different groups in society would then have their overall claims to health care resources assessed on the basis of these different types of claims.

The community might thereafter determine weights for these claims. These weights are born of vertical equity and the fact that the benefits to some disadvantaged groups within the community might be weighted more highly than others even if the benefits are nominally equal. Groups who are very poor for example might have their claims over resources weighted by 1.2 and those who are poor but closer to the average by 1.1. The size of these weightings will be a function of how compassionate the community feels towards the disadvantaged.

The weighted claims would then constitute the bases on which resources would be allocated to different groups in the society. Beyond that, however, it would be for each group to decide for itself how the resources allocated to it were to be deployed.

It is important to recognize that these communitarian claims are not welfarist.

They allow the society or the community to decide who shall have access to what quantities of resources for what purposes. They accept that resources are limited and provide a community-determined mechanism for their allocation to competing groups. They are thus about community provision. There is no need strictly for the recipients to be active in 'claiming' the resources ... The claim establishes the legitimacy of [some] service for that individual (or more likely for a group into which the individual falls). The extent to which that service in practice is provided will in turn hinge on the community's judgement of the strengths of claims involved and the resources available (Mooney and Russell 2003 p. 217).

Three particular advantages perceived for communitarian claims are as follows. First, they do not require that the basis for allocation is consequentialist, which is the basis of much of health economics, both welfarism and extra-welfarism, arguing that only outcomes (or consequences) are valued. Communitarian claims allow for the possibility that processes are also valued. The society, or the community through these claims, sets the components of benefits that are to count, the relative weights to be attached to these types of benefits and the vertical equity weights for degrees of disadvantage for different subpopulations. It is then possible to form judgements about the 'capacity to benefit' of the different subpopulations (see below and Culyer 1991).

Second, the values adopted in the way that resources are allocated between different groups (e.g., different social or cultural groupings) are those of the overall community qua community. To this extent, since both welfarism and extra-welfarism are based on individuals' values, the communitarian-claims approach represents a critique of both these schools of thought. This also means (as indicated above) that an altruistic society that seeks to help the disadvantaged can do so. Significantly, too, in so far as there is benefit to the society as a whole in being or feeling altruistic – in 'doing good' if you like – this is counted as a benefit that neither welfarism or extra-welfarism can incorporate in their respective paradigms.

Third, when deciding how to use the resources that are allocated by the society to any group, it is the different groups' values that are applied to 'their' resources, i.e., the resources that have been allocated to them by the wider community or society. Thus it is the values of the poor, for example, which are used to decide how the resources allocated by society as a whole to the poor are to be deployed by and for the poor.

Culture and economic systems

When one begins to think through the underlying concern in policies on equity, especially across the globe, in addressing the issue of improving the health of the poor or the disadvantaged more generally, it becomes significant that both the construct of health and the values surrounding it are likely to vary from country to country and culture to culture. Even within countries this can happen (e.g., Aboriginal people in Australia have a different construct of health from that of non-Aboriginal Australians). Communitarian claims recognize the need to avoid paternalism, to respect the values of different cultures and thereby to promote self-esteem and, in turn, health.

It is clear that it is not possible to use a single set of values in setting objectives or weights for equity, which is, for example, what the World Health Organization did in its World Health Report (WHO 2000). The WHO used their own criteria to decide what constitutes a good health-care system. Further, they adopted a single set of weights, their, i.e. WHO's, weights to decide how important equity was to be in different member countries. In fact, all member countries were deemed to weight equity equally. This is WHO elitism and universalism on a global scale.

Communitarian claims are based on the idea that it is for the community as a whole to decide on what basis and according to which weights resources for health care should be allocated to different groups. Once such allocations are made, it is then for the different subcommunities or cultural groupings to decide how to use the resources that have been allocated to them and to do this according to *their* values and to *their* construct of health.

For this paradigm to prevail, there is a need to protect local cultures – which many might argue is a worthwhile end in itself. Such protection will foster self-esteem in communities and societies. That, in turn, can have a positive impact on population health. The destruction of local culture – as is apparent in the context of indigenous health in many countries – can be a major factor leading to poor health in those affected.

As Adams (2004 p. 283) indicates: 'Health is a product of social, economic, political, and religious social structures that are themselves shaped and constituted culturally and in contested political terrain.' Health economists have ignored this cultural dimension.

In doing so it may be that they are simply following Western medical models, which 'tend to prioritise the physical and material contours of health ... and to treat cultural phenomena as extraneous,' (Adams 2004 p. 284). It may be more cynical than that, as Adams suggests in another context. 'The marginalisation of cultural issues may be a result of the fact that focussing on "culture" makes visible the ways in which groups of people become incomparable,' (Adams 2004 p. 283). Health economics is conducted primarily within the dominant hegemonic culture and other cultures tend to go 'unseen'. As Shiva (1998) states: 'The dominant [Western cultural] system is also a local system ... It is merely the globalised version of a very local and parochial tradition.'

The best defence of diversity of culture is diversity of economic systems, allied to strong and just social institutions to promote social justice. It follows that there is a need for much greater community autonomy (see below) both for the world community and for local communities. There is a problem here, not solely of the neo-liberalism of globalization, but of the hegemony of neo-liberalism as an economic system.

Where economics comes to the fore here is in the risk that neo-liberalism, which is not neutral in terms of values, or ideologically neutral or, importantly, culturally neutral, endangers the prospects for the diversity of economic systems. Current moves to build a monoeconomic-system world, through the hegemony of neo-liberalism, foster, in turn, a monocultural world. It behoves economists, including health economists, to recognize this and to try first to analyze and second to counter this threat in the interest of promoting population health.

The proposed paradigm for health economics as outlined in the previous section is a macroscopic one based on an expanded version of the social determinants of health and social capital. It points to the need to accept the links between culture and health; between economic systems and culture; and hence the need to allow peoples to be comfortable in their own cultures. That implies respecting the legitimacy of different cultures, protecting the diversity of cultures and, in turn, protecting the diversity of economic systems to allow diversity of cultures to be maintained.

It is a function of neo-liberalism that we have such a dominance of individualism in Western society. Such individualism leaves little room for the building of compassionate societies and, in turn, equitable social institutions. It is given sustenance in the smugness of Francis Fukuyama (1992) in *The End of History*. There he argued that neo-liberalism and the market represent the summit of social and political endeavour. There is, he suggests, nothing better.

Neo-liberalism is, in essence, the acceptance of the ideology of the marketplace, indeed the promotion of the market, in all or as many as possible areas of society. It is opposed to government in all but its most essential aspects and looks to government instead to stay out of the sphere of economic influence. As an ideology it 'asserts that economic growth is by definition good for everyone and that economic performance is optimized when governments refrain from interfering in markets . . . for the good of all citizens, governments should grant the greatest possible autonomy to individual market actors – companies in particular' (Millen *et al.* 2000 p. 7).

The social determinants of health and the theory underlying social capital tell us that individualism and disengagement are bad for our health. One example: in the decade following introduction of the individualism of the market economy in Russia, the resultant excess deaths were equivalent to the numbers killed in Stalin's purges in the thirties (Chomsky 2003). At the still broader level of social institutions and ideologies in a comparative international framework, looking at the WTO for example and its impact on health globally, while this would seem to be important, yet again health economists have been largely absent from the scene.

It is, however, not just that rich nations do not care about the poor; there are elements of exploitation as well. For example, Rosenberg (2002 p. 28) brings out the problems for the poor of the laws that surround patenting, which give rise to 'intellectual property rules that require poor nations to honour drug patents [that] will result in a transfer of $40 billion a year from poor countries to corporations in the developed world.'

The difficulties that neo-liberalism creates in this context stem from the fact that neo-liberalism encourages inequality. This is most obvious in the workplace with the erosion of unions, the increased casualization of the workforce and increasing lack of job security in neo-liberal economies. It can be argued that neo-liberalism not only breeds inequality but needs inequality. It is anti-equity.

There is a need to seek diversity in forms of economic systems and, in particular, to build on those alternative models that already exist. Some of these operate at the level of the nation state. Those that spring to mind immediately are Cuba and the Scandinavian countries. Others are more local, such as the communitarianism of the Mondragón co-operative economy in the Basque region of Spain, which is based on mutuality and sharing, and the Grameen microcredit banking system in the Indian subcontinent, where credit is seen as a human right.

There has been all too little interest by health economists (indeed by health researchers in general) in the Cuban health services and Cuban health. As Cooper *et al.* (2006 p. 217) identify, 'The biomedical literature in English has been almost entirely silent on the Cuban experience.' It may well be that the success of the Cuban health services and society (for some of the equity benefits arise from the social determinants of health in Cuba) is too embarrassing and points up the failings of the neo-liberal societies' health policies.

Again, as Aviva Chomsky (2000 p. 333) notes: 'The Cuban revolution's commitment to the health of the country's population is notable in several respects. First, the government understands health to be the responsibility of the state. Second, the government approaches health as a social issue that includes health-care delivery but is far from limited to it. Thus, the state is responsible not only for building, maintaining and ensuring universal access to doctors, clinics and hospitals, but also for guaranteeing and sustaining the social conditions necessary for health: universal access to education, food, and employment.' There are macroscopic messages here for health economics, even global ones.

Navarro (2000) shows that, in the European Union, it has been possible for some governments, primarily the Scandinavians, to 'throw off' the ties of globalization and follow their own road. What is crucial in Navarro's analysis is that, where this has happened, there have been strong institutions which have provided the framework to allow this. He continues that among these institutions, 'A key element is the existence of a social pact between employers and unions and the government.'

This theme is picked up independently by Drèze and Sen (1989). They argue that avoiding hunger requires analysis not just of food intake but also, 'The person's access to health care, medical facilities, elementary education, drinking water and sanitary facilities.' While again it would be possible to see these purely in resource terms or to 'commodify' them, their argument is based on the premise of the need to have or to create the social institutions to allow these other aspects to be present and indeed to allow such a philosophy to underpin public policy. Just social institutions are again critical.

What is potentially problematical with respect to this view of the possible road to avoiding the neo-liberal excesses of the market forces of globalization is that many poor countries have weak social institutions. Nonetheless, the links between market economics, globalization, increased poverty and worsening distribution of income are such that there is here at least the recognition that there is a way out, not necessarily in economic development per se but in an economic development that respects and fosters the culture of the society which is being developed. This is important for the nature of society in terms of the social determinants of health and, in turn, for equity in health.

Current neo-liberal globalization is leading to resource allocation, income and power in individual countries being dominated by the laws of the neo-classical marketplace. This is most likely to result in the continuing neglect of the standard of living and, in turn, the health of the world's poorest. Sen's thinking on building strong institutions can mean not only that the benefits from globalization are obtained but that they are distributed more fairly across rich and poor.

There is a need to embrace what is best described as social or community autonomy. It has been argued that, '[a]ccording to this principle [of community autonomy] it makes no sense to claim either that we are autonomous beings and the society ought simply to protect our right to act in accordance with this innate gift or that the values expressed in our preferences or choices are our personal creations. Values are common, they are embodied in concrete exemplars of ideal patterns of action which regulate any human community. Our whole moral language – and our ethical concepts of rights and obligations – are acquired in social contexts, as ways of characterising and assessing relationships of power and dependence between individuals' (Jensen and Mooney 1990 p. 11). This social or community autonomy is supported by the Hegelian concept of freedom, where social institutions play a pivotal role (Muller 2003). Such community autonomy stands in juxtaposition to its individual, neo-liberal counterpart, particularly as that latter entity manifests itself in today's market economy.

Applying the paradigm

The communitarian paradigm suggested here is one that, while it is applicable to problems of equitable resource allocation generally, will make most difference as compared with RAWP-type formulations where three considerations apply. First, there are different cultural groupings. Second, there are substantial variations in health across different groupings. And third, there are different reasons for, or causes of, ill health across the different groupings. Here, I examine one particular application – equitable resource allocation between Aboriginal and non-Aboriginal Australians. Thereafter I want to report briefly on how the process of establishing values in support of communitarian claims might proceed.

The health of Aboriginal people is very poor and life expectancy is about 20 years behind that of non-Aboriginal Australians. Lying behind these statistics are historical facts, perpetuated today by important links between economics and culture and culture and health.

An added factor is the racism that is present in Australian society. At an institutional level this inhibits access to health care for Aboriginal people (Henry *et al.* 2004). It highlights the need to create more culturally secure services to promote equity in health and health care.

Such racism is also present in the personal lives of Aboriginal Australians. That almost certainly adds to their health problems, as has been recently demonstrated in New Zealand for Maori. There, for example, (Harris *et al.* 2006 p. 1435) 'self-reported experience of discrimination is associated with various measures of poor health for all ethnic groups, independent of socio-economic position'. Maori are particularly affected.

Culture is important to all people. It is the attempts by white colonial Australia and its racist equivalent today to destroy Aboriginal culture and, in turn, Aboriginal identity that are primarily to blame for the poor state of Aboriginal health.

Most Aboriginal people have a different world-view from other Australians. They have a much more communitarian set of values than Western society. They also have a different construct of health which is not only holistic within an individual but holistic in their community. This involves *inter alia* certain obligations between people in looking after each other's health. Further it embraces not only physical wellbeing but also cultural security, good environment and being poverty-free (Houston 2004).

It would be difficult given such a very different definition of health from that of other Australians to argue for some 'RAWP' type resource allocation formula (DHSS 1976) where health status and, in turn, health need are measured in one single universal way. Communitarian claims, however, allow more than one construct of health as well as other considerations to come into play in deciding on allocations between Aboriginal and non-Aboriginal.

Taking this case as an example, the proposed paradigm has the capacity to help in determining, first, what values or principles the community wants to underpin its health service and, next, what benefits it seeks from its health service. Notice immediately that the emphasis is on the health service being a social institution, i.e., it is the community's health service in the sense that it is for them, the community, to say what values they want to drive health services and what benefits they as citizens want from their health service; in other words what the 'social good' is that they want improved through the use of scarce health care resources. Questions the paradigm throws up include what characteristics of subpopulations will constitute a claim over health care resources, beyond health status (which of course will constitute a claim over resources in any health service). Does patient or community autonomy matter to the community? Does good patient information about service availability count with the community? The claims then have to be weighted according to the preferences of the community regarding how they see equity and the strengths of their desires to help disadvantaged groups as compared with groups which are better-off.

One way of eliciting these claims is through deliberative democracy such as with citizens' juries, four of which have been facilitated by the author on health issues in Western Australia (WA). Such juries comprise randomly selected citizens brought together to reflect on certain issues, presented with relevant information from experts whom they can quiz, and then given time to reflect on the sorts of principles, values or, perhaps, priorities they would want for, say, their health service.

The 'claims' that a jury in Perth in WA (Mooney and Blackwell 2004) sought to take into account in their assessment of how to allocate resources were health, age and remoteness. (The jury were, however, not presented with information about the different cultural constructs of health as, ideally, they should have been.) Additionally, they set out some key principles they wanted to bring to bear on issues of equity. Thus, first and foremost, they were strongly of the view that it was the job of citizens rather than others (such as doctors or health service administrators) to determine what constitutes equity; second, that barriers to be lowered to improve equity should include cultural barriers; and third, the equity definition they endorsed involved vertical equity, thereby expressing a preference for positive discrimination for disadvantaged people. They classified the poor and Aboriginal people as disadvantaged and, as a result, wanted their claims weighted more highly than those of others.

These citizens were very much in favour of involving the community and its values in health and health care policy. They went further and advocated such involvement. They also recognized cultural differences in both health per se and barriers to access to health care. They further acknowledged the value of the health care system as a social institution.

It is also noteworthy that, while no efforts were made to assess this explicitly, nonetheless it is highly likely that the jurists, as a group representing the community, came to a different set of claims and different weights than if they had been approached separately as individuals and their responses aggregated together. It was also clear in this and subsequent citizens' juries in Western Australia that the randomly selected jurists, asked to represent the community, were almost bursting with pride to do so. Nearly all the citizens in all four juries endorsed the process and were keen to be involved, if approached to do so, in further similar work in the future. There is thus some evidence, tentative as of now, that citizens get benefit from the process of playing this role of representing the community. This suggests that an important strand of communitarian claims, as opposed to simply community values, is present in this process, i.e, as quoted above, 'that the carrying out of this duty [of determining claims] is not just instrumental but is good in itself,' (Mooney 1998).

Thus, such deliberative democracy can assist in establishing communitarian claims. It is through the determining of these claims that the nature of the components of benefit is to be defined. These will assuredly include health; probably not as the size of the problem as in the conventional formulation of resource allocation formulae, but rather as capacity for health benefit as originally advocated by Culyer (1991) and with no requirement that the construct of health be constant across all social groupings.

In considering how to apply the new approach, there is a need, after the elicitation of what constitutes claims, to address two questions:

(a) In any geographical area or jurisdiction, what is the capacity to benefit of the people in the area (where the nature of benefit is defined by the relevant community or society overall) with the health service resources available?

(b) Might there be a desire on the part of the community to weight some people's claims more highly than others, thus, for example, weighting nominally equal benefits to some group or groups higher than to others, i.e, vertical equity?

It is to be emphasized that the first of these is concerned with the question of improvement, i.e., doing better, in essence working with whatever concept of benefit is agreed by the community or society at large. How best to measure capacity to benefit remains for debate. In the context of work done for the Indigenous Funding Inquiry for the Commonwealth Grants Commission (2001), it was argued by key representatives of the communities concerned in Western Australia that capacity to benefit was greatest where the most efficient interventions lay, i.e., in environmental health such as air pollution. It was further argued that the second greatest marginal return was likely to be in social health (i.e., where ill health is a result of social circumstances such as land dispossession or social inequalities) and thirdly, the return would be lowest in trying to change individual behaviour (such as diet) which was having adverse effects on health (see

Houston 2004). Additionally, however, there is scope for claims being based on any other factors deemed relevant by the society at large. (How transferable these considerations are to other populations remains to be researched.)

The second component involves a weighting factor for capacity to benefit. This reflects the idea of vertical equity, that according to social preferences, the value attached to nominally equal benefits may be different, depending on who the recipients are. What should constitute 'disadvantage' in this context is also best determined according to the preferences of the community or society. It is then for the relevant society to decide, according to their preferences, the relative weights to be attached to different degrees of disadvantage. In Australia, for example, as between Aboriginal and non-Aboriginal benefits of health care, in various community surveys weights of between 1.2 and 2.5 have been suggested (Mooney 2000).

Conclusion

Freire (1996) in *Pedagogy of the Oppressed* advocates what he calls 'problem-posing education'. He states that in this, 'People develop their power to perceive critically the way they exist in the world with which and in which they find themselves; they come to see the world not as a static reality, but as a reality in process, in transformation . . . [both students and teachers] reflect simultaneously on themselves and the world without dichotomizing this reflection from action, and thus establish an authentic form of thought and action.'

If there is to be a move towards a community autonomy, which can signal a new form of freedom, there is a need, not just for the oppressed, but for everybody, to adopt a problem-posing concept of education to support a new political economy. Thus, in addition to the diversity of economic systems, we need education of the world citizenry along the lines that Freire advocated, allowing people to 'develop their power to perceive critically the way they exist in the world with which and in which they find themselves'. This represents a recognition of the need to move to a political economy that is based more on a clear set of principles established by the relevant communities and the development of the power of communities rather than markets and the erosion of the power of citizens qua citizens. Freire's call is one that has echoes of Hegel's support of social institutions (Muller 2003) but with the emphasis in Freire very much on critical education as a social institution.

An alternative health economics paradigm for equity is needed. It might be based on communitarian economics, building on the notions of social capital and the social determinants of health. In essence it must build on community as opposed to individual values arguing that health services and population health are first and foremost social institutions.

Citizens want to be engaged. Communities do want more autonomy for themselves. Citizens are not stupid; treat them responsibly and they act responsibly.

As Dowbar (1997 p. 8), the Brazilian development economist, argues: 'To the extent that there is a certain gap between the rich and the poor, markets become segmented, and a large part of the world's population is simply kept at the margin of the central process of wealth accumulation led by transnational corporations. The end of all hope for trickling down means that, structurally speaking, neo-liberalism does not respond to modern challenges.'

This is the message that I have tried to convey in the context of a new health economics approach to equity. The microeconomics of health care matters but for those who seek to make a difference to the health of disadvantaged people to think about economic development in terms of cultures and social institutions is important. The social determinants of health and issues around social capital need a major injection of health economics research in the poorer countries of the world. The impact of globalization on health equity and especially of the effects of the hegemony of neo-liberalism need to be researched. The links between economic systems and culture and between culture and health have, to date, barely appeared on the health economics research agenda.

The way forward here is addressed by Sen (2001). It is to build a caring world and especially caring governments and caring institutions. He argues that while economic progress can yield health benefits to a population, 'much depends on how the income generated by economic growth is used,' and even in poor economies, 'major health improvements can be achieved through using the available resources in a socially productive way.' Sen's message is, as ever, optimistic but it does require that governments be good, caring and compassionate, believing that they can be a force for building a better society for the poor and not just a facilitator for market forces to hold sway or a mediator for the worst excesses of modern capitalism.

Paulo Freire's reasoning revolved around a very simple but today much neglected construct: human solidarity. In our search in health economics to try to make a difference in equity, we need to accept the importance of culture, social institutions, the social determinants of health, social capital and the ideas of communitarianism – what Freire calls human solidarity.

REFERENCES

Adams, V. (2004) Equity of the ineffable: cultural and political constraints on ethnomedicine as a health problem in contemporary Tibet. In Anand, S. Peter, F. and Sen, A., eds, *Public Health, Ethics and Equity*. Oxford: Oxford University Press. pp. 283–305.

Avineri, S. and De-Shalit, A. (1992) Introduction. In Avineri, S. and De-Shalit, A., eds, *Communitarianism and Individualism*. Oxford: Oxford University Press. pp. 1–11.

Broome, J. (1991) *Weighing Goods*. Oxford: Basil Blackwell.

Chomsky, A. (2000) The threat of a good example: health and revolution in Cuba. In Kim, J. Y., Millen, J. V., Irwin, A. and Gersham, J., eds, *Dying for Growth: Global Inequality and the Health of the Poor*. Monroe, ME: Common Courage Press. pp. 331–357.

Chomsky, N. (2003) *Hegemony or Survival*. New York: Henry Holt.

Commonwealth Grants Commission (2001) *Report on Indigenous Funding*. Canberra: Commonwealth of Australia.

Cooper, R. S. Kennelly, J. F. and Ordunez-Garcia, P. (2006) Health in Cuba. *International Journal of Epidemiology*. **35**: 817–24.

Culyer, A. J. (1990) *Demand-Side Socialism and Health Care*. Keynote paper presented at the Second World Congress on Health Economics. Zurich: University of Zurich.

Culyer, A. J. (1991) *Equity in Health Care Policy*. Paper prepared for the Ontario Premier's Council on Health, Well-being and Social Justice. Toronto: University of Toronto.

DHSS (1976) *The RAWP Report. Resource Allocation Working Party. Sharing Resources for Health in England*. London: HMSO.

Dowbar, L. (1997) Preface. In Freire, P. *Pedagogy of the Heart*. New York: Continuum Publishing.

Drèze, J. and Sen, A. (1989) *Hunger and Public Action*. Oxford: Oxford University Press.

Freire, P. (1996) *Pedagogy of the Oppressed*. New York: Continuum Publishing.

Fukuyama, F. (1992) *The End of History*. New York: Simon and Schuster.

Harris, R., Tobias, M., Jeffreys, M. *et al.* (2006) Racism and health: the relationship between experience of racial discrimination and health in New Zealand. *Social Science and Medicine*. **63**(6): 1428–1441.

Henry, B., Houston, S. and Mooney, G. (2004) Institutional racism in Australian health care: a plea for decency. *Medical Journal of Australia* **180**(10): 517–520.

Houston, S. (2004) Aboriginal Health Policy: the Past, the Present, the Future. *Ph.D. thesis*. Perth: Curtin University.

Jensen, U. J. and Mooney, G. (1990) Changing values: autonomy and paternalism in medicine and health care. In Jensen, U. J. and Mooney, G., eds, *Changing Values in Medical and Health Care Decision Making*. New York: John Wiley. pp. 1–15.

Millen, J. V., Irwin, A. and Kim, J. Y. (2000) Introduction: What is growing? Who is dying? In Kim, J. M., Millen, J. V., Irwin, A. and Gersham, J., eds, *Dying for Growth*. Monroe, Maine: Common Courage Press.

Mooney, G. (1998) Communitarian claims as an ethical basis for allocating health care resources. *Social Science and Medicine*, **47**(9): 1171–1180.

Mooney, G. (2000) Vertical equity in health care resource allocation. *Health Care Analysis*. **8**(3): 203–215.

Mooney, G. (2001) Communitarianism and health economics. In Davis, J., ed., *The Social Economics of Health Care*. London: Routledge. pp. 24–42.

Mooney, G. and Blackwell, S. (2004) Whose health service is it anyway? *Medical Journal of Australia*. **180**: 76–78.

Mooney, G. and Russell, E. (2003) Equity in health care: the need for a new economics paradigm. In Scott, A., Maynard, A. and Elliott, R., eds, *Advances in Health Economics*. Chichester: Wiley.

Muller, J. Z. (2003) *The Mind and the Market, Capitalism in Western Thought*. New York: Anchor Books.

Navarro, V. (2000) Are pro-welfare state and full-employment policies possible in the era of globalization? *International Journal of Health Services*. **30**(2): 231–251.

Rosenberg, T. (2002) Globalization; the free trade fix. *New York Times*. (August 18): 28.

Sen, A. (1992) *Inequality Re-examined*. Oxford: Clarendon Press.

Sen, A. (2001) Economic progress and health. In Leon, D. and Walt, G., eds, *Poverty Inequality and Health*. Oxford: Oxford University Press. pp. 333–345.

Shiva, V. (1998) *Monocultures of the Mind*. www.resartis.org/index.php?id=74.

UNDP (1999) *Human Development Report*. New York: OUP.

WHO (2000) *World Health Report 2000*. Geneva: WHO.

5

Beware of the libertarian wolf in the clothing of the egalitarian sheep: an essay on the need to clarify ends and means

Alan Maynard

Summary

Ideologies permeate policy debates in health care. However, they do so in an implicit manner and the combatants rarely reveal their underlying objectives. Typically, in both public and private health care systems, policy makers focus on expenditure control and efficiency, paying lip-service to equity issues. A focus on efficiency is clearly merited, as many health care interventions have no evidence base; there are large variations in clinical practice, which have been well evidenced and ignored for decades. Furthermore there is an absence of outcome measurement and evidence that consumers' health is improved by expensive health care systems.

Political frustration about the inefficiency of health care enables policy advocates holding competing libertarian and egalitarian perspectives to debate reform as if it were ideologically neutral. Libertarians seek economic and social structures that maximize individual freedom, minimize the role of government and ensure that health care is delivered by market-orientated insurers and providers. Egalitarians seek to maximize equality of opportunity. They regard government as a means by which the inequalities of market provision and finance can be reduced to provide real opportunities for all, and in particular the disadvantaged.

Reform debates in socialized health care systems are characterized by libertarians advocating reforms to increase individual freedom and undermine equality. In more libertarian systems, the egalitarians seek reforms to increase equality and circumscribe the freedom of the advantaged to experience better care. Rarely do the combatants reveal their ideological preferences. Egalitarians should beware libertarian wolves posing in sheep's clothing.

Introduction

Government intervention in the market for health care has usually been precipitated by concerns about inequity and its effects. The 1911 National Insurance Act

The Economics of Health Equity, ed. Di McIntyre and Gavin Mooney. Published by Cambridge University Press. © Cambridge University Press 2007.

in Britain was, in part, caused by the poor health of potential recruits to fight for 'King and Country' in the South African Boer War. One of Bismarck's concerns when he pushed through health care legislation a quarter of a century earlier was to ensure fit recruits for the German armed forces and for the burgeoning economy. Currently in China the drive for health care reform is based on the desire for a fit population for its army and its industrial revolution, and the concern that the lack of access to basic health care for hundreds of millions in rural areas may also precipitate not only inadequate control of infectious diseases but also social unrest.

Most developed countries now place relatively little emphasis on equity, believing too complacently that inequalities will be resolved by increased affluence (the trickle-down thesis), increased resourcing of health care and a focus on improving efficiency in the provision of care. Such policies tend to mask long-standing inequalities in health, e.g., the Blair reforms in the UK have increased spending by 85% in the last seven years and involved an avalanche of largely evidence-free reforms targeted at improving system efficiency (Maynard and Street 2006), but there is little evidence that health inequalities are declining (e.g., Shaw *et al.* 2005).

This lack of progress in reducing health inequity is unsurprising as even if the distribution of health care utilization were equalized, the impact on health inequalities might be small. If governments were really concerned about reducing health inequalities, they would redistribute other social goods (e.g., income and education), which would probably have a greater impact in terms of health production (Maynard and Sheldon 2002). The reluctance to adopt potentially more effective methods of equalizing health status is, in part, a reflection of current political rhetoric that limits such 'social engineering', a conventional, often evidence-free, view that deems the public sector to be inherently 'bad', owing to its inefficiency (much of which often mirrors the defects of the private sector as epitomized by Enron in the USA and Marconi in the UK) and the reluctance of governments to tax for fear of losing political supporters, who are reputedly enamoured with a 'low tax' philosophy.

These political maxims are a product of long established but often implicit ideological values, initially set out nicely by Donabedian (1970). The two competing ideological positions are outlined in the next section and Tables 5.1 to 5.3. This is followed by a brief analysis of market failures or ubiquitous inefficiencies in health care systems worldwide and the continuous reinvention of often evidence-free advocacy of market-orientated 'solutions' to these problems. The final section addresses the issue of how, given these imperfections in health care delivery, market-type mechanisms can be developed without undermining the equity goals of egalitarian health care systems.

The contention of this chapter is that the focus of the health care industry worldwide is on spending more, with lip-service being paid to improving system efficiency and virtually no real, rather than rhetorical, concern for equity. This rewards powerful health care providers such as the professions and the pharmaceutical industry but does not necessarily produce improved population health, let alone reduce lifetime differences in health status between different social groups. Furthermore, it seems that some libertarian notions have captured decision makers in largely egalitarian health systems and diverted their attention away from the goals of improving equity in health care and health and towards spending on health care. This occurs despite the fact that spending on health care may exhibit diminishing returns in terms of producing health and may not be consistent with ideological goals.

Defining and adopting ideological positions

The policy debate about social provision internationally is permeated with covert ideological values. The egalitarian and libertarian perspectives are both legitimate but, in health care and other 'public' marketplaces, the policy debate often takes place as if values were irrelevant, or did not exist. In fact, they permeate all policy exchanges. Also, they determine the choice of means by which the priorities of the competing ideologies are best achieved. These are set out in Tables 5.1 to 5.3.

The crucial distinction between the egalitarians and the libertarians is different maximands in their utility functions. The libertarian's primary focus is on freedom of choice, regarding health care as part of the reward system of society that should be distributed according to willingness and ability to pay. The goal of the egalitarian is equality of opportunity; where access to care is determined by social judgements about need, i.e., in health care the relative ability of competing patients to benefit in terms of health per unit of cost.

In pursuing their primary goal of freedom of choice, the libertarians prefer and advocate minimal government intervention and regulation and low levels of taxation. Such policies leave money in citizens' pockets, with the freedom to spend it how it suits them, rather than government. Libertarians regard markets as essential means of defending and augmenting freedom. They continually espouse the utopian ideals of perfect competition with free market entry and exit for providers where the supply of goods and services is determined by the preferences expressed in open marketplaces by consumers. They tend to underplay market imperfections and the ubiquitous problems of cartelization and monopolies, which undermine competitive markets. For the libertarians, the problem of the poor and disadvantaged is ideally dealt with by charitable institutions when their own resources are exhausted. Individuals should be self-sufficient as such independence encourages thrift and economic progress.

Table 5.1. Attitudes typically associated with viewpoints A and B

	Viewpoint A (libertarian)	Viewpoint B (egalitarian)
Personal responsibility	Personal responsibility for achievement is very important, and this is weakened if people are offered unearned rewards. Moreover, such unearned rewards weaken the motive force that assures economic wellbeing and in so doing they also undermine moral wellbeing, because of the intimate connection between moral wellbeing and the personal effort to achieve.	Personal incentives to achieve are desirable, but economic failure is not equated with moral depravity or social worthlessness.
Social concern	Social Darwinism dictates a seemingly cruel indifference to the fate of those who cannot make the grade. A less extreme position is that charity, expressed and effected preferably under private auspices, is the proper vehicle, but it needs to be exercised under carefully prescribed conditions, for example, such that the potential recipient must first mobilize all his own resources and, when helped, must not be in as favourable a position as those who are self-supporting (the principle of 'lesser eligibility').	Private charitable action is not rejected but is seen as potentially dangerous morally (because it is often demeaning to the recipient and corrupting to the donor) and usually inequitable. It seems preferable to establish social mechanisms that create and sustain self-sufficiency and that are accessible according to precise rules concerning entitlement that are applied equitably and explicitly sanctioned by society at large.
Freedom	Freedom is to be sought as a supreme good in itself. Compulsion attenuates both personal responsibility and individualistic and voluntary expressions of social concern. Centralized health planning and a large governmental role in health care financing are seen as an unwarranted abridgement of the freedom of clients as well as of health professionals, and private medicine is thereby viewed as a bulwark against totalitarianism.	Freedom is seen as the presence of real opportunities of choice; although economic constraints are less openly coercive than political constraints, they are nonetheless real and often the effective limits on choice. Freedom is not indivisible but may be sacrificed in one respect in order to obtain greater freedom in some other. Government is not an external threat to individuals in the society but is the means by which individuals achieve greater scope for action (that is, greater real freedom).
Equality	Equality before the law is the key concept, with clear precedence being given to freedom over equality wherever the two conflict.	Since the only moral justification for using personal achievement as the basis for distributing rewards is that everyone has equal opportunities for such achievement, then the main emphasis is on equality of opportunity; where this cannot be assured, the moral worth of achievement is thereby undermined. Equality is seen as an extension to the many of the freedom actually enjoyed by only the few.

Table 5.2. Idealized health care systems

	Private	Public
Demand	1. Individuals are the best judges of their own welfare. 2. Priorities are determined by own willingness and ability to pay. 3. Erratic and potentially catastrophic nature of demand mediated by private insurance. 4. Matters of equity to be dealt with elsewhere (e.g., in the tax and social security systems).	1. When ill, individuals are frequently imperfect judges of their own welfare. 2. Priorities are determined by social judgements about need. 3. Erratic and potentially catastrophic nature of demand made irrelevant by provision of free services. 4. Since the distribution of income and wealth is unlikely to be equitable in relation to the need for health care, the system must be insulated from its influence.
Supply	1. Profit is the proper and effective way to motivate suppliers to respond to the needs of demanders. 2. Priorities are determined by people's willingness and ability to pay and by the costs of meeting their wishes at the margin. 3. Suppliers have strong incentive to adopt least-cost methods of provision.	1. Professional ethics and dedication to public service are the appropriate motivation, focusing on success in curing or caring. 2. Priorities are determined by where the greatest improvements in caring or curing can be effected at the margin. 3. Predetermined limit on available resources generates a strong incentive for suppliers to adopt least-cost methods of provision.
Adjustment mechanism	1. Many competing suppliers ensure that offer prices are kept low and reflect costs. 2. Well-informed consumers are able to seek out the most cost-effective form of treatment for themselves. 3. If, at the price that clears the market, medical practice is profitable, more people will go into medicine and hence supply will be responsive to demand. 4. If, conversely, medical practice is unremunerative, people will leave it, or stop entering it, until the system returns to equilibrium.	1. Central review of activities generates efficiency audit of service provision and management pressures keep the system cost-effective. 2. Well-informed clinicians are able to prescribe the most cost-effective form of treatment for each patient. 3. If there is resulting pressure on some facilities or specialties, resources will be directed towards extending them. 4. Facilities or specialties on which pressure is slack will be slimmed down to release resources for other uses.
Success criteria	1. Consumers will judge the system by their ability to get someone to do what they demand, when, where and how they want it. 2. Producers will judge the system by how good a living they can make out of it.	1. Electorate judges the system by the extent to which it improves the health status of the population at large in relation to the resources allocated to it. 2. Producers judge the system by its ability to enable them to provide the treatments they believe to be cost-effective.

Table 5.3. Actual health care systems

	Private	Public
Demand	5. Doctors act as agents, mediating demand on behalf of consumers.	5. Doctors act as agents, identifying need on behalf of patients.
	6. Priorities are determined by the reimbursement rules of insurance funds.	6. Priorities are determined by the doctor's own professional situation, by his assessment of the patient's condition and the expected trouble-making proclivities of the patient.
	7. Because private insurance coverage is itself a profit-seeking activity, some risk rating is inevitable; hence, coverage is incomplete and uneven, distorting personal willingness and ability to pay.	7. Freedom from direct financial contributions at the point of service and absence of risk rating enables patients to seek treatment for trivial or inappropriate conditions.
	8. Attempts to change the distribution of income and wealth independently are resisted as destroying incentives (one of which is the ability to buy better or more medical care if you are rich).	8. Attempts to correct inequities in the social and economic system by differential compensatory access to health services leads to recourse to health care in circumstances where it is unlikely to be a cost-effective solution to the problem.
Supply	4. What is most profitable to suppliers may not be what is most in the interests of consumers and since neither consumers nor suppliers may be very clear about what is in consumers' interests, this gives suppliers a range of discretion.	4. Personal professional dedication and public-spirited motivation likely to be corroded and degenerate into cynicism if others, who do not share those feelings, are seen to be doing very well for themselves through blatantly self-seeking behaviour.
	5. Priorities are determined by the extent to which consumers can be induced to part with their money and by the costs of satisfying the pattern of 'demand'.	5. Priorities are determined by what gives the greatest professional satisfaction.
	6. Profit motive generates a strong incentive towards market segmentation and price discrimination and tie-in agreements with other professionals.	6. Since cost-effectiveness is not accepted as a proper medical responsibility, such pressures merely generate tension between the 'professionals' and the 'managers'.
Adjustment mechanism	5. Professional, ethical rules are used to make overt competition difficult.	5. Because it does not need elaborate cost data for billing purposes, it does not routinely generate much useful information on costs.
	6. Consumers are denied information about quality and competence and, since insured, may collude with doctors (against the insurance carriers) in inflating costs.	6. Clinicians know little about costs and have no direct incentive to act on such information as they have – and sometimes quite perverse incentives

Table 5.3. (cont.)

	Private	Public
	7. Entry into the profession made difficult and numbers restricted to maintain profitability. 8. If demand for services falls, doctors extend range of activities and push out neighbouring disciplines.	(i.e., cutting costs may make life more difficult or less rewarding for them). 7. Very little is known about the relative cost-effectiveness of different treatments and, even where it is, doctors are wary of acting on such information until a general professional consensus emerges. 8. The phasing out of facilities that have become redundant is difficult because it often threatens the livelihood of some concentrated specialized group and has identifiable people dependent on it, whereas the beneficiaries are dispersed and can only be identified as statistics.
Success criteria	3. Consumers will judge the system by their ability to get someone to do what they need done without making them 'medically indigent' or changing their risk rating too adversely. 4. Producers will judge the system by how good a living they can make out of it.	3. Since the easiest aspect of health status to measure is life expectancy, the discussion is dominated by mortality data and mortality risks to the detriment of treatments concerned with non-life-threatening situations. 4. In the absence of accurate data on cost-effectiveness, producers judge the system by the extent to which it enables them to carry out the treatments that they find the most exciting and satisfying.

Libertarian antipathy to government arises from their belief that unearned rewards erode individual and social motivation for improvement. Government intervention in the financing and provision of health care are seen as unacceptable reductions in the freedom of patients as well as health professionals. Thus, libertarians regard private medicine as a bulwark against the totalitarian tendencies of the state. The diversity private activity brings erodes the state's ability to determine the workings of markets.

In Britain currently these views are epitomized by a privately funded 'think-tank' called 'Reform', whose leading advocates are the health economist Nick Bosanquet and the cancer specialist Karol Sikora (www.reform.co.uk) Libertarian think-tanks, including Reform, are usually generously funded by private institutions, in particular the pharmaceutical industry, not only because the think-tanks' aims are consistent with their ideological values but also because unregulated markets and policy instruments (e.g., co-payments) break down expenditure controls such as capped budgets and cash limits. Thus, Reform is chaired by the former Chief Executive of Glaxo, who is now a London University Principal. The financial reforms they advocate would allow the more affluent to exercise their superior buying power and undermine equity.

Whilst the libertarian groups continue to advocate the erosion of public health care systems in their pursuit of freedom of choice, the egalitarians continue to defend their institutions. For this group there is a preference to develop and sustain self-sufficiency by creating efficient social institutions which patients and consumers can access according to explicit and equitable rules of entitlement. For egalitarians, government has to intervene to create real opportunities for the population to exercise choice and is seen as the vehicle whereby choice available to the few is extended to the many.

The logic of the egalitarian viewpoint is that social allocation mechanisms are required in health care. These are based on need, defined as the patient's capacity to benefit per unit of cost (Williams 1974). The application of the need principle in public health care systems requires the ranking of competing therapies in terms of their cost-effectiveness and the targeting of resources at those interventions that give the greatest health gain per unit of cost. With such an allocation mechanism in place, available resources would achieve the largest possible population health gain from the available budget (Maynard 1997). In those health care systems where such a goal is explicit it was initially pursued by attempts to equalize financial capacity to fund health care (e.g., the English Resource Allocation Working Party (RAWP) formula (DHSS 1976), in a capitated formula weighted by differences in local mortality and other indicators of need.

Whilst Donabedian's polarization of the competing ideologies gives a clear definition of competing viewpoints, in most health care systems the dominant ideology has to admit some role for its competing alternative to protect the rights of minorities in democracies. Thus in the UK NHS, the private sector permits the more affluent to opt out of the public system for largely elective care but most emergency, primary and chronic care remains publicly funded and provided. In the USA an ostensibly private system has significant public elements that, in addition to tax subsidies, exceed over 40% of health care spending (e.g., Medicare for the elderly and Medicaid for some of the poor). This moderates the effects of allocation based solely on the willingness and ability to pay of consumers. Such deviations from the dominant ideology are usually highly circumscribed and politically contentious as the majority reluctantly give some consideration to the views of the minority.

This is nicely further illustrated by China. With rates of economic growth nearing 10% annually, China has become the 'workshop of the world'. The opening of its economy has led not only to increased affluence but also increased inequality. Whilst the new manufacturing sector has prospered, the old State Enterprises have largely collapsed and the rural sector remains very poor. Some 640 million people live in rural China, where the barefoot doctor system has collapsed and health care providers survive by charging full costs to patients, complemented by often high profits from inappropriately prescribed pharmaceuticals. These problems pose considerable political, social and economic challenges. For instance the recent SARS epidemic illustrated graphically to the Chinese Government and the world that public health surveillance and controls were inadequate.

These rural health deficiencies have led to significant new Government investment in the form of expenditure subsidies to encourage local communities to band together in new social insurance schemes. However, the variations in income both between and within Provinces is considerable and progress, whilst significant, is slow.

Meanwhile, in the urban sector existing social insurance and often inequitable medical savings account mechanisms (Yi *et al.* 2005) are being complemented by the development of private insurance. The World Bank has been working with the Chinese Government to increase understanding of the health care market and the essential need to ensure it is adequately regulated. To control health care institutions and ensure consistency with egalitarian principles, market regulation is essential.

This was epitomized by the succinct advice to Chinese colleagues given by some visiting health economists over a decade ago (Evans *et al.* 1994). They proposed four principles to govern health care reform:

- Established market economies do not use the market mechanism to govern their health care sectors. Market forces may be used to complement health care systems where it is safe to do so but no market economy, including the USA, leaves resource allocation to the market.
- 'Competition' and 'markets' are means to an end, not ends in themselves. If they are treated as ends the social goals of efficiency, equity and expenditure control will not be achieved.
- Better health is a major objective of investing in health care. The provision of good health at low cost requires a focus on preventable ill health and this requires strong government action.
- Commercial health insurance would create inefficiency, inequity and expenditure inflation. If the insurance principle is used (usually on a pay as you go basis), what is required is highly regulated public or non-commercial social insurance. Those who ignore this 'rule' will accrue all the negative consequences of commercial insurance as evidenced in the USA.

Sadly such advice to be explicit about the definition and ranking of policy goals such as efficiency, equity and expenditure control is often ignored worldwide and countries, affluent and not so affluent, repeat well documented errors in policy formation and execution (Maynard 2005).

Policy advocacy involving changes in public–private boundaries is always politically contentious and in countries where public systems dominate (e.g., Australia and the UK) these usually involve reforms consisting of greater use of co-payments, which redistribute expenditure from the healthy affluent to the sick who tend to be old and poor, who are ill most often. This, and the subsidization of private insurance, redistributes resources to the more affluent (and usually more healthy) whose tax burdens are reduced (Hall and Maynard 2005).

Egalitarians favour taxation as the means by which to extend health care systems. However, they may compromise with regard to the choice of taxation and its redistributive impact. In France, the Socialist government in the late 1990s changed funding away from a dependence primarily on social insurance with its proportional tax rates, to general taxation (Rochaix and Hartmann 2005). Similar proposals have been made by the current Government in Germany. These movements from a Bismarckian system to a Beveridge system have not been emulated by the British who, under Blair, have increased the extent of NHS funding from social insurance rather than from income taxation, which is more progressive.

The policy battleground of the competing ideologists is often the demand side of the health care market, i.e., funding. However, that is now complemented to an increasing degree by advocacy of market incentives as a means of improving supply-side efficiency. The language of the consumer society is permeating the management of public services with politicians emphasizing concepts such as competition and 'choice'. For some, for instance egalitarians, choice may be seen as a means rather than an end, i.e., may be a mechanism that can be used to improve efficiency. For libertarians, choice may be an end, which increases individual freedom and undermines collective provider mechanisms.

Competition is difficult to create and sustain as capitalists are always the enemies of capitalism and anxious to undermine competition by protecting themselves in monopolies. All markets have to be regulated. The regulation of health care markets is problematic where, for instance, physicians and hospitals may be local monopolists and provider groups such as drug firms are given protection and implicit subsidies. Patent and other legislation gives providers the power to restrict the market entry of competing rivals. Consequently, regulation is both difficult to design and costly to implement. Sometimes the need for regulation is neglected, as in England, but in the Netherlands, for instance, strict rules have been adopted to control the excesses of market incentives (Schut and Van de Ven 2005).

For egalitarians the challenge is to determine whether competitive markets can be developed so that they do not undermine the achievement of their primary goal of equality of opportunity. In relation to health care this involves demonstrating the successful use of competition as a means of reducing inequalities in lifetime health. There is no evidence base for such an effect. Furthermore, in principle, any moves towards a two-tier system are likely to be treated with suspicion by egalitarians. They view us all as one community and there should be no opting out for the affluent. Enhancing the freedom of choice for some by developing market alternatives and privileged access as a result of superior purchasing power shifts the distribution of health care to a more inequitable outcome that does not serve well the pursuit of equality of opportunity. Giving social priority to some, more affluent, citizens diminishes social welfare in an egalitarian system.

In the frenzy of policy debates, often inflamed by short-term crises in the performance of an economy or often poorly evidenced assertions of the imminent 'collapse' of the local health care system, it is crucial to have these two ideological perspectives in mind. Any policy change has to be challenged firstly by clarification of its objective and secondly by the evidence base that informs any proposed change.

To lose sight of the ultimate goal of the health care system inevitably allows the protagonists of the competing ideologies to confuse the policy debate. The egalitarians tend to proffer their system in terms of its ideal characteristics and criticize their opponents for failures in the libertarian market systems. The libertarians proffer their ideally performing system as the solution to failures of the egalitarian system. The 'ideal' and 'actual' characteristics of the two systems have been described by Williams (1988) and can be found in Tables 5.2 and 5.3 together with an elaboration of the competing ideological viewpoints. The ideological competition inherent in this policy debate wastes considerable resources by reiterating 'solutions' that are incompatible with the objective of the ideological system for which they are proposed. For beneficiaries of the status quo this ensures that system reform is often modest and protective of the income and employment of major provider groups, which may be inefficient in their use of society's scarce resources.

Avoiding obvious inefficiencies in the delivery of health care

As the egalitarians and libertarians wrestle worldwide to increase the influence of their ideologies on health care policy, long-standing inefficiencies in the delivery of health care are sustained. Even though the protagonists may at varying levels recognize their failure in their own systems to implement change, they are concerned largely with tilting at their opponents' windmills in a manner reminiscent of Don Quixote.

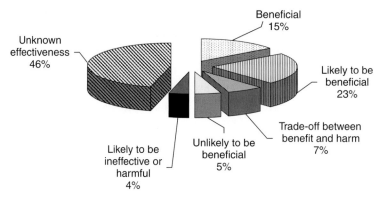

Figure 5.1   Uncertainty about clinical effectiveness (BMJ 2005)

In all developed countries, health care systems are generally large and expensive but the evidence base in terms of proven effectiveness and cost-effectiveness of interventions is far from complete. The data in Figure 5.1 are indicative of the incompleteness of evidence of the effectiveness of commonly used diagnostic and therapeutic interventions (BMJ 2005). Whilst the evidence base indicates that perhaps 38% of interventions are beneficial or likely to be beneficial for patients, over 45% of therapies are of unknown effectiveness. The remainder (about 16%) are a mix of therapies that may be harmful, or are unlikely to be beneficial, or involve a trade-off between benefit and harm. Examples of the last category would include a 'standard' treatment for high blood pressure, beta blockers, which increase the risk of developing diabetes, and the breast cancer drug Herceptin which retards tumour growth but increases the risk of cardiac disease.

All health care decision makers recognize first that death is inevitable, although Western social norms exhibit a preference to not deal with this certainty explicitly. Second, it is recognized that resources are scarce. However, in dealing with these certainties there is also a need to be more sceptical about the evidence base about 'what works' and how best to use scarce resources to delay death and improve patients' quality of life. Unfortunately, this is largely absent. The desire to live longer and better lives leads providers and consumers to use interventions that may or may not be beneficial, and with little investment in determining which of these two outcomes is achieved.

This uncertainty about what works in health care is further enhanced by the unusually blinkered nature of performance measurement and management in medicine. Health care systems worldwide, to the extent that they are interested in patient outcomes, focus on data on mortality and complications. This obsession with failure in medicine can be useful. Indeed many of the public concerns in Britain in the last decade have been concerned about failing practitioners. For instance, a paediatric cardiac surgeon in Bristol used the wrong technique for over a decade and killed over two dozen children as well as damaging many more. A gynaecological surgeon in Kent damaged scores of women, rendering them incontinent after hysterectomy. A GP systematically killed over 200 women over 30 years by lethal morphine injection.

Appalling incidents such as these have been explored retrospectively with routine mortality and complication data. It has been shown, however, that their practices were well evidenced at the time but no one analyzed the data and acted on the results. This retrospective discovery is causing improvements in policy focus on outcomes. However, this focus is still on failure, in particular on avoidable mortality, post-operative complications and medical errors, of which the latter in particular are often poorly measured and managed (e.g., Kohn *et al.* 2000). Although there is now increased awareness of mortality and error magnitudes and variation in countries such as basically libertarian USA and egalitarian UK, the management response has been less than complete.

Thus, one deficit common in all health care systems, regardless of their ideological perspectives, has been the failure to measure success as opposed to failure in systems' performance. For most patients or consumers passing through primary and hospital care, death is generally not the immediate relevant end point; rather it is whether they 'feel better' as a consequence of health care delivery. Such a feeling has both physical and mental dimensions and their measurement has been the subject of considerable investment over the last three decades.

This investment effort is not novel. For hundreds of years medical professions have been advocating and investing in better systems of medical management. For instance the nineteenth-century British nurse, Florence Nightingale, advocated the measurement of patient outcomes in terms of whether patients were dead, relieved or unrelieved. She argued:

I am fain to sum up with an urgent appeal for adopting this or some uniform system of publishing the statistical records of hospitals. There is a growing conviction that in all hospitals, even those which are best conducted, there is a great and unnecessary waste of life . . .

In attempting to arrive at the truth, I have applied everywhere for information, but in scarcely an instance have I been able to obtain hospital records fit for any purpose of comparison. If they could be obtained, they would enable us to decide many other questions besides the ones alluded to. They would show subscribers how their money was being spent, what amount of good was really being done with it, or whether it was doing more harm than good. (Nightingale 1863)

Sadly, over 140 years later, and after high levels of investment in libertarian and egalitarian health care systems, nowhere are there systems of measurement and management that routinely collect over time, and particularly before and after medical interventions, patient-reported outcomes, in particular assessments of personal mental and physical functioning. The generic quality of life instrument short form 36 (www.sf36.org) produces a profile of patients' health states. Another generic measure, EQ5D, can be used to produce a health index (www.euroqol.org). Both of these instruments have been adopted in thousands of clinical trials and have been translated into dozens of languages. Despite the fact that clinicians use them extensively in research, they are not routinely used to appraise, for instance, the level of success and variability between providers in improving patient functioning after, for instance, hip replacements, hysterectomies or cancer therapy.

It is essential if consumer choice is to work efficiently in private markets that information about the cost and quality of goods and services is available. But all private health care markets fail to produce such information, leaving consumers reliant on the word of 'experts', who themselves are relatively ignorant of the clinical effectiveness of many interventions in their armoury (see Figure 5.1). Furthermore these markets are yet more corrupted by the biased marketing techniques of other providers, such as pharmaceutical companies (e.g. Angell 2004, Moynihan and Cassels 2005).

Consumers and providers in egalitarian systems of health care are exposed to similar problems of imperfect information and biased marketing. Rationing in this type of health care system is determined, in principle, by need or the relative cost-effectiveness of treatments competing for limited resources. Despite the clear definition of this principle, egalitarians have generally been tardy in investing in better systems of technology appraisal.

The causes of this are not difficult to discern. In egalitarian systems, information about the cost-effectiveness of competing technologies would make the practice of rationing more explicit and politically even more difficult to manage. Rationing involves depriving patients of care from which they would benefit and, as patients even if not as citizens, they would wish to have available. Bowel and skin cancer patients who have been told in the NHS that the latest cost ineffective interventions will not be provided make formidable political opponents, especially when supported by vibrant patient lobbies funded by the drug industry.

To augment such technology assessment with the measurement and management of specialist and general practitioner success in terms of improving, or even maintaining, the functional status of patients would also be controversial. However, if the role of the UK NHS and similar health care systems is to meet need cost-effectively, both technology appraisal and performance management of health care professionals is essential if currently noticeably absent. Consumer ignorance and provider inflexibility prevents public markets from working efficiently.

Furthermore, the technology appraisal that takes place to inform and prioritize health care investments, for instance in the English National Institute for Health and Clinical Excellence (NICE), focus on clinical and cost-effectiveness and offers no more than lip-service to the issue of equity weights. Given that it may be less efficient to intervene and save the life of a poor person who smokes, is obese, has a poor diet and takes little exercise in comparison with a middle-class person with more health-protecting habits, the pursuit of efficiency discriminates against the poor and disadvantaged. The NICE policy issue is whether health gains for such poor people should be weighted higher than equivalent health gains for the middle classes. Such issues are discussed in technology appraisal literature but not operationalized, thereby ensuring that efficiency is pursued and investments in health care are selected that advantage the relatively well-off.

Libertarian systems are no better at delivering care cost-effectively, let alone equitably. Private insurance companies compete on price for varying finite and often highly constrained packages of benefits, which may be difficult to identify and quantify *ex ante*. Consumers may be driven into bankruptcy when their utilization exceeds the often well disguised limits of their insurance, even though the care they have received may be neither clinically nor cost-effective. As in public systems, there are no effective systems of consumer protection that ensure that providers are of good quality. The absence of such mechanisms for the efficient working of competitive markets leads us to ask why some insurer does not break ranks and compete for market share on the basis of making patients 'feel better' by using providers with demonstrably good outcomes in terms of patients' mental and physical functioning. That no insurer has acted efficiently in the USA is indicative of the fact that these markets are as cartelized and inefficient as those in egalitarian systems.

It is unsurprising, therefore, that these markets, public and private, exhibit similar defects in their functioning. With many interventions of unknown clinical effectiveness, individual practitioners inevitably offer patients different levels and types of intervention, even though their personal and health characteristics may be similar. There is a long established literature on this from the United States in particular. Wennberg and his colleagues at the Dartmouth Medical School in New Hampshire have charted the variations in care delivered to Medicare patients for 30 years (Iglehart 2004). Wennberg's collaborators summarized these variations recently by pointing out that expenditure per Medicare enroller in 2000 varied from $10 500 in Manhattan to $4823 in Portland, Oregon. These differences were the product of volume effects rather than difference in illness rates, socioeconomic status or the price of services. They concluded:

Residents in spending regions received 60% more care but did not have lower mortality rates, better functional status or higher satisfaction. (Fisher 2003)

These variations in the egalitarian part of the US health care systems can be seen in other public health care organisations (e.g., Bloor and Maynard (2002); Maynard and Bloor (2006)). Both types of system also exhibit similar inefficient characteristics in delivering types of care, for instance, chronic care. There is a good evidence base to inform the delivery of care to patients with chronic illness such as high blood pressure, diabetes, cholesterol and asthma. Furthermore, the monitoring and treatment interventions are not complex and the pharmaceuticals needed are usually cheap, being out of patent. But public and private health care systems fail to deliver these interventions, thereby inducing avoidable morbidity and premature mortality. For instance, in the USA, the Rand Corporation estimate that only 55% of patients received appropriate care (Kerr *et al.* 2004). Inevitably, such inefficiencies exhibit social class variations with the disadvantaged, who usually have higher levels of incidence and prevalence of chronic disease, being provided with inferior service delivery.

Despite the common failures in public and private systems of health care, a common belief amongst some egalitarians is that the problems of public provision of care can be mitigated by emulating private sector mechanisms, many of which can already be seen to have failed. This illogicality is sustained by libertarians proffering the ideal nature of the marketplace in health care, whilst seemingly egalitarian politicians exploit the ignorance of the electorate by holding out to them a mythical and evidence-free version of an improved system of delivering health care.

This is epitomized by the recent English NHS reforms, where after increasing funding by 50%, the Government became frustrated that the service had not 'acted smarter' and delivered productivity gains but had instead diverted funding into provider rents, in particular higher pay (Maynard and Sheldon 2002; Maynard and Street 2006). In this case, reform policies have included public funding of increased private provision, now at about 10% of elective capacity, a national tariff system for the reimbursement of hospitals, thereby inhibiting price competition, and the funding of capital projects by the Private Finance Initiative, a route of ambiguous efficiency gain.

These and other policies are ambitious and not integrated into a coherent strategy, e.g., reimbursement on the basis of national tariffs (known as DRGs in other countries) may be incompatible with the pursuit of geographical equity through capitated budgets and the traditional cash limits of the NHS. However they are advocated as market 'solutions' to the failures of the NHS. That the NHS has failed to deliver care efficiently is true but these mechanisms internationally have not proved to be 'magic bullets' and in the English NHS they may undermine expenditure control and equity, while having little effect on inefficiency. Those who reject this pessimistic scenario offer little evidence to support their optimism.

The production of health is a complex business often clouded by the evidence-free claims of self-interested provider groups exploiting asymmetry of knowledge between them and a populace unreconciled with the inevitability of death. It is generally accepted that health is a production of genetic endowments and lifetime behaviours, the adverse effects on health capital of which can be mitigated by health care and other inputs. As has been shown (Figure 5.1) the evidence for the effectiveness of much of health care is poor. This is, in part, a product not so much of inadequate investment in research and development but of poor research and development expenditure in terms of the design of clinical trials and their reporting (Maynard and Chalmers 1997). The rigidities in these investment choices is indicative of the fact that some research and development is targeted not at knowledge creation but at marketing products of marginal clinical and cost-effectiveness.

These problems with research and development and the magnitude of uncertainty about what works in health care should induce caution in those involved in investing further in health care. Undoubtedly, there are interventions that are cost-effective and are inadequately provided to patients (e.g., Nolte and McKee 2004). Furthermore, it is likely that some of the interventions in the 'unknown effectiveness' category will be shown to be effective. However, there are other areas of health care in which further investment is not merited and in which reductions in investments may be efficient, e.g., hysterectomies, tonsillectomies and antibiotics. Inducing greater scepticism in society about the limits of medicine is difficult, as noted by Skrabanek and McCormick (1989), who regard 'scepticaemia' as a health-promoting state. They defined this condition as, 'an uncommon generalised disorder of low infectivity. Medical school education is likely to confer life-long immunity!'

The challenge for health care delivery is to focus on the supply of what is cost-effective, eradicate what is inefficient and examine carefully whether population health could be enhanced more effectively if governments focused more on non-health-care inputs such as behaviours (e.g., alcohol and tobacco consumption and nutrition), education and income distribution. Health care providers in both egalitarian and libertarian systems might resist this redistribution of resources but consumers and patients might be better-off in terms of health and disposable resources.

Using market mechanisms in egalitarian health care systems

Political frustration arising from expenditure inflation and inefficiency in health care delivery has led to unevaluated and usually evidence-free adoption of market mechanisms in egalitarian health care systems. Is there evidence that such mechanisms are cost-effective?

In the USA, concern about expenditure inflation is often correlated with political discontent with access to care for the forty-five million uninsured and the many millions who are underinsured. Reform proposals from the more liberal quasi-egalitarians are usually designed to provide universal access in a market structure that is highly regulated to induce both improved system efficiency and cost control.

There are many examples of such proposals. For instance, Enthoven and his colleagues (Ellwood *et al.* 1992) proposed the provision of a basic benefit package for all, with the poor being funded to access such care by the abolition of tax breaks for the more affluent and Federal funding. This structure involved creation of institutions for the regulation of insurance premiums, including coverage of small employers, an Outcomes Management Board responsible for providing quality data, a National Health Board to regulate all insurance purchasers and providers, and a board to ensure the supply of technology assessment.

These proposals influenced President Clinton's reform efforts but they failed, in large part because of the regulatory complexities they proposed and the resistance of key private sector players who would have been financially affected by such a regulated market. However, such ideas are once again being resurrected by more liberal US reformers and will undoubtedly be a key part of the post-Bush political agenda (e.g., Emanuel and Fuchs 2005).

These plans represent a major challenge to the orthodox libertarian ideology of the Bush Government as they involve a major expansion in the role of government and the direction of increased support to the disadvantaged, who have increasing problems accessing health care but who libertarians believe should be incentivized to be independent. They also rely on the conviction of liberal reformers that the proposals they are advocating can be translated efficiently from principles into practice. This optimism may be misplaced as competition like that envisaged by Enthoven and others is difficult to create, let alone sustain, as providers seek to cartelize the marketplace (Reinhardt 1993). The Enthoven proposals had little impact on the managed care revolution that overtook the American health care system in the 1990s. After its failure to curb inflation, let alone improve efficiency and access, the advocates of 'proper' managed care structures, such as Enthoven, continue to reiterate the proposals in a manner reminiscent of the novelist G. K. Chesterton who argued that Christianity had not failed, it merely had not been tried. Translating principles into practice where people are concerned whether it involves personal beliefs or health care, and especially when change threatens their power and incomes, is always difficult.

The mid-term US elections in 2006 restored Democrat party control of Congress. Reinhardt (2006) has once again addressed the question of whether there was any hope for the US uninsured? He summarized negatively: 'It is safe to conclude that any flurry of activity on uninsurance will be just another instalment in the never ending series of America's national conversations on the topic – a conversation that resembles nothing so much as the rambling of a drunken lover at the bar: big talk, little action.' This pessimism is a product of the power of libertarian interest groups that dominate the 'American way' in social policy.

This American perspective also affects European policy advocacy, although so far it has failed to undermine the dominance of tax or social insurance funded universal benefits, largely free at the point of consumption. The strongest advocates of competition in egalitarian health care in Europe are the Dutch. Following the Dekker proposals in 1987, they tried to introduce competition into both the demand and supply sides of their health care markets. The State health insurance fund was to compete with private alternatives, and these purchasers of care could contract with competing public and private providers. The initial reform effort failed but in recent years a second attempt to introduce regulated competition is being made. This has involved complex mechanisms to equalize insure risks across competing public and private insurers and the extension of copious regulation of insurers and providers, including the application of anti-trust legislation to groups of physicians (Schut and Van de Ven 2005).

The Dutch cycle of market-orientated health care reform has been emulated in England. The Thatcher government published proposals in 1989 for an internal NHS market with continued public funding of the NHS. Its attempt to create market-like institutions led to the evolution of new structures, in particular the purchaser–provider split in management, but little substantive change in the way health care was delivered or access improved.

After dismissing the Thatcher reforms as a 'failure', the Blair government initially retained many of the changes and has subsequently back tracked and readopted most of its predecessor's reforms and developed them even further in a market-orientated fashion. For instance, in an effort to reduce apparent public sector expenditure and accrue alleged but un-evidenced based efficiency gains, the Private Finance Initiative (PFI) has been used to fund NHS capital expenditure from private sources. This re-establishment of the Thatcher reforms has been augmented with a plethora of other changes in an ad hoc and fragmented manner.

Perhaps the most radical aspect of these policies has been NHS investment in the private provision of elective, diagnostic and primary care. The investment in electives has focused on small DTCs: diagnostic and treatment centres where private providers have been given contracts for three to five years for procedures such as hip replacements and hernia operations and at national tariffs with a 15% uplift. Such contracts oblige commissioning Primary Care Trusts (PCTs) to direct patients to these facilities as the contracts are set and PCTs have to pay even if patients do not use the facilities. Similar contracts, but without the 15% tariff premium, are emerging for diagnostics and primary care. The Government's stated intention is to limit this private activity to 15% of NHS total activity.

The impact of this policy on efficiency is difficult to determine in the absence of evaluation. Presumably these companies are making a profit but whether their costs are lower and their outcomes are as good as NHS competitors is unclear. The policy, like much else of the New Labour NHS agenda, requires careful evaluation (Maynard and Street 2006).

However, evaluation alone is inadequate because what the English reforms lack is regulatory framework, like that proposed for the USA by Enthoven and implemented in the Netherlands. Such a framework is needed to determine and enforce market entry and exit rules and provider behaviour, in particular anti-trust activity. It seems that the UK Government prefers anarchy rather than market rules as a means of inducing public sector reform. In doing this, there is a risk that expenditure control will fail (NHS deficits are increasing and amounted to over £500 m net in 2005–6), with unknown effects on efficiency. As ever this focus on the 'redisorganization' of delivery structures means that policy makers fail to confront inequalities in health and health care, except in their breast-beating rhetoric around election times.

This use of quasi-libertarian market mechanisms to improve the performance of egalitarian systems of health care is increasingly common across the globe as costs inflate and efficient performance is seen to be at best unclear and at worst demonstrably absent. The lack of focus on the clinical and cost-effectiveness of care and its distribution to the different parts of the population is ubiquitous as is a real, rather than vacuous, focus on equity. As adherents to the competing ideologies compete for political dominance, there is a lack of attention to the common failures of all types of health care systems, in particular the health of disadvantaged groups. Until both libertarians and egalitarians focus on translating evidence into practice and on the reform of the deficiencies in their systems, it will be difficult for them to achieve their goals. For egalitarians, it is essential that they are clear about their goal of equality of opportunity and ensuring that 'market' innovations are consistent with the more efficient pursuit of improving care for the disadvantaged. They should always beware of the packs of libertarian wolves dressed up as egalitarian sheep.

Where to now?

With libertarian wolves prowling ubiquitously in egalitarian sheep's clothing it is essential to confront all reform proposals with scepticism. All too often such efforts are poorly disguised attempts to redistribute resources from sometimes weakly performing collective health care systems to rich interest groups served by libertarian advocates (e.g., Evans and Vujicic 2005). As Campbell argued over three decades ago, all reforms are social experiments (Campbell 1969). As such, their design should be informed by logic and the evidence base, and their implementation should be evaluated carefully to build up international knowledge of the effects of reform on macroeconomic expenditure control, efficiency and equity. Sadly, in health care and other social programmes affecting health, such as education, policing and court sentencing, there are too few randomized controlled trials and a wholly inadequate knowledge base to inform reform (e.g., Figure 5.1).

Expenditure control and efficiency, as well as current fashions of the time such as 'choice' and 'competition' are, for egalitarians, means to an end. That end is the presence of real opportunities to make choices and requires distributing rewards so that everyone has equal opportunity for achievement. Reducing inequalities in lifetime opportunities caused by ill health requires radical action that will redistribute income and jobs and be resisted by vested interests in the health care industry.

As argued when the British Government decided to increase NHS funding by 85% in real terms over eight years, spending on health care may not be the best way to improve health, let alone reduce lifecycle inequalities in health (Maynard and Sheldon 2002). The human capital theorists, in particular Michael Grossman (Grossman 2000), have emphasized the roles of income and education in improving the health capital stock and increasing lifetime health.

Such investment issues have clear intergenerational aspects: the health and other behaviours of one generation clearly affect the health of the next generation. This is not only a genetic issue, the health of the mother during reproduction has marked effects on the health of the child (Eriksson 2005). Thus whilst manipulating DNA problems may be a thing of the future, policies to improve mothers' health and compensating programmes to improve the health of low-birth-weight babies improve health more efficiently than some health care interventions.

The international evidence on the cost-effectiveness of health care in producing health is impressive but very uneven (Nolte and McKee 2004 and Figure 5.1). The cases for targeting health care resources on those activities that are demonstrably cost-effective, facilitate expenditure control and improve equity have been well documented for decades. However, service delivery fails to reflect this evidence base.

For egalitarians, there are two related problems with this evidence. First, how can change be incentivized so that efficient health improving interventions are provided regardless of whether they are in the health care sector or in other sectors that contribute to lifetime health? The second issue is how to use that evidence to provide not only that which is efficient but also that which reduces inequalities in lifetime opportunities related to income, wealth and power.

As in all things, progress towards this goal will be slow, i.e., it can only be pursued in small steps that incentivize the use of evidence as a means of dissipating ignorance and ideological power. In health care this requires much more emphasis, not on spending and measures of process such as waiting times, but on improved measures of outcome (e.g., Kind and Williams 2004). This medium-term enterprise, to determine whether generic quality-of-life measures are sufficiently sensitive and valid for routine use to appraise the effects of health care, has to be accompanied with incentives that induce providers, be they individual doctors or organizations, to use routine administrative and other data to make practice more transparent and accountable. Hopefully, such scrutiny will inform prioritization and the targeting of scarce resources.

The clashes between libertarian and egalitarian ideologies are unlikely to diminish. However without continued careful clarification and ranking of policy objectives (e.g., expenditure control, efficiency and equity) and appraisal of policy, much of the reform efforts worldwide will be little more than 'jumping on the spot'. The then President of the English Royal College of Physicians criticized the Thatcher NHS reforms by saying that, 'Instead of ready, take aim and fire, the Government chose to make ready, fire and then take aim.' Sadly for the disadvantaged, the premium payers and taxpayers health care reform worldwide has this characteristic and thereby ensures neither efficiency nor equity in health care and health production.

REFERENCES

Angell, M. (2004) *The Truth about the Drug Companies: How They Deceive Us and What to Do About it*. New York: Random House.

Bloor, K. and Maynard, A. (2002) Consultants: managing them means measuring them. *Health Service Journal*. **112**: 10–11.

BMJ Publishing Group (2005) *Clinical Evidence Concise*. (14)

Campbell, D. T. (1969) Reforms as experiments. *American Psychologist*. **24**(4): 409–429.

DHSS (1976) *The RAWP Report. Resource Allocation Working Party. Sharing Resources for Health in England*. London: HMSO.

Donabedian, A. (1970) Social responsibility for personal health services: an examination of basic values. *Inquiry*. **8**(2): 3–19.

Ellwood, P. M., Enthoven, A. C. and Etheredge, L. (1992) The Jackson hole initiatives for the twenty-first century American health care system. *Health Economics*. **1**(3): 149–168.

Emanuel, E. J. and Fuchs, V. R. (2005) Health care vouchers: a proposal for universal coverage. *New England Journal of Medicine*. **352**: 1255–1260.

Eriksson, J. G. (2005) The fetal origins hypothesis – 10 years on. *British Medical Journal*. **330**: 1096–1097.

Evans, R., Maynard, A., Preker, A. and Reinhardt, U. (1994) Health care reform. *Health Economics*. **3**: 359.

Evans, R. and Vujicic, M. (2005) Political wolves and economic sheep: the sustainability of public health insurance in Canada. In Maynard, A., ed., *The Public–Private Mix for Health: Plus ça Change, Plus C'est la Même Chose*. Oxford: Radcliffe Publishing. pp. 117–140.

Fisher, E. S. (2003) Medical care: is more always better? *New England Journal of Medicine.* **349**(17): 1665–1667.

Grossman, M. (2000) The human capital model. In Culyer, A. J. and Newhouse, J., ed. *Handbook of Health Economics*, Vol. 1A, Amsterdam: North-Holland.

Hall, J. and Maynard, A. (2005) Healthcare lessons from Australia: what can Michael Howard learn from John Howard? *British Medical Journal.* **330**: 357–360.

Iglehart, J. K., ed., (2004) Variations revisited. *Health Affairs.* supplement, web exclusive (7 October). http://content.healthaffairs.org/cgi/content/full/hlthaff.var.5/DC1.

Kerr, E. A., McGlynn, E. A., Adams, J., Keesey, J. and Asch, S. M. (2004) Profiling the quality of care in twelve communities: results from the CQI study. *Health Affairs.* **23**(3): 247–256.

Kind, P. and Williams, A. (2004) Measuring success in health care: the time has come to do it properly. *Health Policy Matters.* **9** www.york.ac.uk/healthsciences/pubs/hpmindex.htm.

Kohn, L. T., Corrigan, J. M. and Donaldson, M. S., eds, (2000) *To Err is Human: Building a Safer Health System*. Washington DC: National Academies Press.

Maynard, A. (1997) Evidence based medicine: an incomplete method for informing treatment choices. *Lancet.* **349**: 126–128.

Maynard, A., ed., *The Public–Private Mix for Health: Plus ça Change, Plus C'est la Même Chose*. Oxford: Radcliffe Publishing. pp. 117–140.

Maynard, A. and Chalmers, I., eds, (1997) *Non-Random Reflections on Health Services Research: on the 25th Anniversary of Archie Cochrane's Effectiveness and Efficiency*. London: BMJ Publishing.

Maynard, A. and Sheldon, T. (2002) Funding for the National Health Service. *Lancet.* **360**: 576.

Maynard, A. and Bloor, K. (2006) Consultant clinical activity is key to improving productivity. *Health Service Journal.* **116**: 18–19.

Maynard, A. and Street, A. (2006) Seven years of feast, seven years of famine: boom to bust in the NHS. *British Medical Journal.* **332**: 906.

Moynihan, R. and Cassels, A. (2005) *Selling Sickness: How Drug Companies Are Turning Us All Into Patients*. Australia: Allen and Unwin.

Nightingale, F. (1863) *Notes on Hospitals*. 2nd edn. London: Routledge.

Nolte, E. and McKee, M. (2004) *Does Health Care Save Lives? Avoidable Mortality Revisited*. London: Nuffield Trust.

Reinhardt, U. E. (1993) Comment on the Jackson Hole initiatives for the twenty-first century American care system. *Health Economics.* **2**(1): 7–14.

Reinhardt, U. E. (2006) Uninsured Americans and the new Democratic Congress. *British Medical Journal.* **333**: 1134.

Rochaix, L. and Hartmann, L. (2005) Public–private mix for health in France. In Maynard, A., ed., (2005) *The Public–Private Mix for Health: Plus Ca Change, Plus C'est la Même Chose*. Oxford: Radcliffe Publishing. p. 141

Schut, F. T. and Van de Ven, W. P. M. M. (2005) Rationing and competition in the Dutch health care system. *Health Economics.* **14**: S59–S74.

Shaw, M., Davey-Smith, G. and Dorling, D. (2005) Health inequalities and New Labour: how promises compare with real progress. *British Medical Journal.* **330**: 1016–1021.

Skrabanek, P. and McCormick, J. (1989) *Follies and Fallacies in Medicine.* Glasgow: Tarragon Press.

Williams, A. (1974) Need as a demand concept (with special reference to health). In Culyer, A. J., ed., *Economic Policies and Social Goals: Aspects of Public Choice.* London: Martin Robertson.

Williams, A. (1988) Priority setting in public and private health care: a guide through the ideological jungle. *Journal of Health Economics.* **7**(2): 173–183.

Yi, Y., Maynard, A., Liu, G., Xiong, X. and Lin, F. (2005) Equity in health care financing: evaluation in the current urban employee health insurance reform in China. *Journal of the Asia Pacific Economy.* **10**(4): 506–527.

Health service access

6

Exploring the dimensions of access

Michael Thiede, Patricia Akweongo and Di McIntyre

Summary

Equity in health care is often defined in terms of access to health services. Yet, in the literature and in policy, the extent to which the concept of access has been taken beyond the realms of principle is limited. This chapter explores the multi-faceted concept of access to health services and indicates how it can be operationalized to address health system inequities. Access is interpreted as the freedom to use health services. Whilst health policy efforts to improve equity in access to services have been guided by a focus on the health system, we propose that household or individual aspects of access deserve more attention than they have received to date. The quality of interaction between an individual and the health system's attributes in terms of delivery and financing lies at the core of access. It is argued that, with a view to health policy, these interactions can be meaningfully and comprehensively presented in three dimensions: availability, affordability and acceptability. Each of these captures distinct interactions between the health system and individuals. There is a set of factors that describes each dimension and that can be represented by a set of clearly defined and measurable variables. Within and across the access dimensions, information is an important determinant of the quality of health system and individual interaction. This approach makes it possible to measure and to map access.

Using a Ghanaian case study, this chapter illustrates the health policy relevance of this conceptual approach. The case study shows how geographical differences in the access dimensions correspond to inequities in access to health services within a mainly rural district in northern Ghana. The findings provide a set of starting points for future health policy in Ghana with an equity goal. This chapter speculates on how this approach can be applied to other health care systems where equity is a major goal.

The Economics of Health Equity, ed. Di McIntyre and Gavin Mooney. Published by Cambridge University Press. © Cambridge University Press 2007.

Introduction

Many countries have health policy goals relating to equitable access to health care. While there has been widespread debate about the concept of health care access since the early 1970s (Aday and Andersen 1975; Penchansky 1977; Penchansky and Thomas 1981; Aday and Andersen 1981; Andersen 1995; Gulliford *et al.* 2002; Gulliford and Morgan 2003; Oliver and Mossialos 2005), there remains considerable confusion and little consensus on how access should be defined. There has been no attempt to identify a common concept that may be applicable in different environments, particularly in a low-income and middle-income context. Without greater clarity on the concept of access, it is impossible to pursue accessible health systems actively.[1] This is particularly so in the current context of evidence-informed decision-making; if the access concept is not well understood, comprehensive evidence on what should be done to promote equitable health systems cannot be gathered.

This chapter discusses the concept of access and argues that, given the multi-faceted nature of access, it is necessary to identify dimensions of access to serve as 'entry points', not only for evaluating access in a systematic and inclusive way but also for comprehensively defining an equity-oriented health policy agenda. A set of access dimensions is put forward, and its implications for assessing access directly (rather than inappropriately focusing only on health care utilization as a proxy for access) are discussed. The final section presents a case study from Ghana, illustrating how the dimensions of access can be measured and mapped in a meaningful and policy relevant way.

What is access?

Although there is considerable debate about the concept of access, most of the literature agrees that access is not the same as health service use (Penchansky 1977; Mooney 1983; Oliver and Mossialos 2005). Access has been described as the *opportunity* to use health services, reflecting an understanding that there is a set of circumstances that *allows for* the use of appropriate health services. At the same time, however, the definition of access should also incorporate the notion of empowerment to make well-informed decisions about health service use. Beyond the objective opportunity, individuals and communities need to be in a position

---

[1] The term health system is used here to denote what is sometimes referred to as 'supply side'. Our narrow definition of the health system encompasses aspects of service delivery as well as broader aspects of health system organization, such as financing arrangements, but not the clients. These individuals or households are regarded as forming the conceptual counterpart, the 'demand side'.

to choose when to use which health service is appropriate in a given context. For that reason, we define access as the *freedom* to use health services (Thiede 2005).

The mere opportunity to use health services exists as soon as acceptable and affordable services are made available to the health system's clients. We argue that this is not sufficient if the level of information about health and health services is poor at the community level. Yet the reality in many developing country settings is that health information is not equally distributed across the population. Only if adequate information on health, information on appropriate health care responses and on the opportunities to use health services accordingly is effectively communicated across communities, can equitable access to health services be established. This is the core idea of promoting access as the freedom to use.

Access may or may not translate into service utilization, as '[f]or various acceptable reasons (for example, varying individual preferences), those in equal need and with equal ... access [to] health care may not make equal *use* of these opportunities,' (Oliver and Mossialos 2005 p. 655). From a health policy perspective, it is more appropriate to seek to promote access, and thus ensure equal *freedom* to use services, than to strive for equal use, which would imply overriding personal preferences. Health systems discriminate against groups of people in different ways. The results of this are generally perceived to be reflected in the degree to which services are used by these groups. Utilization patterns across different socio-economic groups, groups of different educational background or different ethnic background have been interpreted as an indication as to the degree of inequity in health care. We would like to challenge the viewpoint that utilization patterns convey lessons for equity-orientated health policy. We argue that utilization is insufficient as an indicator of equity in health care, even if, for example, the analysis of utilization patterns according to socio-economic status is widely used to demonstrate the importance of making health services work better for poor people (Gwatkin *et al.* 2005).

Frequently, inequalities in health services uptake across different groups of people have been considered a manifestation of inequities in access to health services (Whitehead *et al.* 1997; Waters 2000). While it is true that fundamental inequities in the health system result in skewed utilization patterns, the reverse is not necessarily true: patterns of service utilization may have different underlying causes, not all of them linked to aspects of equity. Specific services may be skewed towards the better-off because the prevalence of the particular health condition is higher within the wealthier groups. Conversely, the utilization of another service can be skewed towards the poorer groups, which at a first glance may suggest a pro-poor, i.e., positive, achievement. The underlying causes for this utilization pattern, however, may be deficiencies of the particular service in terms of its acceptability, driving those who can afford it away, e.g., from public services to an expensive private sector provider. Consequently, utilization patterns, as such, can potentially provide a first pointer towards equity challenges, but they cannot be interpreted as indicators of equity per se. Equal utilization as a proxy for equal access does not acknowledge preferences and degrees of risk aversion as points of departure leading to differences in service uptake. Utilization does not fully consider the quality or quantity of care provided (Burstrom 2002). Seemingly low utilization of health services observed in a health care system may be as a result of the use of other alternative therapies or providers outside the formal health system and not actually differential access to health care (Puentes-Markides 1992; Goddard and Smith 2001). Hence, utilization is not only an inappropriate proxy of access; describing use as 'realized access' (Aday and Andersen 1981) appears similarly inappropriate.

It may not be immediately obvious why utilization should not serve as the marker for equitable health services. Yet, utilization per se neither says anything about the process of interaction between the health system and the users that brought about a particular socio-economic pattern of utilization nor does it reflect the adequacy or appropriateness of the services utilized. The first aspect addresses the role of choice in health care: if a utilization pattern results from people's informed choices on health services that fulfil a set of criteria, such as adequacy and appropriateness, the provision of health care may be considered equitable, even though the pattern of utilization may be skewed towards one or other socio-economic group. The second aspect reflects the principle that a utilization pattern should not just be considered equitable because it appears to favour the poor. The underlying reasons may be that the types of health care under investigation are characterized by low quality or are inappropriate, but are still used by poorer segments of the population because the alternatives are unaffordable.

Although some authors focus exclusively on health care provision and financing (Mooney 1983; Goddard and Smith 2001), we see access as relating to the interaction between the health system and individuals or households (Gulliford et al. 2002; Oliver and Mossialos 2005). After all, access of someone to something describes a relationship. This position was, in fact, put forward in the early 1970s by Donabedian (1973) and refined by Penchansky (1977), who argued that access is the 'degree of fit' between the health system and its clients. This concept refers to a dynamic interaction, with the potential for both the health system and individuals to adapt and address or improve the interaction between the two sides (Ricketts and Goldsmith 2005). It is a relational concept with two-directional interaction, that is, it refers to both the health system's interaction with individuals and individuals' interaction with the health system. It reinforces the notion of access as the freedom to use health services, whereby individuals should have the right 'to do' rather than 'to be done to' in terms of their engagement with the health system. The interactive process is centred around the exchange of information. Thus, the quality of communication between the actors determines the dynamics of access.

There is one issue on which there is consensus in the literature; that access is a multidimensional concept. However, there is considerable debate about the number and nature of the dimensions to access. It is important to achieve greater clarity on these dimensions so that access can be evaluated directly, to inform policy interventions. There is a wide range of health system and individual or household level factors that influence access. To explore these in a systematic way, it is necessary to group together factors that are closely associated with each other into dimensions, each of which focuses in an integrated way on a clearly distinguishable issue. The dimensions should ideally be coherent and comprehensive, i.e., should collectively cover all the relevant factors that constitute access. These key dimensions can then act as 'entry points' for empirically investigating access in an inclusive way within specific country contexts and for developing health policy strategies that separately address the access dimensions. Whilst there will always be some interdependence between the dimensions, they should, conceptually, be clearly separable.

An 'A-frame'

Figure 6.1 summarizes our understanding of the concept of access. The three access dimensions of availability (sometimes referred to as physical access), affordability (often referred to as financial access) and acceptability (sometimes referred

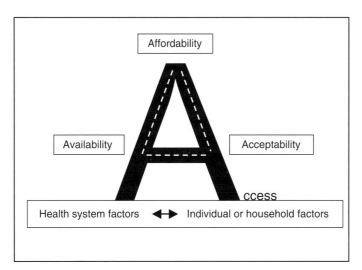

Figure 6.1   Access framework

to as cultural access, although the term 'cultural' provides too narrow a focus) are those that appear most frequently in the literature (e.g., Penchansky 1977; Gulliford and Morgan 2003) and are consistent with the approach outlined earlier. In Figure 6.1, these three dimensions are presented as the three points of a triangle, which together constitute access. The linkage lines in the triangle highlight that the dimensions are interrelated (yet deal with distinct issues). For example, poor availability of services in relation to geographic distribution of providers impacts affordability. The figure also highlights that the foundation of the access concept is the *interaction* between health system and individual or household factors within each dimension. In the following detailed descriptions of each access dimension, it will be seen that specific health system factors always correspond with associated individual or household factors, and vice versa.

Availability

This access dimension deals with the question of whether or not the appropriate health services are available in the right place and at the time that they are needed. It includes issues such as:

- The relationship of the location of health care facilities (health system factor) to the location of those who need these services (distance) and their transportation options (individual or household factors);
- Health care providers' transport resources and willingness to provide mobile services or undertake home visits relative to the location of those in need;
- The 'degree of fit' between the hours of opening of health care facilities (and the related issue of whether or not an appointment system operates) and the time when it is feasible to attend these facilities (especially for working adults) or the time when services are needed (as in emergencies); and
- The relationship between the type, range, quantity and quality of health services provided (which is, in turn, influenced by policy on service packages within different types of facilities; the number, skills, experience and mix of staff within a particular facility; regulations on scope of practice; availability of equipment and medical supplies; etc.), both at the point of first contact as well as at referral facilities (with appropriate referral systems), and the nature and extent of the health needs of the community being served.

The geographic aspect of availability has been studied in different settings (e.g., Rosero-Bixby 2004; Tanser *et al.* 2006). Research on geographic availability and health services planning from a spatial perspective has received a dramatic boost with technical progress in the field of Geographic Information System (GIS) mapping. Health care facilities of different types with different numbers and cadres of staff, and the communities they serve, can be recorded in a spatial context using this technology. Physical distance and travel times from the catchment communities to the facilities can be tracked. This technique allows a focus on particular geographic features (e.g., mountains and rivers) and the existence of certain types of infrastructure (e.g., roads).

Other authors have separated out some of the factors described above, such as appointment systems and walk-in facilities into a different dimension called accommodation, and geographic location into a dimension termed accessibility, leaving only volume and type of services in the availability dimension (Penchansky 1977). It appears appropriate, however, to incorporate in one dimension the aspects that refer to the physical 'ease of use' of health services or the degree of fit between the health system and its clients around space and time.

Affordability

The affordability dimension concerns the 'degree of fit' between the cost of utilizing health care services and individuals' ability to pay. Discussions of the affordability of health services have dominated the debate around equity in health care, particularly in recent times. This is the access dimension that is linked to the discussions around financial risk of ill health and health service use, and the role of the health system in protecting households and communities from this risk. This access dimension, therefore, ties the discussion to the broader field of health care financing. Affordability describes people's financial access to health services in the broadest possible sense. Thus, on the one hand, there are a range of costs that would be incurred if health care is to be sought, including:

- Health care costs such as consultation fees (comprising both official fees and in many low-income and middle-income countries, unofficial or 'under-the-counter' fees), costs of diagnostic tests, costs of medicines and, for inpatient services, pre-admission deposits, ward fees, theatre fees, etc.;
- Other direct costs such as the cost of transportation and special food; and
- Indirect costs such as lost income or productivity while travelling to, and waiting to be seen by, a health care provider.

On the ability-to-pay or individual side of the affordability dimension, the range of factors influencing affordability includes:

- The eligibility of individuals to benefit from different health care financing mechanisms that protect them, in part or in full, from the costs of health care at the time of service use (e.g., eligibility to benefit from public funding – and the associated issue of who is eligible to be exempted from out-of-pocket payments and eligible for services that are fully funded from public resources, the distribution of health insurance beneficiaries, etc.);
- The amount, timing and frequency of income payments within a particular household (both from work activities and in the form of social transfers),

and the extent to which individual household members can access this income, influences ability to make insurance contributions or out-of-pocket payments;

- The extent of cash savings that can be drawn on for health care related payments;
- The number and type of assets owned by the household and whether these assets can be easily and rapidly translated into cash;
- The extent and nature of social networks that would enable households to mobilize cash (either from gifts or loans) from relatives and friends;
- Access to credit and the conditions of loans (e.g., repayment period and interest rate charges); and
- The individual's ability to incur indirect costs (e.g., whether or not an employed individual has sick leave benefits, whether or not subsistence farmers are able to mobilize other family members to work in their fields, etc.).

A core 'ability-to-pay' issue that cuts across all of these factors is the potential impact on household livelihoods of using household resources (income, savings and assets) or incurring debt in order to make health care related payments.

The relational aspect of affordability rests on the interaction of health service costs and household ability to pay. An associated issue is the suitability of the form of payment to both the health care provider and the potential user. For example, affordability is influenced by whether an immediate cash payment is required or whether an account will be sent at a later stage or a credit facility provided and, in low-income contexts, whether payment in kind (e.g., a chicken or some grain, or provision of a reciprocal service) is acceptable. This is a clear example of the relational aspect of access; payment mechanisms must be agreeable to both the provider and the potential user.

Acceptability

Acceptability refers to the nature of service provision and how this is perceived by individuals and communities. The way in which health services are delivered and in which patients are attended to may accommodate patients' beliefs and sensitivities or it may deter them from using services to the desirable extent. The degree of fit between attitudes of providers and individuals, which are influenced by age, sex, ethnicity, language, cultural beliefs, socio-economic status, etc., defines the acceptability dimension. Health services offered and the environment in which they are being offered should be sensitive to the cultural needs and understandings of those seeking or potentially seeking health care. Acceptability may vary in response to cultural beliefs and the nature of the illness.

The interaction between the expectations of providers and patients also influence acceptability of health services, such as:

- Providers' expectations that patients will have respect for their professional status and comply with their prescribed treatment and the extent to which this is forthcoming from patients;
- Patients' expectations that providers will treat them respectfully, will listen attentively to their symptom description, undertake a thorough examination, explain their illness and discuss treatment alternatives, etc. and the extent to which providers meet these expectations; and
- Patients' expectations about health service organization, e.g., the expectation that when arriving at a health facility they will be directed to the appropriate entry point to obtain the care needed, relative to how health services are organized in reality.

A key issue in relation to acceptability is that of respect. The extent to which there is a good fit between the attitudes and expectations of health care providers and users depends on whether or not there is mutual respect for each other.

Information and the degree of fit between health system and individual factors

Information is not only crucial in the understanding of access as freedom to use, it is also neccssary for each of the access dimensions. Good information facilitates a good fit between the health system and individual or household access factors. It cuts across the access dimensions. Being well informed is the outcome of communication processes between the health system and its clients. To achieve informed and empowered communities, communicative interaction needs to abide by certain principles that guarantee fair involvement of both sides in the dialogue (Thiede 2005).

In relation to availability, it is necessary for health planners to have information on the geographic distribution of the population in order to identify the appropriate location for fixed facilities and whether or not mobile or home-based services are necessary. It is also essential that the community has information on where health care providers are located, what types of services they provide, their operating hours and whether or not an appointment is required.

Similarly, in relation to affordability, it is essential for the health system to be aware of the population's ability to pay for health care in order to assess the extent to which general tax resources are required, whether health insurance mechanisms are feasible and sustainable, the extent to which out-of-pocket payments should be seen as viable and who should receive specific protection from contributing to health care costs (either through out-of-pocket payments or health insurance contributions). The general public requires information on the cost of various services, acceptable forms of payment, whether or not they are eligible for payment exemptions and how to secure such exemptions.

Information also influences the acceptability dimension. For example, information on patients' rights will influence patient expectations of providers and the extent to which providers meet these expectations. Also, if providers have information on cultural beliefs in the local community (e.g., that a female patient should only be examined by a female health worker) they may be able to be more sensitive in interactions with patients. As indicated previously, mutual respect is critical to translating the potential benefits of information into acceptability in reality.

Implications of the 'A-frame' for evaluation of access

Many of the studies that claim to consider health care access in fact focus on health service use, partly because utilization can be easily observed or measured (Whitehead *et al.* 1997; Waters 2000; Goddard and Smith 2001). In general, researchers have considered differences in health service utilization between different groups, and have evaluated the extent to which a limited number of factors (related to access) have contributed to these utilization differences. The access-related factors that have featured most prominently in such evaluations are geographic distance or travel time to a health facility and health insurance membership. A key problem that arises is that by adopting measurement of utilization as the starting point, access issues are not explored in a comprehensive way. Yet these are critical to understanding the reasons underlying utilization differences between socio-economic or other defined groups.

There are two broad reasons why utilization differences may arise. First, it may be due to differences in access to – or the freedom to use – health services. Second, given equal access to services, fully informed individuals may make different choices in relation to the use of a particular service, on the basis of deep-seated fundamental beliefs in different healing systems and types of services and *not* as a result of inadequate information on the effectiveness of that service or because they feel it is too far from their place of residence or because they have previously been subject to abusive treatment by that provider.

It is important to distinguish between these two underlying reasons for differences in utilization from a policy perspective as policy interventions should be directed to addressing inequities, i.e., differences in access that are not only unfair but are unnecessary and avoidable. This is where the access framework presented earlier is particularly helpful. It enables researchers and health sector officials to explore in detail where access constraints exist, in order to identify appropriate policy interventions.

Figure 6.2 illustrates how the framework can be used to explore access, using the three dimensions as entry points. It again highlights that access can be conceptualized in relation to three main dimensions, and that there is a range of relational factors that influence each access dimension (the major factors for each dimension were outlined previously). These clearly distinguishable factors

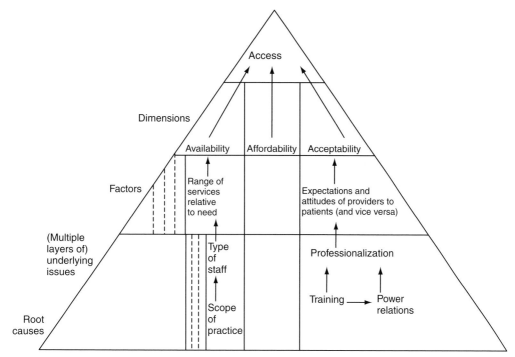

Note: dotted lines indicate the existence of other factors for each dimension, and other issues influencing each factor in addition to those used for illustrative purposes in the Figure.

Figure 6.2   Using the 'A-frame' to explore factors and issues influencing access

serve as indicators of access, while at the same time they allow some form of measurement. Access factors could be the distance between an individual's home or place of work and the location of the health facility or the health service costs in relation to the ability to pay. The access factors speak to the different dimensions of access. In turn, there are multiple layers of issues underlying each factor. The root causes for the functional or dysfunctional interactions between the health system and the individual or household form the bottom of the pyramid. Within this conceptual framework, improvements in access overall depend on the communicative interaction between the health system and its clients. Communication is a two-directional process. In order ultimately to achieve equitable access, the interpretation of the degree of fit between the health system and individual or household access factors needs to become a matter of common understanding. This requires a form of communication that allows for mutual recognition of both sides' perspectives of health and health care.

Attempting to evaluate access by considering all of the underlying issues that could possibly impact on health service access, or beginning the evaluation at the bottom of the pyramid, would be an overwhelming task. Instead, a more systematic and comprehensive evaluation can be undertaken if one begins with each of the dimensions (i.e., at the top of the pyramid), and methodically explores whether there are access constraints in relation to each possible factor that contributes to that dimension. For example, one can assess whether availability constraints are due to the location of the facility relative to the distribution of the population or due to the types of services provided at the facility relative to the health needs of the local community. In the latter case, what underlies the inadequacy of the range of services relative to the health needs of the population? It may be related to the type of staff employed at the facility and, in turn, the type of services provided by those categories of staff may be influenced by their regulated scope of practice. Figure 6.2 illustrates this and other examples of issues relating to the acceptability dimension of access.

A case study of access to malaria control and treatment in Northern Ghana

The following case study illustrates how the approach to addressing access by focusing on the proposed framework of access dimensions, and the cross-cutting issue of information, can be used for empirical research. Although the emphasis in this case study is on quantitative analysis, we recognize that a combination of quantitative and qualitative methods should be used to explore health service access issues fully.

This study was conducted in the Kassena-Nankana District (KND) on the northern border of Ghana, adjacent to Burkina Faso. The district, which has a population of roughly 140 000 people, lies within the Guinea savannah woodland area of Ghana. The district has two main ethnic groups, the Kassenas and the Nankanis, who live in dispersed settlements. Traditional beliefs dominate people's lifestyles, and the literacy rate is generally low.

Methods

The study set out to understand access to malaria control interventions in the mainly rural north of Ghana and to gain an understanding of equity issues in malaria care. The research was conducted with the objective of deriving concrete policy guidance by exploring each access dimension in detail and from mapping the geographical patterns of each dimension across the study area. The findings are based on a cross-sectional survey of 1880 households. As the concept of a household is quite alien in the Kassena-Nankana district and people live in extended compounds (which can accommodate one or several households), a household was defined as a group of people living together and sharing the same food budget. The household questionnaire collected data on a broad range of socio-economic variables, including consumption patterns, as well as on malaria episodes, malaria-related knowledge, health service utilization and perceptions around different types of health services.

The locations of all households were mapped with Geographic Information System technology. This allows for the geographical mapping of socio-economic status and the spatial presentation of each of the access dimensions. The analysis of the household data focuses on factors that influence access. Models using principal component analysis (PCA) were developed for the access assessment. (Kline 1994; Tabachnick and Fidell 2006). Each dimension was modelled separately because of the fact that, even though access to health care is multidimensional and the factors interrelate, each dimension substantively influences access on its own.

The first step in undertaking the analysis was to identify those access factors (or data variables) likely to be relevant for each dimension of access, based on the conceptual understanding of these dimensions. Factors such as the physical distance to certain types of health facilities and opening and waiting times were assigned to the availability dimension. Fees for certain services, eligibility for exemptions, membership of health insurance, transportation costs, household wealth and household size were assigned to the affordability dimension. Generally, qualitative research methods are required to complement quantitative data, in order to explore the acceptability of services dimension fully. In this study, only quantitative variables referring to cultural and religious beliefs, perceptions of the effectiveness of services, health seeking behaviour and perceptions of health worker attitudes, as well as the educational status of household members, have been incorporated in the analysis of acceptability.

The initial steps in identifying appropriate access factors also involved conducting regression analyses. Factors that turned out to be statistically significant in explaining each dimension were retained as explanatory variables for the particular dimensions. Using principal component analysis, factor scores were generated for the access factors in order actually to 'measure' the respective dimensions of access. Disadvantage indices were then generated, with different weights for each access factor. These weights ensure that the importance of each access factor in contributing to access is reflected in the design of the index for each dimension.

Separate maps for the three dimensions show the degree to which areas across the Kassena-Nankana district are disadvantaged in terms of the availability, affordability or acceptability of malaria-related health services (Figures 6.3 to 6.5). Dark shading indicates areas with lowest access scores and light shading represents areas with very high access scores. Mapping the dimensions of access to health services provides insights into areas with relatively high or low overall access as well as the dimensions contributing to differential access. As information is crucial to each dimension of access, the information score is also mapped (in Figure 6.6). Comparison with the access score distribution may provide insights into which access dimensions are influenced by communication interventions.

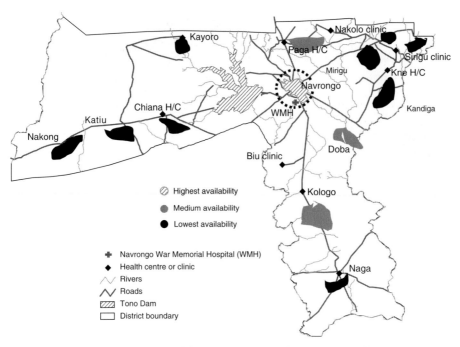

Figure 6.3   Distribution of the availability dimension in the Kassena-Nankana district (KND)

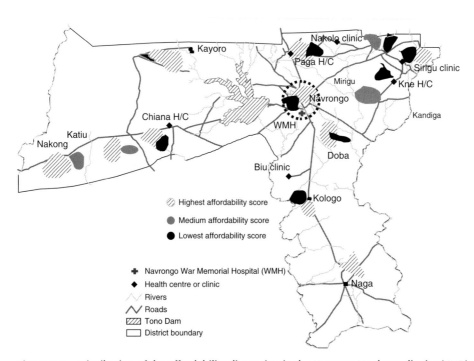

Figure 6.4   Distribution of the affordability dimension in the Kassena-Nankana district (KND)

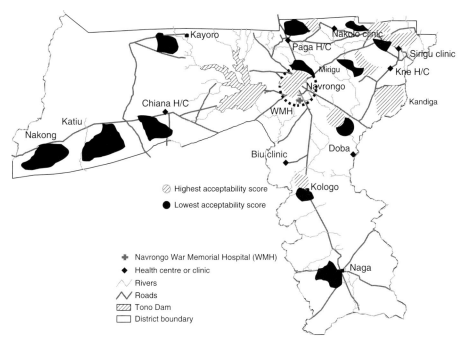

Figure 6.5   Distribution of the acceptability dimension in the Kassena-Nankana district (KND)

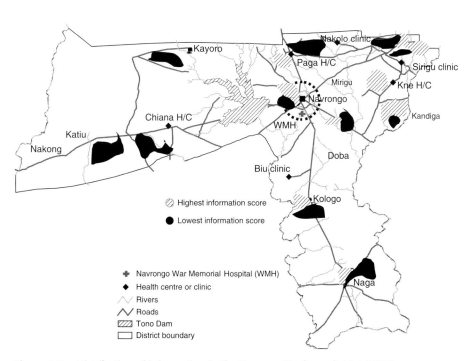

Figure 6.6   Distribution of information in the Kassena-Nankana district (KND)

Results

The statistical approach to designing the disadvantage indices reveals the relative weight of different access factors for each dimension. For example, in the Ghanaian context it turns out that the variables 'distance to health facility' and 'area of residence' are by far the most important in determining availability of health care. It appears, therefore, that in addressing availability of health care, policy makers need to pay priority attention to further developing 'close-to-client' services. Figure 6.3 shows the spatial distribution of availability of health care in the district. Many areas in the district are disadvantaged when it comes to the availability of malaria services. The urban area of the district, where the main hospital is located, unsurprisingly turns out to be most advantaged.

The interplay of a composite 'household factor' on the one hand, describing household composition, economic dynamics incorporating consumption, house-hold size, sex of the household head, as well as marital status, and 'user fees' on the other hand, explain affordability of care to the greatest extent. The greatest weight in this particular study setting turns out to rest on the household character-istics. User fees, however, were of greater importance to affordable care than transport costs. The advantage of this statistical approach is that it makes explicit some of the trade-offs in the interaction between the health system and house-holds. It therefore provides different entry points for health policy.

In contrast to the map of health care availability, the affordability of services turns out to be high in some remote parts of the district (see Figure 6.4). This can be explained by the existence of large forests and farmlands in those areas. Here, farm yields are higher than in many other areas in the district. However, some areas are disadvantaged in both dimensions, and the lowest availability coincides with the lowest affordability scores.

Acceptability is explored in this study with reference to households' preferred treatment choices and preferred management of malaria at different severity levels, as well as religious and cultural beliefs of household members. These factors are interpreted in relation to the management of different severity levels of malaria. The variables with the highest explanatory value turned out to be those reflecting 'revealed acceptability'. Thus, the primary determinant of acceptability was gen-erally related to households' readiness to engage in home treatment with anti-malarials (which is a WHO recommended strategy where anti-malarials are obtained directly by households from trained drug distributors). Readiness to engage with health professionals for severe cases of malaria or disease was a secondary explanatory factor for acceptability, as seeking professional care was a last resort for most households. Preference for treatment with herbal medicines was the factor with the lowest weight in the analysis, which indicates that tradi-tional practices do not necessarily impede the use of effective modern malaria treatment. Misconceptions, previously encouraged by traditional healers, in respect of the inability of Western medicine to treat convulsions effectively, are increasingly being dispelled in the district. Health care providers and traditional healers now jointly promote the use of rectal artesunate for the treatment of convulsions in children. The preference for treatment of mild and severe malaria in adults and children by qualified health providers as an explanatory factor in this dimension indicates the level of knowledge of the household with regard to appropriate malaria treatment methods. Households have a high probability of relying on information from professional health providers if the first source of information on managing malaria was obtained from health professionals.

Areas with the lowest acceptability scores are also areas where the availability of health services is lowest (Figure 6.5). This may indicate that people tend to use traditional methods of managing malaria if modern health services are not available – not necessarily because they do not accept treatment of malaria with antimalarials or refuse to use the services of health professionals. Thus, in the Ghanaian case socio-cultural factors may not be the most important factors impeding access to effective treatment. The primary factor rather appears to be the availability of health services. The findings for the Kassena-Nankana district also show that the areas where the acceptability of health services appears lowest tend to be economically better-off with high affordability scores. Yet households in these areas more frequently use herbal medicines for treating malaria rather than attend health services. This again suggests that low utilization of effective anti-malarial treatment in these areas is not primarily related to cultural beliefs but rather to lack of service availability.

The study interprets information rather narrowly and focuses on the malaria context. Factors taken into account for the generation of an information index were derived from household-reported malaria treatment methods and from stated sources of information on the appropriate treatment of the disease.

The pattern of information scores derived in this way shows that areas with a concentration of households with a disadvantage in information are likely to be further away from the centre of the district (Figure 6.6). Remote areas tend to be more disadvantaged in terms of the availability of health care and the acceptability of health services as well as being characterized by the lowest information levels. Some of these areas are, however, economically better-off than areas with better availability, accessibility and information.

The information index derived in the Ghanaian study is not sufficiently comprehensive to reflect fully the extent to which households are informed across the access dimensions, so that they are empowered to choose whether or not to use health services. Nevertheless, it highlights the need for the health system to engage with communities across the region. The findings particularly suggest that if general socio-economic variables were used as a proxy for information needs, communication interventions may be inappropriately targeted.

Lessons from 'access mapping'

Despite constituting a key element of common definitions of equity, access is an ill-defined concept. Health system and policy research so far has largely failed to promote strategies to address access in its multiple dimensions. Studies that claim to be evaluating health service access have overwhelmingly focused on only one or two factors, most frequently physical distance to a facility or health insurance membership. We recognize that the interpretation of access variables in Ghana as factors feeding into the respective access dimensions, albeit informed through preliminary qualitative and quantitative analyses, is very specific to the study context, is partly based on normative assumptions and could be open to debate. This case study is an illustration of how the complex concept of access can be broken down into different dimensions, which can be analyzed on the basis of household survey data. It shows that access can be meaningfully described as a composite concept that can even be measured. It is not necessary to reduce access to health care to something as narrow as the distance to a facility or indeed to any single factor. At the same time, a purely quantitative approach to access will never be enough. To understand the reality of access to health services in a particular study context, quantitative research will always require a qualitative complement. But the approach to mapping access reveals a whole range of policy-relevant issues that would have been hidden by restricting the analysis to distance to services or by adopting a purely qualitative approach.

The most striking finding revealed by the different access maps is that geographical patterns of one dimension of access may differ from those of another access dimension. In the Ghanaian example, areas suffering from disadvantages in terms of service affordability do not necessarily show disadvantages with respect to the availability of services. In other words, there may not be areas of poor overall health service access as such. Whereas this insight may not come as a surprise, it certainly appears to be contrary to common perception, which tends to categorize disadvantaged and less disadvantaged areas rather than areas disadvantaged in terms of one access dimension and areas disadvantaged in terms of another. The findings also illustrate the need to improve the communication processes between the health system and its clients across the district. Only if the communities have a full understanding of their own health and of the choices that exist within the health system and only if there is an awareness on the delivery side of people's needs and expectations, i.e., if there is a common level of information and understanding, will access as the freedom to use health services be achieved.

Consequently, there is not just one policy to address access to health care. Improving access requires a diverse set of policies. Addressing problems of availability requires completely different policy tools from those for improving the acceptability of a specific type of service. 'Access mapping' may turn out to be an extremely useful tool for health policy development and implementation. Not only does the exercise distinguish between the various dimensions that may be interpreted as areas of action, it also highlights the magnitude of the problem and, therefore, assists in prioritizing. 'Access mapping' turns equity-orientated health policy development into a concrete and actionable task.

The challenge lies in achieving a balance between the different dimensions. 'Access mapping' may, as the case study shows, imply the need to address different challenges in different geographical areas, yet there is no immediately evident way to prioritize between the different access dimensions. For example, how can the benefits of allocating resources to improving acceptability in area A be compared to the benefits of allocating resources to improving availability in area B? In practice, however, the question may not need to be posed. First, geographical priorities may already have been set on the basis of other policy imperatives. In this case, 'access mapping' helps to identify the dimension of access that shows the greatest relative disadvantage in order to address this dimension in the prioritized area. Second, priorities for action may already have been set. Here, 'access mapping' helps to identify the geographical areas that need preferential attention. However, where there are extremely limited resources, it may be necessary to view this as an efficiency question and to seek to identify the most cost-effective way to promote greater health service access.

'Access mapping' on the basis of composite indices, irrespective of the statistical technique used to generate them, does not suffice for formulating policies. Once the dimensions have been evaluated and degrees of disadvantage in each area determined, further attention needs to be devoted to the root causes underlying relative disadvantage in the access factors. Here, the pyramidal conceptual model that was introduced earlier can be of help in structuring the investigative framework. Policy action to address the access dimensions must be based on sound qualitative information. Communicative processes between the health system and its clients, and vice versa, do not only empower individuals and communities, they can also guide policy action to improve access through its dimensions.

Conclusions

There is considerable scope for promoting equitable access to health care, but only if the concept of access is better understood and is 'unpacked' into its constituent parts so that it can be evaluated comprehensively. The framework suggested here can serve as a useful basis for such evaluations; it suggests three key dimensions of access which can serve as entry points for analyzing the interaction between the health system and individuals or households and it spells out some of the factors that influence each dimension. This chapter has also illustrated how household survey data can be used to assess the relative importance of different factors in each dimension, which should be followed up with a thorough consideration of issues underlying, and ultimately the root causes of, 'lack of fit' between the health system and individuals in terms of the most important factors. This can then be used to identify appropriate policy interventions, which should not be restricted to the health system side of the access equation, but should also include policies that empower individuals and households in their interactions with the health system. Information was also highlighted as being core to each of the access dimensions.

In focusing on inequalities in service use, equity research has not made much progress in identifying appropriate policy interventions. There is likely to be considerably more success if greater energy is devoted to evaluating access directly and comprehensively (i.e., focusing on all dimensions of access) and identifying appropriate ways to promote equitable access.

REFERENCES

Aday, L. A. and Andersen, R. (1975) *Development of Indices of Access to Medical Care*. Ann Arbor: Health Administration Press.

Aday, L. A. and Andersen, R. (1981) Equity of access to medical care: a conceptual and empirical overview. *Medical Care*. **19**: 4–27.

Andersen, R. (1995) Revisiting the behavioural model and access to medical care: does it matter? *Journal of Health and Social Behaviour*. **36**: 1–10.

Burstrom, B. (2002) Increasing inequalities in health care utilization across income groups in Sweden during the 1990s? *Health Policy*. **62**: 117–129.

Donabedian, A. (1973) *Aspects of Medical Care Administration*. Cambridge, MA: Harvard University Press.

Goddard, M. and Smith, P. (2001) Equity of access to health care services: theory and evidence from the UK. *Social Science and Medicine*. **53**: 1149–1162.

Gulliford, M., Figueroa-Munoz, J., Morgan, M. *et al.* (2002) What does 'access to health care' mean? *Journal of Health Services Research and Policy*. **7**: 186–188.

Gulliford, M. and Morgan, M., eds., (2003) *Access to Health Care*. London: Routledge.

Gwatkin, D., Wagstaff, A. and Yazbeck, A., eds., (2005) *Reaching the Poor With Health, Nutrition, and Population Services*. Washington, DC: World Bank.

Kline, P. (1994) *An Easy Guide to Factor Analysis*. London: Routledge.

Mooney, G. (1983) Equity in health care: confronting the confusion. *Effective Health Care*. **1**: 179–185.

Oliver, A. and Mossialos, E. (2005) Equity of access to health care: outlining the foundations for action. *Journal of Epidemiology and Community Health*. **58**: 655–658.

Penchansky, R. (1977) *The Concept of Access: a Definition*. Hyattsville: National Health Planning Information Center.

Penchansky, R. and Thomas, W. (1981) The concept of access. *Medical Care*. **19**: 127–140.

Puentes-Markides, C. (1992) Women and access to health care. *Social Science and Medicine*. **35**: 619–626.

Ricketts, T. and Goldsmith, L. (2005) Access in health services research: the battle of the frameworks. *Nursing Outlook*. **53**: 274–280.

Rosero-Bixby, L. (2004) Supply and access to health services in Costa Rica 2000: a GIS-based study. *Social Science and Medicine*. **58**: 1271–1284.

Tabachnick, B. and Fidell, L. (2006) *Using Multivariate Statistics*. 5th ed. Needham Heights, MA: Allyn & Bacon.

Tanser, F., Gijsbertsen, B. and Herbst, K. (2006) Modelling and understanding primary health care accessibility and utilization in rural South Africa: an exploration using a geographical information system. *Social Science and Medicine*. **63**: 691–705.

Thiede, M. (2005) Information and access to health care: is there a role for trust? *Social Science and Medicine*. **61**: 1452–1462.

Waters, H. (2000) Measuring equity in access to health care. *Social Science and Medicine*. **51**: 599–612.

Whitehead, M., Evandrou, M., Haglund, B. and Diderichsen, F. (1997) As the health divide widens in Sweden and Britain, what's happening to access to care? *British Medical Journal*. **315**: 1006–1009.

7

Acceptability, trust and equity

Lucy Gilson

Summary

This chapter seeks to tease out the key elements of acceptability from evidence on health care seeking behaviour, as well as discussing its relevance and importance to health care equity. The chapter also considers the influences over patient and provider behaviour, as well as the policy actions required to address acceptability barriers and so improve health care access for disadvantaged social groups.

Understood as the social and cultural distance between health care systems and their users, the evidence suggests that the acceptability dimension of access is closely tied to patient–provider trust. It comprises the fit between lay and professional health beliefs, provider–patient engagement and dialogue, and the ways in which health care organizational arrangements frame patient responses to services. Acceptability and trust barriers are clearly disproportionately faced by socially disadvantaged groups in all societies, and influence both the distributional and procedural justice of health care. As structural and power relations influence patient and provider behaviour, and the interactions between them, an examination of acceptability barriers demonstrates, moreover, how social inequality is embedded within health care.

The chapter argues that it is important to take acceptability and trust seriously in policy debates about health care equity, notwithstanding the important physical and cost barriers also facing health care users. Tackling acceptability and trust barriers requires three sets of actions: those that strengthen the provision of care to the benefit of all groups whilst offering particular gains for socially disadvantaged groups; those that prioritize the specific needs of these groups; and those that are necessary to enable and sustain the other interventions. Together these policy actions can strengthen universal health care systems and ensure delivery of interventions tailored to the needs of socially disadvantaged groups.

Introduction

The importance of access in discussion of health care equity is well established (Gulliford *et al.* 2002). Access is, in essence, a function of the 'degree of fit' between

The Economics of Health Equity, ed. Di McIntyre and Gavin Mooney. Published by Cambridge University Press. © Cambridge University Press 2007.

clients (patients, citizens) and health care provision (Pechansky and Thomas 1981). Although often seen as a purely supply-side phenomenon, there are always supply-side and demand-side influences over access (see Chapter 6). Commonly identified access dimensions include availability, covering factors such as geographical location, transportation availability, as well as organizational factors such as opening hours or waiting time to appointment, and affordability, combining concern for the costs of seeking care, households' ability to manage these costs and their impacts on household livelihoods. Consideration of these access barriers generate health policy conclusions around the need to improve geographic availability, strengthen health care organization, reduce prices and introduce financing mechanisms to protect patients from the costs of seeking care.

A third access dimension is that of acceptability, that is, the social and cultural distance between health care systems and their users (Hausmann-Muela *et al.* 2003). Such barriers are identified as underpinning the systematic differences in health care utilization patterns that exist in many European settings between socio-economic groups and between other population groupings (e.g., non-migrants and minority groups or immigrants; men and women), despite the wide geographic availability of health services and well established financial risk protection mechanisms (Tamsma and Berman 2004). The need for culturally appropriate health services is also discussed in relation to lower socio-economic and minority groups in the United States (Anderson *et al.* 2003) and in relation to indigenous peoples worldwide (Stephens *et al.* 2006). Poor provider–patient interactions, an element of social and cultural distance, are, moreover, often raised as an important access barrier in low-income and middle-income countries (Palmer 2007).

However, there remains unclarity about the nature of the acceptability barriers to access, how they influence health care equity, how important they are relative to other barriers, particularly in low-income and middle-income settings, and how they can be addressed.

This chapter, therefore, examines the evidence on health care seeking behaviour in a wide range of contexts, and discusses its relevance and importance to health care equity. It then considers the influences over patient and provider behaviour, as a basis for thinking through the policy action required to address acceptability barriers and so improve health care access for disadvantaged social groups. Overall, the chapter argues that it is important to take acceptability seriously in policy debates about health care equity, notwithstanding the important physical and cost barriers also facing health care users, particularly in low-income and middle-income settings.

In making this argument, the paper draws primarily on empirical evidence (single studies and review papers) collected through a comprehensive and systematic literature review. This evidence was identified through searches of PubMed, the International Bibliography of Social Sciences (IBSS) and Google Scholar for the past 10 years, involving combinations of the following key words: access, acceptability, cultural access, cultural competence, cultural security, equity, health care, health seeking behaviour, social exclusion and trust. A second set of searches in the same databases also sought to identify empirical work specifically considering the influences over provider behaviour, using the key words provider, practice and organizational culture. The reference lists of papers were then reviewed and additional references identified, whilst general web searches were conducted to identify relevant grey literature. The final set of papers included here were those selected as being most relevant to the issues under focus. A few were purposively identified because they are relevant to the policy actions outlined in the last section of the chapter. The papers are drawn from country settings with high, middle and low incomes.

Some conceptual material is also brought into the chapter, drawn from a set of debates identified by the author as relevant to the notion of acceptability. These are the debates around: cultural security and cultural competence of health care; the contribution of a human rights 'lens' in work on health care systems in low-income and middle-income countries; responsiveness as an indicator of health system performance; and, finally, the role of trust within health care.

The elements of acceptability

Table 7.1 identifies the three elements of acceptability, understood as social and cultural distance, most commonly identified in experience. It is based on a comparison of the evidence on general health care seeking behaviour with that which specifically examines the ways in which patient–provider trust influences this behaviour. Patient–provider trust is a relational notion founded on the patient's judgement or belief that the provider will act in the patient's interests (Hall *et al.* 2001), for example, by being respectful and doing his or her best to address the patient's problems. It has clear relevance to the notion of acceptability and has been specifically noted as an influence over health care seeking behaviour in both high-income and low-income settings (Johansson and Winkvist 2002; Watkins and Plant 2004; Kefford *et al.* 2005; Armstrong *et al.* 2006).

The fit between lay and professional health beliefs is the first element of acceptability. Lay understandings of health care and healing systems are often an important influence over the decision of whether and where to seek care. The broad mismatch between lay health beliefs and the biomedical perspectives dominant within health care systems may deter use of allopathic providers and generate patient distrust in them. Lay understandings also influence patient perceptions about the probable effectiveness of the treatments available from different providers,

Table 7.1. Elements of acceptability

Element	General health care seeking behaviour influenced by:	Patient trust influences health care seeking behaviour and is influenced by:
The fit between lay and professional health beliefs	• Lay constructions of health and healing and degree of fit with provider knowledge systems; • Perceived effectiveness of treatment provided and possibility of cure (and perceived importance of drugs to effective care).	• Perceived technical competence of providers, availability of drugs and necessary equipment.
Patient–provider engagement and dialogue	• Patient ability to exercise voice in medical care encounters; • Provider behaviours and attitudes towards patients and, in particular, communication practices and maintenance of confidentiality; • Provider stereotyping of and discrimination towards groups of patients.	• Patients' own characteristics and attitudes; • Levels of provider respect and compassion towards patients demonstrated in attitudes and communication practices, including maintenance of confidentiality; • Lack of bias or discriminatory attitudes towards patient groups.
The influence of health care organizational arrangements on patient responses to services	• Fit between health service structure and routine practices of intended beneficiaries.	• Range of services provided or accessible through provider; • Concern that providers face incentives to pursue profit, not patient need; • Continuity of relationship, and time spent, with provider; • Institutional guarantees, e.g., scrutiny mechanisms, training, ethical commitments.
Sources	Barr 2005; Dixon *et al.* 2003; Golooba-Mutebi and Tollman (private communication); Lau *et al.* 2000; Lonnroth *et al.* 2001; Montenegro and Stephens 2006; Rouse 2004; Stephens *et al.* 2006; Shaikh and Hatcher 2004; Takahashi and Rodrigeuz 2002; Willems *et al.* 2005	Armstrong *et al.* 2006; Bostrom *et al.* 2004; Dibben and Lean 2003; Gilson *et al.* 2005; Greene 2004; Jacobs *et al.* 2006; O'Malley and Forrest 2002; Riewpaiboon *et al.* 2005; Russell 2005; Tendler and Freedheim 1994; Tibandebage and Mackintosh 2005

and the probability of cure. For some illnesses, self-care or traditional healing may be understood as the most appropriate forms of care, and for some conditions use of allopathic medicine may even be deemed dangerous. Patient concerns about the (perceived) technical competence of providers, the availability of drugs and equipment and institutional guarantees of competence (see later) also influence patient trust in providers and affect provider choice. Such judgements are, however, dynamic, influenced by past experiences of care, the perceived appropriateness of care received and past experiences of getting better or worse after care.

The second element of acceptability is the nature of patient–provider engagement and dialogue. Although encompassing provider communication practices and attitudes towards patients, such engagement (and the associated patient–provider trust) is also influenced by patients' own abilities and willingness to enter into dialogue with health professionals and their attitudes towards providers. Providers personally known to the patient, or of the same ethnic group or sex as the patient, may be trusted more than other providers, for example. Providers may, however, only reinforce negative patient perceptions through their practices. The mismatch between lay and professional health beliefs may, thus, be exacerbated by the language and manner providers use to explain health problems to patients. Providers also exercise power through their communication practices and by whether or not they maintain patient confidentiality, and demonstrate bias or impartiality towards different patient groups. Thus, providers commonly, if sometimes unconsciously, stereotype certain patient groups, making assumptions about them, talking to them in particular ways and offering different levels of emotional support and engagement to them compared with other patients (Burgess *et al.* 2004). Such experiences can deter patients from using health care services and cause their distrust of providers.

The final element of acceptability is linked to the organizational arrangements of health care, and how they frame or shape patient responses to care. These arrangements and responses can, first, enable or disable patient access to the full range of needed health services. For example, an investigation of the care seeking experiences of different minority groups (gay men, Latina or Hispanic women who spoke only Spanish, and injecting drug users) living with HIV and AIDS in one area of the USA demonstrates that the ways in which health services are organized do not always reflect the socially accepted practices of the patients seeking care. As a result, two of the three groups routinely accessed health care at places where few HIV and AIDS services were available and so only gained access to these services by chance or through informal encounters with knowledgeable people (Takahashi and Rodriguez 2002). Patient trust of providers may, moreover, specifically result from the comprehensiveness of services provided, ability to secure access to referral care and providing services in response to patient needs and demands (Tendler and Freedheim 1994; O'Malley and Forrest 2002).

Another organizational factor noted in Table 7.1 as particularly important in building or undermining patient trust in the provider is the provider payment mechanism. In many contexts, patients see fee-based payment systems as encouraging providers to act against the patient interest and in pursuit of financial gain (Gilson 2005). However, in some instances, patients may see free care as an indicator of poor care, discouraging use of services (Lonnroth *et al.* 2001). Other influences over patient–provider trust include the opportunity for repeated interactions of reasonable duration and the availability of institutional guarantees of trustworthy provider behaviour. In general, therefore, the trust literature suggests that organizational arrangements can influence the acceptability of care by providing institutional signals about whether providers will act in the patients' interests, institutional opportunities to generate enough knowledge of the provider to build such trust or institutional influences that shape provider behaviour (Gilson 2003; 2005). Similarly, Rouse (2004) argues that managers and providers shape patient access to care through their influence over staff education, personnel decisions and resource management, as well as their own sense of responsibility towards patients.

The identification of these three sets of issues as aspects of acceptability is, finally, supported by wider conceptual literature and debates. All three elements reflect key concerns about the cultural competence of health care systems. Anderson *et al.* (2003) and Tamsma and Berman (2004), for example, argue that cultural incompetence is commonly demonstrated by the dissonance between the health beliefs of minority patient groups and dominant medical knowledge, racial predjudice or other discrimination towards patients, communication barriers between patients and providers, poor information provision and mistrust of health care providers. The second and third elements identified in Table 7.1 also reflect seven of the eight domains of the World Health Organization's responsiveness indicator (see Box 7.1); one of the very few efforts to codify such aspects of health care performance. From a human rights perspective, moreover, Gostin and Hodge (2003) and Freedman

---

Box 7.1 The eight domains of responsiveness

(a) Respect for dignity of person;

(b) Autonomy to participate in health-related decisions;

(c) Confidentiality;

(d) Prompt attention;

(e) Adequate quality of care;

(f) Communication;

(g) Access to social support networks;

(h) Choice of health care provider.

Source: Gostin and Hodge 2003

(2001) argue that the right to dignity is a basic human right linked both to being free from disease and to the ways in which human beings interact to obtain and maintain a good standard of health. Being badly treated by providers or the health care system undermines this right.

Acceptability and trust as influences over health care equity

Commonly recognized as reflecting the fairness of health care systems, the degree of (in)equity is assessed in terms of the extent of systematic differences between population groups in their experience of health care. In making equity judgements, comparisons are, moreover, generally made between population groups categorized on the basis of various markers of socio-economic status, whilst the experience of care is generally considered in terms of the distribution of health care benefits and burdens. In this chapter, however, the broader value derived from health care is also considered to be an element of the experience of care, linked to the notion of procedural justice (Mooney 1996; Gilson 2000).

Looking first at the distribution between population groups of acceptability and trust access barriers, the evidence shows that, across countries, these barriers are disproportionately faced by socially disadvantaged groups, compared with other population groups. Very clearly, these groups suffer most from discriminatory provider attitudes and poor communication practices linked to their lower socio-economic status, race or ethnicity, sex or particular health condition. This is true in countries of both high income (O'Malley and Forrest 2002; Wolff *et al.* 2003; Rouse 2004; Tamsma and Berman 2004; Barr 2005; NHMRC 2005; Willems *et al.* 2005; Jacobs *et al.* 2006) and low income (Golooba-Mutebi and Tollman (private communication); Lonnroth *et al.* 2001; Johansson and Winkvist 2002; Greene 2004; Shaikh and Hatcher 2004; Watkins and Plant 2004; Gilson *et al.* 2005; Russell 2005; Tibandebage and Mackintosh 2005). At the same time, socially advantaged groups have greater ability to engage with providers during consultations (Dixon *et al.* 2003; Hausmann-Muela *et al.* 2003). A particular access barrier faced by indigenous peoples, moreover, is the mismatch between their health beliefs and dominant biomedical models of care (Stephens *et al.* 2006).

There is little evidence on whether levels of patient–provider trust differ between population groups. However, the greater discrimination experienced by socially disadvantaged groups may lead such trust to be an access barrier of particular relevance to these groups, as suggested by the African-American and American Indian experience in the USA (Call 2006; Jacobs *et al.* 2006). Patient–provider trust is, moreover, clearly a factor influencing the health care seeking behaviour of low-income patients in countries of both high income (O'Malley and Forrest 2002;

Sheppard *et al.* 2004) and low income (Gilson *et al.* 2005; Riewpaiboon *et al.* 2005; Russell 2005; Tibandebage and Mackintosh 2005).

The evidence suggests that acceptability and trust barriers influence health care utilization patterns among population groups. Acceptability problems deter or delay the use of curative care by a range of socially disadvantaged groups (Johansson and Winkvist 2002; Anderson *et al.* 2003; Hausmann-Muela *et al.* 2003; MacKian 2003; Thorson and Johansson, 2004). Systematic differences in health beliefs, thus, explain the UK evidence that lower-income groups do not use prevention services as much as richer groups, use emergency services rather than general practitioner surgeries and avoid or delay seeking care (Dixon *et al.* 2003). There are also some hints that distrust may act as a particular barrier to the uptake of preventive services among poorer groups. On the one hand, general evidence suggests that immunization uptake is particularly influenced by patient or parental trust in providers and other health services in both low-income (Birungi 1998; Das and Das 2003) and high-income (Brownlie and Howson 2006) countries. On the other hand, two studies point to the particular influence of trust over use of preventive services by groups of lower socio-economic status. A historical study argues that in the nineteenth century smallpox vaccination levels increased more quickly among better educated and more wealthy peasants in one part of Scandanavia because they were better able to acquire and use new information and had a higher level of trust in the authorities providing the information (Dribe and Nysedt 2002). A more recent US study, meanwhile, presents data showing that patient trust in primary care providers is associated with greater use of a range of preventive services by low-income African-American women (O'Malley *et al.* 2004).

Acceptability and trust problems also influence patient decision-making and experience in ways that shape the benefits derived from health care and are likely further to disadvantage socially marginalized groups (given that the problems are disproportionately experienced by these groups). In particular, acceptability and trust problems are linked to:[1]

- Patient unwillingness to reveal past medical history, making diagnosis and treatment difficult (Scott *et al.* 1995; Tamsma and Berman 2004; Jacobs *et al.* 2006);
- Lower rates of referral to secondary and tertiary care, and lower rates of intervention relative to need (Dixon *et al.* 2003);
- Limited patient adherence to advice or treatment, and failure to follow up, particularly in relation to chronic care (Johansson and Winkvist 2002; O'Malley

---

[1] Wallerstein's (2006) thorough review of empirical evidence concerning the links between patient empowerment initiatives and health outcomes reflects these findings. She judges that patient empowerment can improve individual decision-making efficacy, lead to better disease complication management and improved health behaviours, and encourage more efficient use of care.

and Forrest 2002; Dibben and Lean 2003; Dixon *et al.* 2003; MacKian 2003; Greene 2004);

- Lower self-reported health status (Armstrong *et al.* 2005).

As an influence over health care seeking behaviour patterns, acceptability problems have, moreover, a direct influence over the costs of seeking care (Shaikh and Hatcher 2004). Russell (2005), thus, uses Sri Lankan evidence to show that lower-income groups often use private providers for acute outpatient care because they have greater trust in private providers than in public primary care facilities.[2] He then demonstrates that this trust-based choice has cost consequences for those on the lowest incomes, forcing asset depletion and increased debt and threatening their overall livelihood situation. The potentially catastrophic impact of health care costs on poor households in low-income and middle-income countries is widely recognized (Russell 2004; McIntyre *et al.* 2006), as is the potential for health care systems to exacerbate or prevent poverty, poor health and social exclusion in higher-income settings (Tamsma and Berman 2004).

Acceptability and trust problems, finally, influence health care equity through their impact on the broader value derived from health care by socially disadvantaged groups. Tibandebage and Mackintosh (2005), for example, draw on Amartya Sen's work in discussing poor people's experience of health care in Tanzania, using the understanding that impoverishment involves a loss of the capability of claim entitlements to essential services such as health care and to participate in social life. They judge that provider abuse towards patients undermines poor patients' capability of claiming decent health care and adds a lived social element to their material experience of poverty. The denial of dignity implied by abusive provider behaviour also represents a denial of the patient's human rights (Freedman 2001) and, some argue, threatens personal identity. The failure to ensure cultural security within the health care system for Aboriginal and Torres Strait Peoples in Australia is, therefore, argued both to compromise their rights, values and expectations, and particularly because culture and identity are central to their perceptions of health, threaten their identity (Houston 2003). Similarly, Williams (1999) has argued that where welfare systems, such as health care, deny people the opportunity to play an active role in decision-making about their care, and to be held responsible for their choices, they deny patients the recognition they need to develop their identity and sense of moral worth.

The way in which people (patients, providers) are treated by health care systems (providers, managers and bureaucrats) is, thus, a central influence over the morality

---

[2] This greater trust is based on their quick service, the greater organizational respect towards patients demonstrated in these facilities, their public sector training (which is recognized as high level), the providers' strong listening skills and opportunities for repeated visits to the same practitioner.

and procedural justice of the system itself (Rothstein 1998). Such treatment is, in turn, strongly influenced by provider practices and health care organizational arrangements: that is, by the acceptability of health care. The trust built and sustained by dignified treatment is, moreover, an integral element of ethical practice within health care systems. Given that sick patients are subject to a unique imbalance of power and knowledge, they are particularly vulnerable and so only grant power reluctantly to health workers to achieve desired outcomes (Goold 2002). Trusting relationships provide for the legitimate exercise of that power. Overall, therefore, through trusting patient–provider relations, health care systems may contribute to building wider social value.

The wider influences embedded in acceptability and access

Before thinking about how to tackle acceptability and access problems, it is important to understand better the various factors underpinning them – that is, influencing the interactions between patients or citizens and providers or health care systems.

On the patient side, these influences are often only considered at the level of the individual (MacKian 2003). Yet, as already noted, patient trust in the provider is not just a function of interpersonal behaviours or patient perceptions of provider competence. Instead, and perhaps more importantly, it represents a response to the degree of fit between lay and professional health beliefs and to the ways in which features of the organizational environment are perceived as likely to influence provider behaviour towards patients. Birungi (1998), for example, tellingly portrays the breakdown of patient trust in the Ugandan immunization services as a result of poor patient experiences of health care, associated with abusive provider behaviour and provider practices that demonstrated little trust in the health care system (providers refused to use state-provided injection equipment), in a context of economic recession, fear about the rising HIV and AIDS epidemic and wider distrust of the Government. The ultimate consequence was that, not being able to afford new syringes for each vaccination, poor patients commonly preferred to share unsterilized injection equipment with their family members than to trust the state-provided equipment (even when sterilized), putting themselves at greater risk of infection.

The social influences over acceptability, and the central place of acceptability within the notion of access, are clearly highlighted in the access definition used by the Nepal Safe Motherhood Programme (see Box 7.2).

The empirical evidence, thus, suggests that in the trial and error search for relief when sick, people nearly always draw on advice from others in the community (Hausmann-Muela *et al*. 2003; Shaikh and Hatcher 2004). Such advice often reflects

> **Box 7.2 Expanded definition of access**
>
> Access is enabled in an environment that encourages people to utilize health services, within any given social context. At its best it is a dynamic, participatory process based on good practice. Access advantageously uses local knowledge, perceptions and values, relevant traditional practices, preferences and beliefs, to enhance knowledge and awareness. Access encourages self-confidence, voice and agency, especially amongst women. Access embraces financial, institutional and infrastructure factors, including but not limited to funding, transportation and education. Access relies upon good provider attitudes, trust, honesty, responsiveness, accountability, and good quality service delivery both at established facilities and through outreach programmes. Access engages socially marginalized and vulnerable communities, is inclusive and is empowering.
>
> Source: Aitken and Thomas 2004 (p. 8)

cultural beliefs about the causes of illness and appropriate approaches to healing, as well as lay knowledge of specific illnesses (e.g., tuberculosis: Watkins and Plant 2004). It also reflects rumours and reputations about providers (Lonnroth *et al.* 2001) as well as pragmatic concerns about factors such as cost and provider behaviours. Judgements about providers may be specifically influenced by wider beliefs, such as some church leaders' condemnation of traditional healers in South Africa (Goolooba-Mutebi and Tollman (private communication)).

Wider social processes also influence patterns of communication, trust, interactions between providers and patients, and health care seeking behaviour (Armstrong *et al.* 2006). The popular and political discourse of public trust in Western medicine, and in the state as a provider of essential services, thus, sustains trust in, and encourages use of, medical practitioners in Sri Lanka (Russell 2005). In contrast, a discourse of distrust in the state has undermined its role as a provider of health information and services in Nigeria (Obadare 2005) and Uganda (Streefland 2005). Socio-economic status also influences trust judgements. Riewpaiboon *et al.* (2005) show, for example, how the varying world-views of different socio-economic groups influence the particular forms of trust mothers see as important in relation to maternal care in Thailand, with consequences for their health care seeking behaviour.

Finally, power relations influence the way patients interact with providers. In Vietnam, for example, patient–provider engagement is constrained by the generally authoritarian nature of social relationships and the established culture of not involving patients in their own care (Johansson and Winkvist 2002; Watkins and Plant 2004). Relations between the sexes within society are particularly important influences in many contexts, as women may not make decisions for themselves (Shaikh and Hatcher 2004) and are less likely than men to seek care or receive family support during treatment episodes (Johansson and Winkvist 2002; Tamsma and Berman 2004).

Overlapping sets of influences also shape health personnel behaviours and attitudes, with consequences for acceptability and patient–provider trust. Medical or clinical protocols, for example, require providers to adopt specific approaches in treating patients presenting with particular conditions or for specific services, influencing patient access to resources (Rouse 2004). Such protocols may also prevent providers from changing the treatment approach to respond to patient difference (thus, the protocol for directly observed therapy for tuberculosis is not easy to adapt to the different factors influencing the adherence to treatment by men and women: Thorson and Johansson 2004). Organizational factors such as workload pressures, the emotional demands of their jobs and the degree of job control can also encourage providers to stereotype particular groups of patients (Burgess *et al.* 2004), and influence provider attitudes towards patients (Tendler and Freedheim 1994; Gilson *et al.* 2005; Russell 2005).

Organizational culture has a particularly strong influence over provider practice. Whilst still contested, this notion reflects the understanding that organizations are socially constructed, comprising sets of institutions (rules, laws, norms and customs) that may reflect but do not fully replicate wider societal institutions and that shape the behaviour and actions of those working within them (Gilson and Erasmus 2004). Emerging evidence, thus, suggests that the culture of health care organizations may:

- Sustain an environment in which patients are dehumanized by providers, given the stress generated by accepted organizational practices (Scott *et al.* 1995);
- Provide an obstacle to implementing patient centred models of care, especially in authoritarian cultures (Johansson and Winkvist 2002; Watkins *et al.* 2004);
- Prevent the co-ordination across services necessary to respond effectively to patient need, given organizational boundaries, medical dominance and bureaucratic hierarchy (Mallinson *et al.* 2006).

Provider practices and organizational culture are, in turn, influenced by power relations within society. Discriminatory provider attitudes and practices towards poor and vulnerable patient groups commonly reflect socio-economic patterning within society as a whole (Greene 2004; Reidpath and Chan 2005). Sexual dynamics in Pakistan are, for example, reflected both in the distance women health workers establish between themselves and their patients, and in the abuses of power to which male managers subject them (Mumtaz *et al.* 2003). The predominantly male health care providers in Vietnam, meanwhile, recognize that sex barriers influence access to TB services but take no action to offset them (Thorson and Johansson 2004). Macroeconomic policies and constraints have, finally, clearly had an impact on provider performance in many lower-income countries, undermining salary levels and professional ethics, prompting abusive behaviour towards patients and breaking down patient trust in the health care system (Owusu 2005; Streefland 2005).

Taking action on acceptability and trust access barriers

In taking action to address acceptability and trust barriers, the evidence so far presented clearly suggests that the first step is to recognize the socialized nature of health care and, in particular, the frequent cultural mismatches between lay and professional health beliefs. Rather than blaming patients for their poor health care seeking behaviour, health professionals need, instead, to understand the beliefs and motivations of the public they seek to serve and to tailor service delivery to their perceptions and needs. Particular attention must be paid to the circumstances of socially disadvantaged groups, given the influence of acceptability and trust access barriers over their health seeking behaviour – in all country settings. Yet action to address these barriers can benefit all patients. As argued earlier, it is a necessary foundation for rebuilding and sustaining the ethical foundations of health care.

Although few intervention studies of relevance are available,[3] the evidence on the nature of acceptability and trust barriers, and their influence over health seeking behaviour, points to three complementary sets of policy actions (Table 7.2): the first set aim to strengthen the provision of care that will benefit all groups, but, given their experiences, particularly socially disadvantaged groups, and those with chronic conditions (Dibben and Lean 2003); the second prioritize the particular needs of socially disadvantaged groups; and the third comprise the actions necessary to enable and sustain other interventions. Taken together, this set of policy actions aims to strengthen universal health care systems and to deliver interventions tailored to the needs of socially disadvantaged groups.

In discussing how to strengthen acceptability and trust, much emphasis is placed on training to improve the communication skills of health workers (doctors, nurses and other staff), as well as their sex and cultural sensitivity (Scott *et al.* 1995; Anderson *et al.* 2003; Dibben and Lean 2003; Shaikh and Hatcher 2004; Tamsma and Berman 2004). Education and training may also assist in encouraging providers to take responsibility for the personal changes that can strengthen their practices (Johansson *et al.* 2000), but careful thought must be given to the educational approach most likely to be effective (Burgess *et al.* 2004).

---

[3] Only one systematic review of relevant interventions was identified. This concludes that, given the lack of before and after or case control studies, there is little clear evidence about the effectiveness of any proposed intervention (Anderson *et al.* 2003).

Table 7.2. Taking action on acceptability and trust barriers

Actions for all groups	Specific actions to address the barriers faced by socially disadvantaged groups	Actions necessary to enable and sustain other interventions
Provider training to improve communication skills Develop client-centred approach to service provision: • Allow greater time for consultations and continuity of patient–provider contact; • Improve co-ordination of primary care and referral services.	Develop client-centred approach to service provision: • Employ members of these groups within the health care system; • Ensure availability of signage in different languages, and of interpreters; • Improve co-ordination of health care and wider social services. Address time and convenience costs: • Provide mobile outreach services to, or patient transport for groups living in, remote areas; • Relocate staff to rural, remote areas. Patient empowerment: • Employ patient care advisors; • Establish peer support mechanisms.	Underpinning actions: • Build supportive organizational culture within health care systems; • Strengthen leadership and management, particularly human resource management, within health care systems; • Establish dedicated funding sources or new funding mechanisms; • Develop accountability mechanisms that develop shared citizen–system responsibility; • Take wider political action to enable and support change.

In strengthening ethical practice, it is certainly critical to develop a health workforce that is reflective and critical, compassionate and caring, and that has integrity, creativity and sensitivity (Shaikh and Hatcher 2004). However, provider education is simply not enough by itself. As health workers are often merely the messengers of the system in which they work (Reidpath and Chan 2005), policy action to tackle acceptability and trust barriers must extend 'beyond individual providers to include organizational settings and administrative procedures, the manner in which technologies are used, the way in which health care is funded, and the elements of health care that are emphasized' (Scott *et al.* 1995 p. 91). Many writers, therefore, call for the adoption of a 'client-centred approach' in the way that health care systems are organized (Shaikh and Hatcher 2004), encompassing concern both for geographic *and* social distance in the provision of care.

Particularly at the primary care level, such an approach should include more time for personalized encounters between provider and patient (O'Malley and Forrest 2002; Thorson and Johannson 2004) and for continuity of contact between patient and provider (Russell 2005; Armstrong *et al.* 2006), or the health care system (Johansson and Winkvist 2002). The structural changes enabling such encounters, such as in staffing levels and practices, could also reduce workloads and provider fatigue, building provider contexts in which provider discrimination towards particular patient groups might be reduced (Burgess *et al.* 2004) and enabling the development of trusting relationships (Gilson 2005). Other actions to build patient trust in the health care system include improving access to a comprehensive range of services through co-ordination of primary and referral services (O'Malley and Forrest 2002) or packaging services in ways that build on patient preferences for curative services (Tendler and Freedheim 1994; Das and Das 2003).

However, these general actions must be complemented by those actions that are tailored to the particular circumstances of socially disadvantaged groups. These include employment strategies that ensure diversity within the health workforce and so allow patients to be served by providers of the same sex or cultural community, reducing cultural distance and enabling patient–provider trust (Shaikh and Hatcher 2004; Barr 2005). Ensuring that signage and literature is available in different languages and that there are interpreters within health facilities might be important for some groups of patient (Anderson *et al.* 2003). Better co-ordination between health and other social services may also be necessary to address the wider health needs of particularly vulnerable patient groups (Mallinson *et al.* 2006).

A client-centred approach to health care organization that recognizes the particular circumstances of socially disadvantaged groups is, however, likely to require action outside existing health care facilities. Addressing these wider access barriers may also build such groups' trust in the health care system by demonstrating care for them in times of vulnerability (Macintyre and Hotchkiss 1999). For example, it might be possible to tackle the time and convenience costs that often deter them from using health care by providing mobile outreach services in the areas where people live and work (Das and Das 2003; Wolff *et al.* 2003; Stegeman and Costongs 2004), tailored to meet their particular needs (Tamsma and Berman 2004). Alternatively, policy action could be taken to reduce transport costs, by improving patient transport or supporting the development of community-based emergency funds (Aitken and Thomas 2004). A Ghanaian project has also demonstrated the potential of locally based services to reduce childhood mortality as well as improve immunization coverage and service use, although scaling up the experience is proving difficult (Nyonator *et al.* 2005). In the Community-based Health Planning and Services Initiative, community nurses are being relocated into villages and out of more distant facilities, in combination with strengthening the social networks that can support local action to promote health.

This experience also points to the potential influence of patient empowerment strategies over health care seeking behaviour, including strengthening patient education about, and self-management of, disease (Hausmann-Muela *et al.* 2003; Wallerstein 2006), especially chronic diseases, as well as actions intended to empower vulnerable patient groups in their interactions with providers. For example, health care workers could be given the specific task of supporting patients in accessing health care by providing information on provider and treatment options, helping to address specific transport or language needs, making appointments with providers and providing support for self-management (Dixon and Le Grand 2006).

Another set of patient empowerment interventions currently receiving particular attention are peer-support mechanisms (MacKian 2003; Aitken and Thomas 2004; Tamsma and Berman 2004). Given the influence of family and friends over health care seeking behaviour as well as patient disempowerment in relation to providers, there is a growing focus on enabling trusted local people or organizations to provide community education and informed support to community members in the initial stages of responding to ill health – be they former tuberculosis patients for tuberculosis care (Johansson and Winkvist 2002), traditional healers (Hausmann-Muela *et al.* 2003) or community organizations (Wolff *et al.* 2003). Two recent studies demonstrate the potential usefulness of this approach in relation to maternal care, although neither identify whether impacts vary between socio-economic groups. In Uganda, training local resource people to encourage the use of intermittent preventive treatment for malaria during pregnancy, together with wider community mobilization efforts, increased access to, and compliance with, the treatment, compared with delivery through existing health facilities. The critical factor in this success was identified as the trust that poor rural women had in the local resource people (Mbonye *et al.* 2007). Meanwhile, a cluster randomized control trial in Nepal has demonstrated significant gains from similar approaches. Participatory peer-support groups were established in poor, rural communities to develop strategies to address local perinatal problems, at the same time that efforts were made to strengthen local health care provision. Compared with control sites, significant reductions in neonatal and maternal mortality rates were achieved, as well as significantly higher levels of antenatal service use, delivery in a health facility and the application of hygienic practices in home delivery (Manandhar *et al.* 2004).

Some argue that participation is an essential feature of strategies intended to empower poor and marginalized groups, whether implemented within or outside the health care facilities (Wallerstein 2006). Such participation enables those involved to recognize their own ability and capacity to improve their personal circumstances (Stegeman and Costongs 2004). Empowerment strategies should, therefore, build on and respect the judgements of the beneficiary groups, respond to their self-identified needs and involve them in implementation. However, the strategies must also take account of societal-level prejudice and stigma, perhaps bringing different groups of people together to confront prejudice (Wolff *et al.* 2003; Stegeman and Costongs 2004) and building participants' capacity to challenge existing power relations (Wallerstein 2006).[4]

Sustaining the implementation of any of these proposed actions, however, requires broader action. First, the dominant organizational culture of health care systems must be reoriented. Many analysts argue that the central processes through which organizational culture is sustained and replicated, or changed, are organizational leadership and management practices, particularly human resource management (HRM) practices (Scott *et al.* 1995; Grindle 1997; Mannion *et al.* 2005). A wider body of literature similarly emphasizes the influence of HRM practices over worker trust in the workplace and worker morale and motivation (Nyhan 2000), sometimes arguing that such practices are likely to have consequences for behaviours and attitudes towards patients (Tendler and Freedheim 1994; Gilson *et al.* 2005). This literature highlights the particular importance of non-financial incentives in encouraging caring and ethical behaviour (Owusu 2005). These might be provided through the group structures and social supports that also help health workers deal with stress (Scott *et al.* 1995) and, importantly, are derived from relationships with supervisors and managers (Albrecht and Travaglione 2003;

---

[4] As the Latin American conditional cash transfer programmes incentivize poor patients to use health services, they are very different from empowerment interventions, and so are not included in this discussion. There is, however, strong evidence that these programmes can encourage greater use of preventive services (e.g., Morris *et al.* 2004), although there are also concerns about their potential effects on provider–patient and community relationships, and replicability in other settings.

Watkins and Plant 2004; Owusu 2005). Financial incentives do, however, influence provider behaviour, as well as signalling those behaviours and values promoted by the wider system of care (Gilson 2005). Scott *et al.* (1995) argue, for example, that the US reimbursement mechanisms that reward medical and surgical procedures more generously than the (informational, educational and management) services vital to caring could be adapted to give greater weight to the caring services.

Changing organizational culture is, however, a difficult task, requiring a wide-ranging set of interventions and having the potential for unexpected and unwanted consequences (Scott *et al.* 2003). In their examination of how organizational culture undermines women health workers employed to reach out to women patients, Mumtaz *et al.* (2003) highlight the need not just for more respectful management, but also career paths for female staff, support for women employees to speak out about managerial abuse, training in sex-related issues for all employees and deliberate action to secure the support of senior male managers. Yet simply employing women empowered them and enabled some, at least, to begin to challenge the dominant power relations in their organizations. This example clearly shows that, 'In many places promoting human rights means making fundamental changes in the interactions between people – easy to say, but fraught with difficult questions about power, rank and (professional, class, and social) hierarchy,' (Freedman 2001 p. 57).

Two further levers that can assist in bringing about client-centred services and organizational change are funding and accountability mechanisms. Dedicated funding for policy actions that address acceptability barriers could both ensure their effective implementation and demonstrate their importance, in both ways leveraging change in organizational culture. Importantly, moreover, such actions may not always require additional resources. Patient care advisors, for example, could be drawn from among existing staff and encourage resource savings as well as better use of expensive hospital care (Dixon and Le Grand 2006). In lower-income settings, some of the existing funding available for training could be used to develop provider communication and wider human resource management skills. Patient-centred care models may, moreover, represent a cost-effective option compared with conventional strategies of service strengthening. The Nepalese peer support groups, for example, were shown to be a cost-effective strategy for address-ing neonatal mortality in developing countries, even when the costs of wider health care strengthening were considered (Manandhar *et al.* 2004). Finally, accountabil-ity mechanisms are important in bridging the gap between health care systems and the community. They have the potential to encourage the development of shared responsibility for services (NHMRC 2005), strengthen service provision (Freedman, 2001), empower marginalized groups (Stegeman and Costongs 2004) and build patient trust in health care (Birungi 1998).

The existence of accountability mechanisms may also create some political space to demand the funding and leadership changes critical in bringing about necessary changes in organizational culture. However, political action will be necessary to sustain such changes – including developing the wider macroeconomic and policy strategies required to address social inequality (Navarro *et al.* 2006).

Conclusions

The acceptability dimension of access comprises the fit between lay and professional health beliefs, provider–patient engagement and dialogue, and the ways in which health care organizational arrangements frame patient responses to services. Acceptability and trust barriers are disproportionately faced by socially disadvantaged groups in all societies, and so influence both the distributional and procedural justice of health care. As social factors and, in particular, structural and power relations influence patient and provider behaviour and interactions, an examination of acceptability barriers also demonstrates how social inequality is embedded within health care.

In tackling health care inequity it is, therefore, important to recognize the socialized nature of health care – and to take acceptability access barriers and embedded social inequality seriously. The definition of access presented in Box 7.2 is very helpful as a starting point for this recognition. As acceptability and trust barriers have an invidious influence over health care equity in all contexts, even lower-income countries, tackling these barriers must be a central element of action to promote health care equity. Addressing the barriers, and the wider inequalities they reflect, is, however, neither simply about developing provider listening skills nor about ensuring patient education. Instead it is particularly important to promote ethical practices by providers, requiring, in turn, the development of organizational environments that encourage ethical behaviour and promote health care provision that is responsive to patient circumstances, particularly to those of socially disadvantaged groups. Multifaceted interventions are required, within which change in management practices and organizational culture have a central role. Most critically, building on human rights' frameworks, the interventions must redress the power imbalances within health care systems, and build patient–provider trust.

REFERENCES

Aitken, J-M. and Thomas, D. (2004). *Synthesis of Final Evaluation Findings from the Nepal Safe Motherhood Project*. Report to HMGN, DfID, Options. www.nsmp.org/publications_reports/index.html.

Albrecht, S. and Travaglione, A. (2003). Trust in public-sector management. *The International Journal of Human Resource Management.* **14**: 76–92.

Anderson, L. M., Scrimshaw, S. C., Fullilove, M. T., *et al.* (2003) Culturally competent healthcare systems: a systematic review. *American Journal of Preventive Medicine.* **24**: 68–79.

Armstrong, K., Rose, A., Peters, N., Long, J. A. and McMurphy, S. (2005) Distrust of the health care system and self-reported health in the United States. *Journal of General Internal Medicine.* **21**: 292–297.

Armstrong, K., Hughes-Halbert, C. and Asch, D. A. (2006) Patient preferences can be misleading as explanations for racial disparities in health care. *Archives of Internal Medecine.* **166**: 950–954.

Barr, D. A. (2005) Listening to patients: cultural and linguistic barriers to health care access. *Clinical Research and Methods.* **37**: 100–204.

Birungi, H. (1998) Injections and self-help: risk and trust in Ugandan health care. *Social Science and Medicine.* **47**: 1455–1462.

Bostrom, B., Sandh, M., Lundberg, D. and Fridlund, B. (2004) Cancer-related pain in palliative care: patient's perceptions of pain management. *Journal of Advanced Nursing.* **45**: 410–419.

Brownlie, J. and Howson, A. (2006) Between the demands of truth and government: health practitioners, trust and immunisation work. *Social Science and Medicine.* **62**: 433–443.

Burgess, D. J., Fu, S. S. and van Ryn, M. (2004) Why do providers contribute to disparities and what can be done about it? *Journal of General Internal Medicine.* **19**: 1154–1159.

Call, K. (2006) Barriers to care among American Indians in Public Health Care Programmes. *Medical Care.* **44**: 595–600.

Das, J. and Das, S. (2003) Trust, learning and vaccination: a case study of a North Indian village. *Social Science and Medicine.* **57**: 97–112.

Dibben, M. R. and Lean, M. E. J. (2003) Achieving compliance in chronic illness management: illustrations of trust relationships between physicians and nutrition clinic patients. *Health, Risk and Society.* **5**: 241–258.

Dixon, A., Le Grand, J., Henderson, J., Murray, R. and Poteliakhoff, E. (2003) *Is the NHS Equitable? A Review of the Evidence.* LSE health and social care discussion paper No 11. London: London School of Economics and Political Science.

Dixon, A. and Le Grand, J. (2006) Is greater patient choice consistent with equity? The case of the English NHS. *Journal of Health Services Research and Policy.* **11**: 162–166.

Dribe, M. and Nysedt, P. (2002) *Information, Trust and Diffusion of Smallpox Vaccination.* Lund papers in economic history No 77. Lund: Department of Economic History, Lund University.

Freedman, L. P. (2001) Using human rights in maternal mortality programmes: from analysis to strategy. *International Journal of Gynaecology and Obstetrics.* **75**: 51–60.

Gilson, L. (2000) Re-addressing equity: the importance of ethical processes. In Mills A., ed., *Reforming Health Sectors.* London: Kegan Paul. pp. 103–122.

Gilson, L. (2003) Trust and the development of health care as a social institution. *Social Science and Medicine.* **56**: 1453–1468.

Gilson, L. (2005) Editorial: building trust and value in health systems in low and middle income countries. *Social Science and Medicine.* **61**: 1281–1284.

Gilson, L. and Erasmus, E. (2004) *Values in Use and Organisational Culture: Exploring the Relevance to Health Systems Development.* Paper prepared for the UN Millennium Project's Task Force on Child Health and Maternal Health. Johannesburg: Centre for Health Policy.

Gilson, L., Palmer, N. and Schneider, H. (2005) Trust and health worker performance: exploring a conceptual framework using South African evidence. *Social Science and Medicine.* **61**: 1418–1429.

Goold, S. D. (2002) Trust, distrust and trustworthiness. *Journal of General Internal Medicine.* **17**: 79–81.

Gostin, L. and Hodge, J. G. (2003) *The Domains of Responsiveness: A Human Rights Analysis.* EIP discussion paper No 53. Geneva: World Health Organization.

Greene, J. A. (2004) An ethnography of nonadherence: culture, poverty, and tuberculosis in urban Bolivia. *Culture, Medicine and Psychiatry.* **28**: 401–425.

Grindle, M. S. (1997). Divergent cultures? When public organisations perform well in developing countries. *World Development.* **25**: 481–495.

Gulliford, M., Figeuero-Munoz, J., Morgan, M. *et al.* (2002) What does 'access to health care' mean? *Journal of Health Services Research and Policy.* **7**: 186–188.

Hall, M. A., Dugan, E., Zheng, B. and Mishra, A. (2001) Trust in physicians and medical institutions: what is it, can it be measured and does it matter? *Milbank Quarterly.* **79**: 613–639.

Hausmann-Muela, S., Muela Ribera, J. and Nyamongo, I. (2003) *Health Seeking Behaviour and the Health System Response.* Disease Control Priorities Project working paper No 14. www.dcp2.org/file/29/wp14.pdf.

Houston, E. S. (2003). *The Past, the Present, the Future of Aboriginal Health Policy.* Unpublished Ph.D. thesis, Division of Health Sciences, Curtin University of Technology.

Jacobs, E. A., Rolle, I., Ferrans, C. E., Whitaker, E. E. and Warnecke, R. B. (2006) Understanding African Americans' views of the trustworthiness of physicians. *Journal of General Internal Medicine.* **21**: 642–7.

Johansson, E., Long, N. H., Diwan, V. K. and Winkvist, A. (2000) Gender and tuberculosis control. Perspectives on health seeking behaviour among men and women in Vietnam. *Health Policy.* **52**: 33–51.

Johansson, E. and Winkvist, A. (2002) Trust and transparency in human encounters in tuberculosis control: lessons learned from Vietnam. *Qualitative Health Research.* **12**: 473–491.

Kefford, C. H., Trevena, L. J. and Willcock, S. M. (2005) Breaking away from the medical model: perceptions of health and health care in suburban Sydney youth. *Medical Journal of Australia.* **183**: 418–421.

Lau, J. T., Cheung, J. C. and Leung, S. S. S. (2000) Studies on common illnesses and medical care utilisation patterns of adolescents in Hong Kong. *Journal of Adolescent Health.* **27**: 443–52.

Lonnroth, K., Tran, T-U., Thuong, L. M., Quy, H. T. and Diwan, V. (2001) Can I afford free treatment? Perceived consequences of health care provider choices among people with tuberculosis in Ho Chi Minh City, Vietnam. *Social Science and Medicine.* **52**: 935–948.

Macintyre, K. and Hotchkiss, D. R. (1999) Referral revisited: community financing schemes and emergency transport in rural Africa. *Social Science and Medicine.* **49**: 1473–1487.

MacKian, S. (2003) *A Review of Health Seeking Behaviour: Problems and Prospects*. University of Manchester: Health Systems Development Programme HSD/WP/05/03. www.hsd.lshtm.ac.uk/publications/hsd_working-papers/05-03_health_seeking-behaviour.pdf.

Mallinson, S., Popay, J., Kowarzik, U. and MacKian, S. (2006) Developing the public health workforce: a 'communities of practice' perspective. *Policy and Politics*. **34**: 265–85.

Manandhar, D. S., Osrin, D., Shrestha, B. P. *et al.* (2004) Effect of a participatory intervention with women's groups on birth outcomes in Nepal: cluster-randomised controlled trial. *The Lancet*. **364**: 970–979.

Mannion, R., Davies, H. T. O. and Marshall, M. N. (2005) *Cultures for Performance in Health Care*. Maidenhead: Open University Press.

Mbonye, A., Bygberg, I. and Magnussen, P. (2007). Intermittent preventive treatment of malaria in pregnancy: evaluation of a new delivery approach and the policy implications for malaria control in Uganda. *Health Policy*. **81**: 228–241.

McIntyre, D., Thiede, M., Dahlgren, G. and Whitehead, M. (2006) What are the economic consequences for households of illness and of paying for health care in low- and middle-income country contexts? *Social Science and Medicine*. **62**: 858–865.

Montenegro, R. A. and Stephens, C. (2006) Indigenous health in Latin America and the Caribbean. *The Lancet*. **367**: 1859–1869.

Mooney, G. (1996) And now for vertical equity? Some concerns arising from Aboriginal health in Australia. *Health Economics*. **5**: 99–103.

Morris, S. S., Flores, R., Olinto, P. and Medina, J. M. (2004) Monetary incentives in primary health care and effects on use and coverage of preventive health care interventions in rural Honduras: cluster randomised trial. *The Lancet*. **364**: 2030–2037.

Mumtaz, Z., Salway, S., Waseem, M. and Umer, N. (2003) Gender-based barriers to primary health care provision in Pakistan: the experience of female providers. *Health Policy and Planning*. **18**: 261–269.

Navarro, V., Muntaner, C., Borrell, C. *et al.* (2006) Politics and health outcomes. *The Lancet*. **368**: 1033–1037.

NHMRC (National Health and Medical Research Council), Australian Government (2005) *Cultural Competency in Health: A Guide for Policy, Partnerships and Participation*. www.nhmrc.gov.au/publications/synopses/hp25syn.htm

Nyhan, R. C. (2000) Changing the paradigm: trust and its role in public sector organisations. *American Review of Public Administration*. **30**: 87–109.

Nyonator, F. K., Awoonor-Williams, J. K., Phillips, J. F., Jones, T. C. and Miller, R. A. (2005) The Ghana Community-based Health Planning and Services Initiative for scaling up service delivery innovation. *Health Policy and Planning*. **20**: 25–34.

O'Malley, A. S. and Forrest, C. B. (2002) Beyond the examination room: primary care performance and the patient-physician relationship for low-income women. *Journal of General Internal Medicine*. **17**: 66–74.

O'Malley, A. S., Sheppard, V. B., Schwartz, M. and Mandelblatt, J. (2004) The role of trust in use of preventive services among low income African-American women. *Preventive Medicine*. **38**: 777–785.

Obadare, E. (2005) A crisis of trust: history, politics, religion and the polio controversy in Northern Nigeria. *Patterns of Predjudice*. **39**: 265–284.

Owusu, F. (2005) Livelihood strategies and performance of Ghana's health and education sectors: exploring the connections. *Public Administration and Development*. **25**: 157–174.

Palmer, N. (2007) Access and equity: evidence on the extent to which health services address the needs of the poor. In Bennett, S. Gilson, L. and Mills, A., eds, *Health, Economic Development and Household Poverty*. London: Routledge.

Pechansky, R. and Thomas, W. (1981) The concept of access. *Medical Care*. **19**: 127–140.

Reidpath, D. D. and Chan, K. Y. (2005) HIV discrimination: integrating the results from a six-country situational analysis in the Asia Pacific. *AIDS Care*. **17** (suppl. 2): S195–S204.

Riewpaiboon, W., Cheungsatiansup, K., Gilson, L. and Tangcharoensathien, V. (2005) Private obstetric practice in a public hospital: mythical trust in obstetric care. *Social Science and Medicine*. **61**: 1408–1417.

Rothstein, B. (1998) *Just Institutions Matter: the Moral and Political Logic of the Universal Welfare State*. Cambridge: Cambridge University Press.

Rouse, C. M. (2004) Paradigms and politics: shaping health care access for sickle cell patients through the discursive practices of biomedicine. *Culture, Medicine and Psychiatry*, **28**: 369–399.

Russell, S. (2004) The economic burden of illness for households in developing countries: a review of studies focusing on malaria, tuberculosis, and human immunodeficiency virus/ acquired immunodeficiency syndrome. *American Journal of Tropical Medicine and Hygiene*. **71** (suppl.2): 147–155.

Russell, S. (2005) Treatment-seeking behaviour in urban Sri Lanka: trusting the state, trusting private providers. *Social Science and Medicine*. **61**: 1396–1407.

Scott, R. A., Aiken, L. H., Mechanic, D. and Moravcsik, J. (1995) Organizational aspects of caring. *The Milbank Quarterly*. **73**: 77–95.

Scott, T., Mannion, R., Davies, H. T. O. and Marshall, M. N. (2003) Policy roundtable: implementing culture change in health care: theory and practice. *International Journal for Quality in Health Care*. **15**: 111–118.

Shaikh, B. T. and Hatcher, J. (2004) Health seeking behaviour and health service utilisation in Pakistan: challenging the policy makers. *Journal of Public Health*. **27**: 49–54.

Sheppard, V. B., Zambrana, R. E. and O'Malley, A. (2004) Providing health care to low income women: a matter of trust. *Family Practice*. **21**: 484–491.

Stegeman, I. and Costongs, C. (2004) *Promoting Social Inclusion and Tackling Health Inequalities in Europe: an Overview of Good Practices From the Health Field*. Brussels: EuroHealthNet.www.eurohealthnet.eu/content/view/97/137/.

Stephens, C., Porter, J., Nettleton, C. and Willis, R. (2006) Disappearing, displaced and under-valued: a call to action for Indigenous health worldwide. *The Lancet*. **367**: 2019–2028.

Streefland, P. (2005) Public health care under pressure in sub-Saharan Africa. *Health Policy*. **71**: 375–382

Takahashi, L. M. and Rodriguez, R. (2002) Access redefined: service pathways of persons living with HIV and AIDS. *Culture, Health and Sexuality*. **4**: 67–83.

Tamsma, N. and Berman, P. C. (2004) *The Role of the Health Sector in Tackling Poverty and Social Exclusion in Europe.* Dublin: European Health Management Association. www.eurohealthnet.eu/content/view/97/137/.

Tendler, J. and Freedheim, S. (1994) Trust in a rent-seeking world: health and government transformed in Northeast Brazil. *World Development.* **22**: 1771–1791.

Thorson, A. and Johansson, E. (2004) Equality or equity in health care access: a qualitative study of doctors' explanations to a longer doctor's delay among female TB patients in Vietnam. *Health Policy.* **68**: 37–46.

Tibandebage, P. and Mackintosh, M. (2005) The market shaping of charges, trust and abuse: health care transactions in Tanzania. *Social Science and Medicine.* **61**: 1385–1395.

Wallerstein, N. (2006) *What is the Evidence on Effectiveness of Empowerment to Improve Health?* Copenhagen: WHO Regional Office for Europe (Health Evidence Network report). www.euro.who.int/Document/E88086.pdf

Watkins, R. E. and Plant, A. J. (2004). Pathways to treatment for tuberculosis in Bali: patient perspectives. *Qualitative Health Research.* **14**: 691–703.

Watkins, R. E. , Rouse, C. R. and Plant, A. J. (2004) Tuberculosis treatment delivery in Bali: a qualitative study of clinic staff perceptions. *International Journal of Tuberculosis and Lung Disease.* **8**: 218–225.

Willems, S., De Maesschalck, S., Deveugle, M., Derese, A. and De Maeseneer, J. (2005) Socio-economic status of the patient and doctor-provider communication: does it make a difference? *Patient Education and Counselling.* **56**: 139–146.

Williams, F. (1999) Good-enough principles for welfare. *Journal of Social Policy.* **28**: 667–687.

Wolff, M., Bates, T., Beck, B. *et al.* (2003) Cancer prevention in underserved African American communities: barriers and effective strategies – a review of the literature. *Wisconsin Medical Journal.* **102**: 36–40.

Equity and health systems

8

International migration and extreme health inequality: robust arguments and institutions for international redistribution in health care

Maureen Mackintosh

Summary

The international migration of health professionals from low-income understaffed health systems worsens the extreme global inequality in health services. The politics and economics of these migration patterns challenge neat boundaries around 'national', 'international' and 'aid', bringing into focus the embeddedness of national health services in internationally integrating markets and cross-border social relationships. This chapter uses the challenging aspects of health professionals' migration as a 'lens' for examining aspects of the economics of international redistribution in health care.

The chapter first demonstrates the distributive consequences of migration of health professionals: a perverse redistribution of resources from poor to rich. This is examined within a policy framework that takes as an assumption that labour markets are populated by individuals with equal human rights, and considers the implications for international obligations of rich countries' governments and citizens. It then provides evidence that health services financing and provision *within* countries is typically progressive, including public health care in much of sub-Saharan Africa, a fact obscured by international emphasis on its shortcomings. In most rich countries, the embedding of redistributive processes within institutionalized commitments to universalist health service provision has long stabilized governmental and social commitment to economic redistribution, while within federal countries and the EU, labour migration is often associated with cross-border redistributive transfers to enhance efficiency and equity.

It follows that as labour markets integrate between rich and poor countries, the economic arguments for sustained redistribution across borders become stronger, while the experience of stable redistribution within health services suggests that health may be an excellent site for progressive international fiscal transfers. This chapter proposes mechanisms for embedding *international* redistributive fiscal

The Economics of Health Equity, ed. Di McIntyre and Gavin Mooney. Published by Cambridge University Press. © Cambridge University Press 2007.

relationships within treaty-based institutionalized commitments to restitutive compensation for the perverse subsidies arising from health professional migration, and within governance mechanisms drawing on long-term international health service relationships such as those between the UK NHS and a number of lower-income Commonwealth countries' health services.[1]

Introduction

This chapter analyzes three economic processes that are important influences on equity in health care, and on social and economic inequality more broadly, yet are normally analyzed in isolation from one other. The international migration of health professionals from low-income under-staffed health systems throws into relief, and at the same time worsens, the extreme global inequality in health services and conditions of employment. The organization of the financing and provision of health services is economically redistributive in many countries, that is, its net effect is to shift resources from the better-off to those who are poorer. And development aid transfers resources from high-income and middle-income countries to, among other recipients, the health services of much poorer countries. These three health-related processes – international migration, health services' financing and provision, and development aid to health services – thus have major distributive effects on health equity and inequity. There is a very large amount of literature on each topic. On the relations *between* the three processes, the health economics and development economics literature is largely silent.

The silence partly reflects boundaried political positioning and policy making around these processes. Development aid in most countries occupies a government ministry of its own, and has its own focused non-governmental actors. National health services – still largely, if in many senses misleadingly, conceived in policy terms as nationally bounded services – again have their own ministries and political worlds. Migration of health professionals is, however, rather different, since in wealthy countries it brings the messy and often racially discriminatory politics of immigration into association with health care provision and development aid. The politics of migration challenge neat boundaries between what is 'national', what is 'international' and what is 'aid', bringing into focus some of the ways in which national health services are necessarily embedded in internationally integrating markets and cross-border social relationships. At the time of

[1] The paper draws on continuing collaborative work partly summarized in Mackintosh *et al.* (2006a). Particular thanks to Kwadwo Mensah, Richard Biritwum, Leroi Henry, Meri Koivusalo, Pam Smith, Parvati Raghuram, Paula Tibandebage, Tausi Kida, Mike Rowson and Matt Gordon for research collaboration. This chapter is the sole responsibility of the author.

writing this chapter[2] the UK had just made a very sharp switch in immigration rules that shifted the country from welcoming doctors and nurses trained in developing countries, effectively to shutting them out; in the context of apparent NHS financial constraint, even doctors halfway through specialist training may find themselves without the staff positions needed to complete it (Mackintosh *et al.* 2006b; Raghuram 2006).

This chapter uses the challenging aspects of health professionals' migration as a 'lens' for examining the economics of international redistribution in health care. It begins by examining migration of health professionals as both result and cause of international labour market integration in health, a process that is generating perverse redistribution of resources from poor to rich. This is explored within a policy framework that takes as an assumption that labour markets are populated by individuals with equal human rights whatever their nationality, and considers the implications for the international obligations of rich countries' governments and citizens.

The next two sections then consider the distributive context within which this perverse redistribution of resources is taking place. I make the case that health services financing and provision is progressive – that is, redistributive of resources in cash and kind from the well-off to those who are less well-off or poor – in most rich countries and that the public sector health services of many low-income and middle-income countries are also progressive in their effects. In particular, the progressiveness of public sector health care provision in much of sub-Saharan Africa has been obscured by the weight of recent multilateral commentary on its shortcomings. I argue that in most rich countries, the embedding of redistributive processes within institutionalized commitments to universalist health service provision has stabilized governmental and social commitment to major economic redistribution over a long period, while sustaining health care access, despite repeated political contestation. This is in good part because of the close interlinking between insurance, efficiency and redistribution that 'social' health service expenditure offers. Finally, I argue, drawing on evidence from federal countries and the European Union, that labour migration across borders is often associated with – and indeed proposed as part of the rationale for – cross-border redistributive transfers including those to allow some common health care standards. Such transfers can enhance both efficiency and equity.

It follows, the next section argues, that as labour markets – and markets for services – integrate across borders between rich and poor countries, the economic arguments for sustained redistribution across borders become stronger. Furthermore, the experience of stable institutionalization of redistribution within health services suggests that health services may be an excellent site for progressive

---

[2] July 2006.

international fiscal transfers. The chapter ends with proposals for mechanisms for embedding *international* redistributive fiscal relationships within treaty-based institutionalized commitments to restitutive compensation for the perverse subsidies arising from health professional migration, and within governance mechanisms drawing on long-term international health service relationships, such as those between the UK NHS and a number of lower-income Commonwealth countries' health services.

Health professionals' international migration: labour market integration, impact and policy options

Scale, trends and context

The migration of health professionals from lower-income to higher-income contexts has become in recent years a major international policy concern, since it is associated with – and has publicly highlighted – the grotesquely unequal global distribution of health professionals in relation to need (WHO 2006). The formulation and monitoring of the UN Millennium Goals[3] has furthermore focused international attention on the importance of access to trained health professionals' services for the attainment of a number of these goals. The most severe impact of the out-migration of doctors and nurses is felt in already labour-short, low-income health services, where the capacity to employ skilled staff is in any case insufficient, and where out-migration generates huge vacancy rates weighted towards areas where needs are highest and conditions of life and work worst. In these contexts, out-migration worsens both in-country and international distribution of health care availability and quality; recognition of this has generated public debate in the UK.[4]

Migration patterns are complex and not well documented, with quite a lot of 'step' migration in which migrants move to one country as a stepping stone to another with higher incomes. However, a number of generalizations seem well supported by evidence. A substantial upward shift in migration of health professionals from developing countries to, notably, the USA and the UK among high-income countries, seems to have occurred in the early twenty-first century. This followed earlier flows to the Middle East. It also followed on from longer-term reliance on overseas-trained doctors and on fluctuating in-migration of nurses within the UK health services over many years (Raghuram 2006; Smith

---

[3] www.un.org/millenniumgoals.

[4] Mensah *et al.* (2005) *Whose Charity? Africa's Aid to the NHS*. Save the Children Briefing www.medact.org/content/Skills%20drain/Whose%20charity%204%20page.pdf; NHS 'being subsidised by Africa'. *The Guardian* (22.2.05); Parasite NHS. *The Sun* (22.2.05); Laurance, J. Medical staff quit for the West leaving Africa's health service in crisis. *The Independent* (27.05.05).

Table 8.1. Percentages of doctors and nurses in selected OECD countries who trained abroad

Country	% doctors trained abroad	% nurses trained abroad
Australia	21	n/a
Canada	23	6
France	6	n/a
Germany	6	3
Ireland	n/a	14
New Zealand	34	21
UK	33	10
USA	27	5

n/a not available

Source: WHO (2006 p. 98); year of reporting not provided.

and Mackintosh 2007), and on long-term reliance on trained staff from the Philippines in particular within the United States (Choy 2003; Ball 2004). While the UK is now shifting from reliance on staff trained in high-income and low-income Commonwealth countries and other developing countries towards more EU nationals and locally trained staff, the USA, which has by far the largest market, employing over 300 000 registered doctors and nurses trained abroad (WHO 2006 p. 98), plans to expand in-migration of health professionals trained overseas, as do other rich countries including Canada.[5] Table 8.1 shows some data on current reliance on overseas-trained staff in selected OECD countries.

Of these overseas-trained staff, a substantial number were trained in low-income labour-short health systems in sub-Saharan Africa, and also in other low-income and middle-income countries where rural and deprived areas have far too few trained staff. In the UK in 2004, 4.3% of registered doctors trained in sub-Saharan Africa and 11.5% in South Asia (GMC 2004); in the USA 64% of overseas-trained doctors trained in low-income or lower-middle-income countries including 5334 from sub-Saharan Africa (Hagopian *et al.* 2004). During the upsurge in recruitment of overseas-trained health professionals in the early 2000s in the UK, new registrations from doctors and nurses trained in low-income Africa rose sharply and in the case of nurses overtook new registrations from high-income countries (Figures 8.1 and 8.2). Furthermore these figures understate true numbers, since in 2005 there was a 'queue' of trained nurses working for low wages in care homes in the UK while waiting for adaptation courses and

[5] Sources: Canadian presentation to British Medical Association Conference on the Global Health Workforce May 2005; brief conference details on www.bma.org.uk/ap.nsf/Content/skillsdrain; Cooper and Aiken 2005.

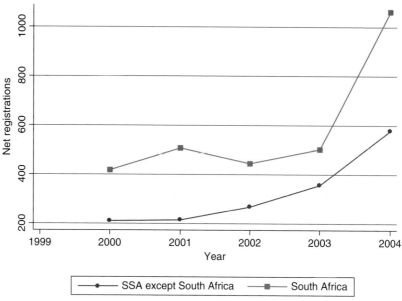

Source: GMC (2004)

Figure 8.1   Net annual change in numbers of doctors on UK register, at first of January each year: doctors trained in South Africa, and in the rest of sub-Saharan Africa (2000–2004)

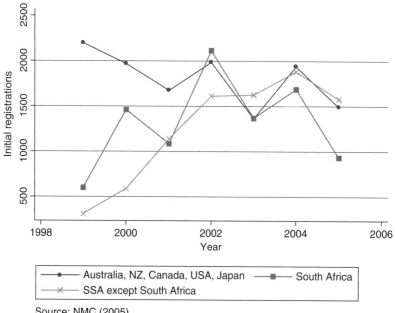

Source: NMC (2005)

Figure 8.2   Initial UK registrations of nurses and midwives from identified high-income countries, from South Africa, and from other identified sub-Saharan African countries (Nigeria, Zimbabwe, Ghana, Zambia, Kenya, Botswana, Malawi, Lesotho, Swaziland) (1999–2005)

registration; one estimate put the numbers at nearly 40 000 (Parish and Pickersgill 2005; Smith *et al.* 2006).

The UK's 2006 retreat from encouragement of overseas-trained staff from Africa is one of several recurrent UK policy fluctuations in overseas recruitment since the 1940s; staff particularly from the Caribbean, South Asia and Africa have repeatedly been treated like a 'reserve army' to be hired at moments of expansion and staff shortage (Mackintosh *et al.* 2006a; Smith and Mackintosh 2007). Underlying this instability, and responding to the UK's changes of policy, however is a broader global labour market in the skills of health professionals, which has become much more integrated and commercialized over the last ten years, especially in nursing, and has underpinned migration worldwide.

Commercial investment in nursing employment agencies has been extensive in the 1990s (Hardill and MacDonald 2000) and 2000s, and there has been a huge growth in online recruitment sites, such as Worldwide Health Care Exchange and Nursingnet UK.[6] The 'internationalization' of the profession of nursing in the 1980s, including integration of qualifications within the EU and increased international migration for training (Iredale 2001) underpinned the market response to changes in policy and visa systems in the UK, the USA and Japan and inter-governmental agreements to encourage recruiting.

In Ghana, for example, agencies have helped to formalize the process of obtaining visas, work permit application and job search, making the international job-seeking process more open and impersonal. For Ghanaian nurses the cost of migration appears to have risen, but loans for migration costs have made them more affordable. The internet and cheap telephone calls, and the availability of publications such as the *Nursing Times*, have dramatically increased knowledge of jobs and conditions elsewhere (Mensah 2005; Mensah *et al.* 2005).[7] Migration furthermore is institutionally and socially cumulative: the more people migrate, the more others are encouraged and supported to do so.[8]

Distributive consequences

In low-income countries of origin of migrants, such as Ghana, the effects are two-fold; to reduce health services available to citizens and to put pressure on low-income countries' governments to improve wages and working conditions in an effort to retain staff and in order to avoid strikes (Mensah 2005).[9] Recent estimates[10] suggest, for example, that Ghana has lost to migration around 45% of all

---

[6] www.whe.co.uk and www.nursingnetuk.com.
[7] Sources include interviews by Kwadwo Mensah and Leroi Henry of Ghanaian health professionals.
[8] Vujicic *et al.* (2004) call this a 'herd' or 'network' effect, citing US migration studies.
[9] At the time of writing there had been a lengthy strike of medical and nursing staff in Ghana.
[10] Current research with Richard Biritwum and Kwadwo Mensah.

Table 8.2. Snapshot of Africa/ UK health inequality: selected indicators of health need and health services, 2003 or latest available year

Indicator	South Africa	Nigeria	Ghana	Malawi	UK
Need indicators					
Life expectancy at birth [1]	50.7	48.8	57.6	40.2	78.2
Mortality < 5 / 1000 boys	70	200	99	182	7
Mortality < 5 / 1000 girls	61	197	92	175	5
Estimated TB prevalence/100 000 population	458	546	380	551	12
Service indicators					
Nurses/100 000 population	388	66	64	26	497
Physicians/100 000 population	69	27	9	1	166
Births with a skilled attendant (%)	84	35	47	61	100
Total health expenditure/head ($) [2]	222	15	12	13	1508

Source: Mensah *et al.* (2005), drawn from WHO data www.who.int/countries.
[1] 2002
[2] US$ Atlas exchange rate basis 2002

its doctors ever trained, and around a quarter of its nurses. There is also qualitative and quantitative evidence of acceleration of departure of nurses since the late 1990s, while the departure of doctors has been consistently high since the 1970s. The most common destination of migrant nurses from Ghana in recent years has been the UK, but this may now switch towards the USA.

The effect on service provision is severe. In Ghana, for example, public sector health facilities, on which most of the population rely, are 'grossly understaffed' and health indicators such as infant mortality are showing signs of worsening (Nyonator *et al.* 2004). A majority of current medical and nurse trainees plan to migrate (Gent and Skeldon 2006). Cuban doctors work in some of the most deprived districts, but this is no permanent solution. And even Ghana's situation is dwarfed by the staffing crisis in relation to the scale of need in Malawi: Table 8.2 shows a snapshot of need and staffing/population ratios, comparing the UK with several African countries of origin of migrants. In these circumstances, the out-migration of professionals is cumulatively driven by deteriorating and dangerous working conditions and despair at being unable to do a good job, as well as a desire for an income that allows saving for old age and investment and conditions that support education for children (Mensah 2005; WHO 2006).

Health professionals' migration from sub-Saharan Africa is thus an increasingly organized response to acute international inequality and generalized poverty. It further undermines struggling African health services and widens the international gulf in mortality, morbidity and service availability (Stilwell *et al.* 2004;

House of Commons 2004; WHO 2006). In cross-country comparisons, health service staffing is associated with better health outcomes after controlling for income. Increased funding and staff are essential to deliver even basic services and meet the UN Millennium Goals (Anand and Baernighausen 2003).

Migration from Africa to high-income countries, therefore, worsens an already intolerable gulf. Its distributive effects may be measured by the perverse subsidy generated. A 'perverse' subsidy is a subsidy from poor to rich. Migrant African health care professionals were trained in sub-Saharan Africa at public and private expense; the benefits of that training are then experienced in the UK and lost to those dependent on African health services. The subsidy arises because UK health care users benefit from skills the UK did not create through investment; it is perverse because it worsens global health inequity.

Using Ghana–UK migration as a case study, we can measure the perverse subsidy by the training costs avoided in the UK (Mensah *et al.* 2005; Mackintosh *et al.* 2006a). Training costs in the UK are estimated at £220 000 for a doctor[11] and £37,500[12] for a nurse. This implies a one-off saving in training costs (at current replacement cost) of about £64.5 million from hiring the 293 Ghanaian trained doctors in the UK in 2004, and about £38 million from an estimated 1021 nurses trained in Ghana.[13] For migrant professionals from the whole of sub-Saharan Africa, the training cost savings would be over £2bn from 9151 migrant doctors and £518 million from hiring an estimated 13 825 nurses (GMC 2004; NMC 2004).

A better way to value investment in training, however, is in terms of the stream of benefits produced by the services of the trained staff. One measure of the value placed on these services is the salaries the staff earn. Making reasonable assumptions about employment, grading and salary scales,[14] the *annual* value of the services of Ghanaian-trained staff calculated on this basis was £39 million in 2004. For all UK-registered doctors and nurses trained in sub-Saharan Africa, the estimate for the annual subsidy is £595 million for doctors and £285 million for nurses. In 2004, total UK official development aid to Ghana was £65 million; we cannot identify the proportion spent on health, but if we subtract our estimate of the perverse subsidy, then the implied net UK aid flow to the Ghanaian health services may well have been negative in that year.

Policy responses: punishment, exclusion, restitution or redistribution?

There are essentially four categories of policy response to this widening of inequality: punitive (punishing those who do not stay), exclusion (keeping out migrants

---

[11] Source: British Medical Association estimate.   [12] Source: Department of Health estimates.
[13] Calculated from new registrations from 1998–9 to 2003–4, allowing for an annual wastage rate calculated from the register as a whole.
[14] See Mackintosh *et al.* (2006a) for details of the assumptions and calculations.

from low-income countries), restitution (repaying the benefits from migration in high-income countries to those who lose), or a sustained process of redistribution of resources to low-income health services to rebuild working and living conditions and prospects and raise salaries. Useful tests of those policies are to ask, first: are they compatible with equality of human rights for all citizens regardless of their nationality? Second, do they 'work' in terms of sustaining health professionals' commitment to their country of origin?

Punitive approaches often take the form of 'bonding' those whose training is paid for by governments to work in government service for a given number of years, particularly in deprived areas, with fines for those who do not do so. They may also include withholding or charging highly for certificates of qualification of early out-migrants or requiring repayment of fees. Staff who wish to leave, especially nurses, may be publicly denigrated. The record of 'success' is poor (Mensah 2005). Bonding may be a reasonable contract in return for training support but will work only when it is regarded as legitimate. Where training opportunities, career prospects and working conditions are not perceived as reasonable it may cause resentment, encourage early exit and make return – an aspiration of many migrant African professionals – difficult. Withholding certification and engaging in forms of harassment of those who wish to leave or who return are incompatible with fundamental human rights and are also likely to motivate departure and remaining abroad (Mensah *et al.* 2005).

Exclusion takes the form of blocking immigration in the employing country by selected nationals, notably from low-income African countries. The Codes of Conduct for 'ethical recruitment' pioneered and promoted by the UK government and supported by the UK medical and nursing associations have a contradiction at their heart. They can be said to 'work' only if they indeed reduce migration from the targeted countries; yet selective exclusion of this kind appears effectively discriminatory, targeted at mainly black African and Caribbean migrants, and selectively contravenes those migrants' right to leave their country of origin (Bueno de Mesquita and Gordon 2005; Mensah *et al.* 2005). UK government ministers recognize this right:

Some have said that we should ban health sector professionals in developing countries from getting jobs in Britain. But we believe that is morally wrong. People, whatever their profession, should be able to go where they choose and apply for jobs they want in a global economy. (Winterton and Thomas 2006)

The third and fourth alternatives within this global context, restitution and redistribution, are the subject of the rest of this chapter. These are both responses to the perverse distributive effects of migration and to the extreme health care inequalities that underlie it, and both seek to contribute to (re)building health services that can retain professional staff and meet the most pressing needs and rights of the population. While they differ in their logic, they both imply a considerable rethinking of the framework and institutions shaping international financial transfers in health.

Health care and redistribution in unitary and federal contexts

Health systems can and do constitute an effective basis for redistribution *within* countries. Their organization has often been designed – in both low-income and high-income contexts – to tackle both inequity in health care access and broader economic inequality. Furthermore, in federal countries and semi-federal groupings, mobility of labour is a key argument for fiscal redistribution between states and for minimum standards of social provision. This section elaborates these arguments; the next considers their implications for international health-related redistribution in the context of integration of health professional labour markets.

Health systems as sites of stable intranational redistribution

In rich countries, the health sector is generally highly redistributive, transferring resources from the better-off to the poor. In almost all high-income countries – the United States is the major exception – a political and social commitment to reasonably equitable access to health care financed largely through social insurance or general taxation has provided a politically stable combination of insurance against the costs of illness and redistribution of resources since the 1950s (Barr 1998).

In high-income countries, Wagstaff *et al.* (1999) found, using 1980s data, that in those which finance health care largely through taxation, funding was progressive, that is, the income distribution is more equal after payment (the main exception was Portugal). In most social-insurance-based countries (e.g., Germany, the Netherlands) funding was mildly regressive, leaving the income distribution rather more unequal (the exception was France). In private insurance systems (Switzerland and the USA) funding was unequivocally regressive: the poor paid relatively more.

However, health care provision in most rich countries was highly progressive. Van Doorslaer *et al.* (2000) found that physician visits in high-income countries were distributed fairly closely according to an independent assessment of need; the exceptions were the USA, Portugal, Greece and Austria. In the USA, however, the impact of differential private insurance coverage on inequality of access to doctors is very marked. In the USA, the better-off spent more on their care relative to need; the data could not establish whether this translated into better treatment, though that seems likely to be the case (van Doorslaer *et al.* 2000).

Taken together, these findings imply that health care in almost all rich countries is highly progressive: financing is progressive or mildly regressive, while delivery

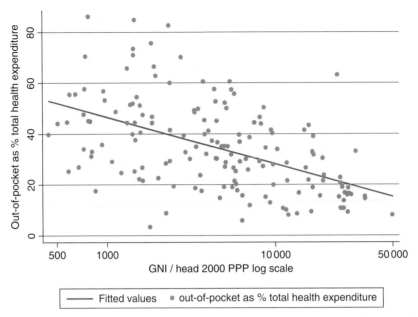

Figure 8.3   Out-of-pocket as per cent of total health expenditure and log gross national income (GNI) per head (PPP)(purchasing power parity) 2000

approaches equity in most of these very unequal societies. Health care, funded largely through taxation or social insurance, is, therefore, a major method of redressing inequality. These large sums of redistributive spending are, furthermore, embedded in quite stable social relationships and political commitments under-pinning national health systems in these countries.

Within poorer countries, the redistributive impact of health systems appears to depend strongly on the balance between private and public spending. In develop-ing countries a higher proportion of total health financing is private expenditure, which implies that those who can pay more receive more care. Higher shares of private in total health spending are strongly associated, across countries, with lower average incomes per head. Among rich countries, only the United States and Singapore have private expenditure shares over 50%, while all but one of the countries with private health expenditure shares over 70% have national incomes per head under $1000 per year. (Mackintosh and Koivusalo 2005)

Worse, the poorer a country, the more likely the population is to face the most inequitable form of health care financing: out-of-pocket expenditure (Figure 8.3).[15] Where this is a predominant means of access to health care across the social scale,

[15] For 155 countries; coefficient is significant at 1% level; horizontal axis GNI/head PPP log scale; regression *x* variable is log GNI per head (PPP); result is unchanged using Atlas method exchange rate data for GNI/head. Source: Mackintosh and Koivusalo (2005).

the extent of care received in response to need will depend on ability to pay on the spot, reducing care for the poor to very low levels and excluding the very poor (Pannarunothai and Mills 1997; Fabricant *et al.* 1999; van Doorslaer *et al.* 2005). In many low-income and middle-income countries but in no rich countries except Singapore, over 40% of health care spending is out-of-pocket; in India 82.4% of *all* health finance is out-of-pocket and this represents over 4% of gross domestic product; in Ghana this is 44.1% and 1.9% respectively. Rich countries are much more likely to have systems that are effectively free at the point of use.

Publicly financed health care, however, appears to be redistributive in most developing countries, and strongly redistributive in some. Developing countries' tax systems are often thought to be less progressive than those of high-income countries, since they tend to rely more on indirect taxes and less on direct taxation (Mirlees 2005). However, a study of Asian countries' health financing systems shows the tax funding to be progressive or proportional, while social insurance funding is generally progressive (O'Donnell *et al.* 2005a).

On the expenditure side, we should distinguish carefully between public health spending that is 'well targeted' and 'pro-poor' (the poorest quintile gaining more absolute benefit than the richest quintile) and that which is 'progressive' (the poorest quintile gains more relative to their income or expenditure than the richest quintile) and inequality-reducing (the post-benefit income distribution is less unequal than before) (Chu *et al.* 2004; O'Donnell *et al.* 2005b). A comparative study of 11 Asian countries (O'Donnell *et al* 2005b) concluded that four (Hong Kong, Malaysia, Thailand and Sri Lanka) achieved 'pro-poor' or even distributions of benefits from public health spending, while in all the others except Nepal the distribution was 'inequality reducing'. In Latin America, benefit incidence calculations suggest that public health spending tends to be pro-poor (Gwatkin 2001).

Sub-Saharan African countries' distributional public health performance has been extensively criticized; Davoodi *et al.* (2003 pp. 24, 33) for example, argue that, 'Spending on primary health care is poorly targeted … the poorest quintile receives the lowest [share] in sub-Saharan Africa …' and that, 'the middle class captures most of the gain from … primary health care, particularly in sub-Saharan Africa.' However, in the profoundly unequal and poverty-stricken context of low-income African countries, health care spending by government does, nevertheless, reach those in the lowest income categories in many countries, and while not egalitarian may still be progressive (Kida and Mackintosh 2005). Chu *et al.* (2004) conclude that although sub-Saharan African health expenditure is not well targeted, 'All thirty available studies find government health spending to be progressive' (Chu *et al.* 2004 p. 255). Indeed as Demery (2002 pp. 2–17) commented in a World Bank document, referring to the case of Ghana,

. . . governments would be hard pressed to find another commodity [other than public spending on health centres] where consumption by the poorest quintile approaches such a large share of total consumption.

Public tax-based expenditure on health thus appears to be generally redistributive in developing countries. Progressive African governments have for this reason repeatedly rebuilt district-level public health care systems (Mackintosh 2001): they are not only needed, they are also a robust method to redistribute resources in a manner that, rather than 'targeting' a desperate minority, provides support for the broad majority of the poor and the vulnerable in very-low-income countries. Similarly, Asian countries such as Sri Lanka and Thailand have allocated substantial public resources to health and achieved wide coverage (O'Donnell *et al.* 2005b). The overall redistributiveness of health systems in developing countries thus depends strongly upon the balance between private and public expenditure, a balance that tends to be least favourable to the poor in the poorest countries.

Inter-state fiscal redistribution with labour mobility in federal and semi-federal contexts

Having established that health systems, and specifically tax-based and social insurance-based health care, can be stable sites for redistribution within countries, we can consider in what contexts that principle might be extended to redistributive transfers between states. One such context is federal countries and systems. While health provision itself is frequently a state-level obligation, for example in India, the national government in many federal countries undertakes fiscal transfers that are directed at improving fiscal equity. Boadway (2005) defines fiscal equity in terms of fiscal capacity to provide a common level of service at common – or comparable – tax rates in the different states. This may include capacity to provide common levels of health services if the individual states wish to do so. The main rich country exception to this redistributive objective is the United States (Boadway 2005 p. 220).

The economic and social rationales for this type of equalizing or semi-equalizing redistributive transfers are well known. In federations and in unions, such as the European Union, without a central government, labour and capital are mobile across state boundaries. As a result, different distributive decisions – for example, different levels of social provision – in different states create incentives to migrate away from taxes for the well-off and towards services for the lower paid, and these responses can make local decisions unsustainable (King 1984). As people and businesses move around, some states can seek to take a 'free ride' on investments made elsewhere; conversely some states may be unable to afford to make investments that would have beneficial external effects for other states (for example, creating a highly educated workforce, cleaning up a water source, creating the basis for economic development that would generate markets for other states in the federation). In these cases, redistributive grants to deal with these external effects, and to encourage development in poorer states, can be agreed between states without a central government (as in the European Union grants to poorer areas in the Union). Factor mobility is, therefore, a basis for some centralized taxation and redistributive behaviour on efficiency grounds, with equitable effects.

Second, redistribution between states in a union or federation may result from a consensus on social citizenship. The citizens of the federation or union may wish to ensure a common minimum standard of services such as education and health not only for efficiency but also for equity reasons based on such sentiments of citizenship and solidarity. These views may be reinforced by mobility of labour, as people come to view as 'close' citizens of states that were previously socially distant.

Health services are an important site of both of these types of redistribution in federations and unions. Public and environmental health policies, and the level and spread of access to high quality health services, create strong externalities especially where people and resources are mobile across boundaries, hence there is a case for redistributive grants to support enforced minimum standards and moves towards fiscal equity. And health services also carry a strong moral weight; they have been repeatedly used by unitary and federal countries as elements of nation building, including response to national crisis as in Europe after 1945, in Africa after independence (Mackintosh 2001) and in South Korea after the 1997 crash (Kwon and Tchoe 2005). While service delivery in health generally remains a state responsibility, many federations exert equalizing leverage over the level of provision (Canada, for example, and Switzerland); the main exceptions seem to be India and the USA, though for the elderly in the US, Medicare is a universalist programme with an equalizing effect. In the European Union, health services are a closely guarded state responsibility, but there has been considerable negotiation and harmonization in areas such as mutual access of European citizens from one country to other countries' health care, and regulation of standards.

Beyond development aid? Arguments and mechanisms for global redistribution in health care

These arguments for redistribution in federations and unions quite clearly have implications in the current context at more global levels. It is possible to envisage, not a *global* solution to the increasing labour market integration in health care and its implications, but a specific and adaptive response starting with the clearest cases of need and reshaping the framework and nature of international financial transfer for health (Mackintosh *et al.* 2006a). The migration of health professionals from sub-Saharan Africa to rich countries creates an opportunity, a challenge, and political and economic motivation for establishing links of fiscal solidarity between health systems in these conditions of extreme inequality (Mensah *et al.* 2005).

First, the migration creates, as argued above, an ethical and moral case for a return flow of resources to countries of origin, and this case is reinforced by human rights obligations on countries of destination. International human rights law creates a moral imperative and a legal framework of obligation which attributes duties to states. States of destination of migrant workers that are parties to the relevant treaties, including the International Covenant on Economic, Social and Cultural Rights – and this includes the UK – have obligations of international assistance and co-operation that require them to ensure that they respect the right to health in other countries. Restitution is a policy that responds to this obligation (Bueno de Mesquita and Gordon 2005).

'Restitution' encompasses financial compensation but carries additional meanings of repair, restoration and the righting of ethical wrongs. In the economic literature, restitution is mainly discussed for property seized by authoritarian regimes and invaders and lost by refugees; for imprisonment, looting and murder by murderous regimes; and for the dehumanization and destruction of the slave trade and slavery.[16] The implication is that flows of aid to health services in countries of origin in sub-Saharan Africa shift, in political and moral terms, from *charity* to *duty*: from a conditional gesture of good will to the fulfilment of international obligations of countries of destination towards, specifically, the health services of countries of origin, and more specifically the health services that serve the poor majority.

Second, the making of that case has been generating a sense of social citizenship and *solidarity* around the interconnections of UK health services with African health services. There is evidence against the existence of 'aid fatigue' (Atkinson 2005) and health, notably African health crises, is a consistent focus of both large-scale and small-scale private giving (Micklewright and Wright 2005). The (Department for International Development) DFID reliance on a recognition of responsibility for the impact of migration when publicizing increases in aid to health systems in Africa suggests that the Department believes this argument to command quite wide public support. This sense of solidarity and responsibility has historically been a basis for public acceptance of redistributive transfers.

Third, health professionals' migration is reinforcing existing institutional links among health services – links between African and European health services, notably UK and France and anglophone and francophone African health services.

---

[16] Source: searches of recent academic and related literature; see for example Barkean (2000) and Vernon (2003); a search for 'restitution and health' and variants on it produces little; 'restitution and migration' largely identifies work on refugees.

Many of these links are long-standing. They include training links, such as post-graduate training, bursaries, exchange programmes, updating, examining and institution-to-institution support in terms of materials and equipment. The training culture is quite similar between the UK and many anglophone African medical and nursing schools – precisely because of this, qualifications are recognized with limited adaptation abroad. There are numerous institution-to-institution links between, for example, individual UK health care institutions and Ghanaian health districts and hospitals, and these are reinforced by Ghanaian medical and nursing staff in the UK supporting such links (Mensah *et al.* 2005). In this context, recognition of the increase in integration between the two services – the blurring of their boundaries – makes the argument for redistribution within the two health services ethically more insistent.

Fourth, there is an economic efficiency case for these redistributive health transfers. Health is an important contributor to development and growth (López-Casasnovas *et al.* 2005). There are also strong externalities in relation to infectious disease epidemics, which are closely associated with extreme poverty and require the rebuilding of effective health systems in order to tackle them, in addition to technological responses, such as new vaccines, which are the focus of large private donations to 'global partnership' approaches to health aid (Micklewright and Wright 2005). Rebuilding African health systems requires a sustained commitment in terms of recurrent transfers; it is not a challenge appropriately addressed by project-based development aid. Health-based redistribution as a long-term commitment to reduce health inequality could represent an important element of a definitive shift away from the refusal of donors to support 'consumption', that is, recurrent costs, a shift which is clearly already occurring in health care as donors such as the DFID agree to support improved wages for health workers in African countries.

Fifth, there is a good case for fiscal transfers to support *government* health expenditure. Evidence that such expenditure is progressive was cited above. Aid has been shown to increase public expenditure by recipients by more than the aid given (McGillivray and Morrissey 2001). Gomanee *et al.* (2005) offer cross-country econometric evidence that aid is associated with higher welfare levels in countries below median levels of the human development index, via its impact on public expenditure on services. Wagstaff (2003) shows that more public spending on health is associated with significantly lower levels of mortality and malnutrition among the poorest children. There is cross-section evidence that more government spending relative to private spending in low-income countries is associated with wider access – less exclusion – for children who are ill (Mackintosh and Koivusalo 2005). It is the redistributive effects of the health system as a whole that matter to poverty reduction, hence where government spending is progressive, more is better.

What then is the mechanism proposed? I and others have suggested that in response to treaty commitments and moral obligation, a fiscal mechanism of redistribution should be established between the UK government and African countries with absolute staff shortages in health, an outflow of staff towards the UK, and a minimum domestic capability to rebuild health systems if the funding were available (Mensah *et al.* 2005). The agreed redistributive transfers should – we have argued – have the following characteristics (Mackintosh *et al.* 2006a):

- They should be *positive*: the perverse subsidy should be repaid and the calculation should ensure a substantial net positive inflow;
- They should be *recurrent*: like redistributive domestic health spending, it should support current expenses such as part of the wage, salary, drugs and supplies bills;
- They should be *ring-fenced* to the health services: see below;
- They should constitute an *institutionalized* commitment: while sovereign governments cannot easily tie the hands of successors, some formal commitment, which would have to be formally unwound, would increase stability;
- They should be *monitored*: see below;
- And if possible they should be *embedded* in exchanges and support between health professionals and health institutions in the UK and Africa, based in the huge variety of links that currently exist.

How should they be funded? The international literature on funding international transfers is now growing rapidly. One long-standing proposal (Bhagwati and Wilson 1989) is that countries of origin of migrants should tax their nationals on the basis of citizenship, not residence. The US already does this and the Philippines has attempted to do so; so, in principle, has Eritrea (Desai *et al.* 2004 p. 678). The practical problems of such a scheme for developing countries with weak tax systems appear, however, 'unimaginable' (Desai *et al.* 2004 p. 683); however tax-sharing schemes between countries of origin and destination for highly skilled migrants are increasingly being considered and have the advantage of not transgressing rights to freedom of movement of migrants (Desai *et al.* 2004 pp. 683–4). Multinational firms are also paying hiring fees e.g. to the Indian government for Indian IT specialists hired under the US H-1B visa scheme for highly skilled foreign professionals.

The principal of tax sharing may be another useful stabilizing element in constructing a regime of redistributive fiscal transfers between health services: for example, a calculation of an agreed share of migrants' tax paid could – along with a calculation of the perverse subsidy – enter into a calculation of the minimum obligated transfer in any year. But it is clearly not sufficient. What are needed are redistributive fiscal transfers large enough to have a serious impact on the condition of the health care system. These need to be undertaken in a context that sustains the concept of shared social citizenship around health service provision beyond the current campaigning era. How could that be done?

It would require, it appears, new institutional mechanisms including broader stakeholders beyond government. The objective of such mechanisms would be to legitimize and stabilize transfers, and this could be assisted by involving, for example, professional associations, diaspora groups and non-governmental health-related organizations in monitoring the effective use of the transfers, alongside recipient governments and donors. The more the transfers are transparent and associated with the growing links among health service professionals across borders, the harder are the commitments to renege upon and the easier it may also be to allay fears within countries such as Ghana that the funds would not be effectively applied to key health service needs.

The basic requirements, using the Ghanaian example, are a commitment to strengthening of the Ghanaian health services (including non-governmental services); a management process that is transparent to donors but under Ghanaian control; and an assurance that the use of transfers would be responsive to Ghanaian priorities. Earlier discussions in Ghana[17] suggested that restitution payments might be particularly focused on supporting training including support for those teaching. Health expenditure in many African countries now includes detailed fiscal mechanisms for tracking the use of donor funds (in Ghana these are the Donor Pooled Funds accounts in hospital and health district accounting), and these could be built on to manage more stable and larger fiscal transfers (Mensah *et al.* 2005).

Finally, such stabilized redistributive transfers do not have to start on a large scale to be both effect and demonstrative of new relationships. Better perhaps to start on a restricted scale, in areas where a strong case exists and the social and professional connections are already in place. Changes to fiscal frameworks can start piecemeal, without the prospect of global solutions, on an individual government to government basis, to redress the worst cases of injustice in poor African countries.

Conclusion: embedding sustained redistribution in mutual obligation and knowledge in health care

The objective of policy response to migration should be, not limitation of mobility, but equity in health care (Mensah *et al.* 2005). The current scale of migrant skilled labour and its implications make a strong ethical case for redistribution between UK and African health services. I, and others, have argued the case for applying the model of domestic redistributive commitments to health services across national borders (Mackintosh *et al.* 2006a). We are arguing, let us be clear,

---

[17] By K. Mensah, with Ghana Health Service and Department of Health officials.

not for a *global* response to the increasing labour market integration in health care, but for a specific, piecemeal and adaptive response to ethical and treaty obligations, starting with the clearest cases of need. Our proposals contribute to the emerging literature arguing for international rethinking of aid, to generate aid governance mechanisms directed at reducing international inequality and rooted in a politics of justice (van der Hoeven 2001; Hickey and Bracking 2005). The arguments may have a utopian air – so did proposals for universal health care in Europe in the early twentieth century.

REFERENCES

Anand, S. and Baernighausen, T. (2003) *Human Resources and Health Outcomes.* Joint learning initiative working paper www.globalhealthtrust.org/doc/abstracts/WG7/Anandabstract.pdf.

Atkinson, A. B. (2005) Over-arching issues. In Atkinson, A. B., ed., *New Sources of Development Finance.* Oxford: Oxford University Press.

Ball, R. B. (2004) Divergent development, racialised rights: globalised labour markets and the trade of nurses – the case of the Philippines. *Women's Studies International Forum.* **27**: 119–133.

Barkean, E. (2000) *The Guilt of Nations: Restitution and Negotiating Historical Injustices.* New York: Norton.

Barr, N. (1998) *The Economics of the Welfare State.* Oxford: Oxford University Press.

Bhagwati, J. and Wilson, J. (1989) *Income Taxation and International Mobility.* Cambridge, MA: MIT Press.

Boadway, R. (2005) National taxation, fiscal federalism and global taxation. In Atkinson, A. B., ed., *New Sources of Development Finance.* Oxford: Oxford University Press. pp. 210–237.

Bueno de Mesquita, J. and Gordon, M. (2005) *The International Migration of Health Workers: a Human Rights Analysis.* London: Medact. www.medact.org.

Choy, C. C. (2003) *Empire of Care: Nursing and Migration in Filipino American History.* Durham, NC: Duke University Press.

Chu, K-Y., Davoodi, H. and Gupta, S. (2004) Income distribution and tax and government spending policies in developing countries. In Cornia, G. A., ed., (2004) *Inequality, Growth and Poverty in an Era of Liberalisation and Structural Adjustment.* Oxford: Oxford University Press.

Cooper, R. A. and Aiken, L. H. (2005) Global human professionals: view from the USA. Paper presented to the British Medical Association Conference on *The Global Health Professional: Improving Health, Fighting Poverty.* (14 April) London.

Davoodi, H. R., Tiongson, E. and Asawanuchit, S. S. (2003) *How Useful Are Benefit Incidence Analyses of Public Education and Health Spending?* IMF working Paper WP/03/227 Fiscal Affairs and Middle Eastern Department. (November) www.imf.org.

Demery, L. (2002) Benefit Incidence Analysis. In *Tool Kit: Techniques for Evaluating the Poverty Impact of Economic Policies.* Washington: World Bank.

Desai, M. A., Kapur, D. and McHale, J. (2004) Sharing the spoils: taxing international capital flows. *International Tax and Public Finance*. **11**: 633–693.

Fabricant, S. J., Kamara, C. W. and Mills, A. (1999) *Why* the poor pay more: household curative expenditures in rural Sierra Leone. *International Journal of Health Planning and Management*. **14**: 179–199.

General Medical Council (GMC) Press Office (2004) *Country of Qualification of Doctors on the Register 1999–2004.* www.gmcpressoffice.org.uk/fileadmin/init_documents/Doctors_on_the_register_1st_January 1999.xls.

Gent, S. and Skeldon, R. (2006) *Skilled Migration: Healthcare Policy Options.* Research Centre on Migration, Globalisation and Poverty briefing no 6 www.migrationdrc.org.

Gomanee, K., Girma, S. and Morrisey O. (2005) Aid, public spending and human welfare: evidence from quantile regressions. *Journal of International Development*. **17**: 299–309.

Gwatkin, D. (2001) Poverty and inequalities in health within developing countries: filling the information gap. In Leon, D. and Walt, G., eds., *Poverty, Inequality and Health*. Oxford: Oxford University Press.

Hagopian, A., Thompson, M. J., Fordyce, M., Johnson, K. E. and Hart, L. G. (2004) The migration of physicians from sub-Saharan Africa to the United States of America: measures of the African brain drain. *Human Resources for Health*. **2**: 17–27 www.human-resources-health.com/content/pdf/1478-4491-2-17.pdf.

Hardill, I. and MacDonald, S. (2000) Skilled international migration: the experience of nurses in the UK. *Regional Studies*. **34**(7): 681–692.

Hickey, S. and Bracking, S. (2005) Exploring the politics of chronic poverty: from representation to a politics of justice? *World Development*. **33**(6): 851–865.

House of Commons, International Development Committee (2004) *Migration and Development: How to Make Migration Work for Poverty Reduction* Sixth report of Session 2003–2004, Vol. 1. Report together with formal minutes, London: The Stationery Office.

Iredale, R. (2001) The migration of professionals: theories and typologies. *International Migration*. **39**(5): 7–26.

Kida, T. M. and Mackintosh, M. (2005) Public expenditure allocation and incidence under health care market liberalisation: a Tanzanian case study. In Mackintosh, M. and Koivusalo, M., eds., *Commercialization of Health Care: Global and Local Dynamics and Policy Responses*. Basingstoke: Palgrave.

King, D. N. (1984) *Fiscal Tiers: the Economics of Multi-Level Government.* London: Allen and Unwin.

Kwon, H-J. and Tchoe, B. (2005) The political economy of national health insurance in Korea. In Mackintosh, M. and Koivusalo, M., eds, *Commercialization of Health Care: Global and Local Dynamics and Policy Responses*. Basingstoke: Palgrave.

López-Casasnovas, G., Rivera, B. and Currais, L., eds. (2005) *Health and Economic Growth: Findings and Policy Implications*. Cambridge, MA: MIT Press.

Mackintosh, M. (2001) Do health systems contribute to inequalities? In Leon, D. and Walt, G., eds., *Poverty, Inequality and Health*. Oxford: Oxford University Press.

Mackintosh, M. and Koivusalo, M. (2005) Health systems and commercialization: in search of good sense. In Mackintosh, M. and Koivusalo, M., eds, *Commercialization of Health Care: Global and Local Dynamics and Policy Responses*. Basingstoke: Palgrave.

Mackintosh, M., Mensah, K., Henry, L. and Rowson, M. (2006a) Aid, restitution and international fiscal redistribution in health care: implications of health professionals migration. *Journal of International Development*. **18**: 757–770.

Mackintosh, M., Raghuram, P. and Henry L. (2006b) A perverse subsidy: African-trained doctors and nurses in the NHS *Soundings*. **34** (Autumn): 103–113.

McGillivray, M. and Morrisey, O. (2001) Aid illusion and public sector fiscal behaviour. *Journal of Development Studies*. **37** (6): 118–136.

Mensah, K. (2005) International migration of health care staff: extent and policy responses with illustrations from Ghana. In Mackintosh, M. and Koivusalo, M., eds, *Commercialization of Health Care: Global and Local Dynamics and Policy Responses*. Basingstoke: Palgrave.

Mensah, K., Mackintosh, M. and Henry, L. (2005) *The 'Skills Drain' of Health Professionals from the Developing World: a Framework for Policy Formulation*. London: Medact. www.medact.org.

Micklewright, J. and Wright, A. (2005) Private donations for international development. In Atkinson, A. B., ed., *New Sources of Development Finance*. Oxford: Oxford University Press.

Mirlees, J. (2005) Global public economics. In Atkinson, A. B., ed., *New Sources of Development Finance*. Oxford: Oxford University Press.

Nursing and Midwifery Council (NMC) (2004) Statistical analysis of the register 1 April 2003 to 31 March 2004. www.nmc-uk.org/aFrameDisplay.aspx?DocumentID=602.

Nursing and Midwifery Council (NMC) (2005) Statistical analysis of the register 1 April 2004 to 31 March 2005. www.nmc-uk.org/aFrameDisplay.aspx?DocumentID=856.

Nyonator, F., Dovlo, D. and Sagoe, K. (2004) *The Health of the Nation and the Brain Drain in the Health Sector*. UNDP Conference on Migration and Development in Ghana (September 14–16 2004) Accra. www.undp-gha.org.

O'Donnell, O., van Doorslaer, E., Rannan-Eliya, R. P. *et al.* (2005a) *Who Pays for Health Care in Asia?* EQUITAP Project working paper No 1. www.equitap.org.

O'Donnell, O., van Doorslaer, E., Rannan-Eliya, R. P. *et al.* (2005b) *Who Benefits From Public Spending on Health Care in Asia?* EQUITAP Project working paper No 3 www.equitap.org.

Pannarunothai, S. and Mills, A. (1997) The poor pay more: health-related inequality in Thailand. *Social Science and Medicine*. **44** (12): 1781–1790.

Parish, A. and Pickersgill, F. (2005) Home Office considers special visa to support overseas nurses. *Nursing Standard*. **19** (46): 12.

Raghuram, P. (2006) *The New Face of Health Provision in the UK*. www.open.ac.uk/socialsciences/staff/praghuram/info.html.

Smith, P. A., Allan, A., Henry, L. W., Larsen, J. A. and Mackintosh, M. M. (2006) *Valuing and Recognising the Talents of a Diverse Healthcare Workforce*. University of Surrey and the Open University http://portal.surrey.ac.uk/reoh.

Smith, P. A. and Mackintosh, M. (2007, in press) Professional, market and class: nurse migration and the remaking of division and disadvantage. *Journal of Clinical Nursing*. In press.

Stilwell, B., Diallo, K., Zurm, P. *et al.* (2004) Migration of health workers from developing countries: strategic approaches to its management. *Bulletin of the World Health Organization*. **82** (8): 595–600.

van der Hoeven, R. (2001) Assessing aid and global governance. *Journal of Development Studies*. **37** (6): 109–117.

van Doorslaer, E. Wagstaff, A., van der Burg, H. *et al.* (2000) Equity in the delivery of health care in Europe and the US. *Journal of Health Economics*. **19** (5): 553–583.

van Doorslaer, E., O'Donnell, O., Rannan-Eliya, R. P. *et al.* (2005) *Paying out of pocket for Health Care in Asia: Catastrophic and Poverty Impact*. EQUITAP Project working paper No 2. www.equitap.org.

Vernon, R. (2003) Against restitution. *Political Studies*. **51**: 542–557.

Vujicic, M., Zurn, P., Daillo, K., Adams, O. and Dal Poz, M. (2004) The role of wages in the migration of health care professionals from developing countries. *Human Resources for Health*. **2**: 3.

Wagstaff, A. (2003) Child health on a dollar a day: some tentative cross-country comparisons. *Social Science and Medicine*. **57**: 1529–1538.

Wagstaff, A., van Doorslaer, E., van der Burg, H. *et al.* (1999) Equity in the finance of health care: some further international comparisons. *Journal of Health Economics*. **18**: 263–290.

Winterton, R. and Thomas, G. (2006) Out of Africa. *Public Finance*. (March 31). www.publicfinance.co.uk.

World Health Organization (WHO) (2006) *The World Health Report 2006*. Geneva: WHO.

9

Pay the piper and call the tune: changing health care financing mechanisms to address public–private health sector mix inequities

Di McIntyre

Summary

This chapter considers health care financing in the African context, particularly the role that financing mechanisms can play in addressing public-private mix inequities. Sub-Saharan Africa has the worst health status indicators of any region in the world. Given many African countries' low level of national income, high poverty levels and low social development, the African experience is a graphic illustration of the social determinants of health. Health services, nevertheless, have a role to play in promoting health improvements, yet the health systems in most African countries are ill-equipped to contribute as they could.

The current health system context in Africa is briefly considered, and then contrasted with the key characteristics of equitable health systems based on a review of evidence from other low-income and middle-income countries. It is argued that a complete reversal of the public-private mix in health care financing and provision is required in African health systems to promote equity. Various ways of potentially achieving this, particularly through health care financing mechanisms, are considered.

A key conclusion of this analysis is that fragmentation in health care financing and provision must be reduced in order for cross-subsidies in income and risk to be achieved. Out-of-pocket payments must be minimized, as they do not permit any cross-subsidies, and linkages between individual voluntary insurance schemes, such as through a risk-equalization mechanism, should be considered. However, the route to equitable health systems lies particularly in increased tax funding and mandatory health insurance. In most African countries, general tax is unlikely to generate sufficient resources to ensure universal care and this form of financing will not dramatically change the public-private mix in health care provision. In contrast, mandatory health insurance integrated with general tax revenue, along with active purchasing of health services, can promote both equitable financing and benefit incidence.

The Economics of Health Equity, ed. Di McIntyre and Gavin Mooney. Published by Cambridge University Press. © Cambridge University Press 2007.

Introduction

Global attention is focused on the Millennium Development Goals (MDGs) and whether or not they will be achieved. The report card currently shows a dismal lack of progress towards achieving these goals. Appropriately, attention has mainly been directed to tackling socio-economic development issues that are not only likely to contribute to achieving the explicit poverty-related goals but also the health-related goals, given the social determinants of health. However, health systems could potentially play a critical role in achieving the goals. Some of the health-related goals, such as reducing maternal mortality by three-quarters and reversing the spread of HIV and AIDS, and malaria and other diseases, require that strong health systems are in place. Moreover, equitable health care financing mechanisms have long been recognized as an important redistributive strategy and could, thus, also contribute to achieving some of the poverty-related goals.

For these reasons, the promotion of health system equity, which is the focus of this chapter, is of considerable relevance to current global concerns. Health system equity is considered here with specific reference to the African context, but the issues raised have broader relevance for other low-income and middle-income countries (LMICs). Particular attention is devoted to considering how to address the inequitable public-private mix that plagues health systems in Africa and in other low-income or middle-income countries, and to critically assessing the potential role of health care financing in this regard.

The chapter begins by briefly contextualizing African health systems, from both a historical and a current situational perspective. It then spells out the equity concepts that guide the analysis presented, and distinguishes equity from poverty alleviation, which is the predominant 'policy-speak' concept in international development initiatives. The main section critically analyzes alternative health care financing mechanisms that could move us forward in our pursuit of equitable health systems, particularly in relation to public-private mix issues.

The African health and health system context

The average health status in sub-Saharan African countries is far worse than the overall average for low-income and middle-income countries (see Table 9.1). Nowhere are the social determinants of health as evident as in African countries. It is no coincidence that the highest infant and maternal mortality rates and the lowest life expectancy, as well as the lowest levels of national income, highest levels of poverty and highest levels of illiteracy, are found in the sub-Saharan African region. These social and economic factors have contributed dramatically to the

Table 9.1. Key macroeconomic, fiscal and health-related indicators for sub-Saharan African countries

	GDP Average annual % growth 2004	Gini Index	Govt. revenue as % GDP 2004	Taxes on income, profits & capital gains % revenue 2004	Taxes on goods & services % revenue 2004	Govt Expend. as % GDP 2004	Total debt service[1] % GNI 2004	Military expend. as % GDP 2004	Public health expend. % GDP 2004	Doctors, nurses & midwives per 1000 pop. 2000–2003	Life expectancy at birth (years) 2004	Infant mortality rate per 1000 live births 2004
Angola	11.1	...	...	...	...	...	11.9	9.1	2.4	...	41	154
Benin	2.7	36.5	...	...	...	...	1.6	...	1.9	...	55	90
Botswana	4.9	63	...	...	...	...	0.6	3.6	3.3	...	35	84
Burkina Faso	3.9	39.5	...	...	...	...	1.2	1.4	2.6	0.3	48	97
Burundi	5.5	42.4	...	...	...	...	13.7	5.8	0.7	0.3	44	114
Cameroon	4.3	44.6	...	...	...	...	4.6	1.5	1.2	...	46	87
Central African Republic	1.3	61.3	...	...	...	...	1.4	1.1	1.5	...	39	115
Chad	29.8	...	...	...	...	...	1.7	1.1	2.6	0.2	44	117
Congo, Dem. Rep.	6.3	...	7.9	25	24	7.8	1.9	...	0.7	...	44	129
Congo, Rep.	3.6	...	30.9	4	16	19.9	10.7	1.4	1.3	...	52	81
Côte d'Ivoire	1.6	44.6	17.1	8	18	17.5	3.7	1.6	1	...	46	117
Eritrea	1.8	...	...	...	...	...	2.1	19.4	2	...	54	52
Ethiopia	13.1	30	18.5	15	12	26.7	1.2	4.3	3.4	0.2	42	110
Gabon	1.4	...	...	...	...	...	3.6	...	2.9	...	54	60
Gambia, The	8.3	50.2	...	...	...	...	8.6	0.4	3.2	...	56	89
Ghana	5.8	40.8	23.8	22	22	20.9	2.7	0.8	1.4	0.9	57	68
Guinea	2.6	40.3	...	...	...	...	4.5	2.9	0.9	0.6	54	101
Guinea-Bissau	4.3	47	...	...	...	...	16.7	...	2.6	...	45	126
Kenya	4.3	42.5	18.2	34	50	20.6	2.3	1.6	1.7	...	48	79
Lesotho	2.3	63.2	49.7	20	17	38	3.2	2.6	4.1	...	36	80
Madagascar	5.3	47.5	60.4	6	16	63	1.9	...	1.7	0.4	56	76

Malawi	6.7	50.3	…	…	…	3.3	…	3.3	0.3	40	110
Mali	2.2	50.5	…	…	…	2.2	1.9	2.8	0.2	48	121
Mauritania	6.9	39	…	…	…	3.5	1.2	3.2	…	53	78
Mauritius	4.2	…	13	43	21.8	4.3	0.2	2.2	…	73	14
Mozambique	7.2	39.6	38	20	…	1.4	1.2	2.9	0.3	42	104
Namibia	6	74.3	…	…	31.1	…	2.4	4.7	…	47	47
Niger	0.9	50.5	…	…	…	1.7	0.9	2.5	0.3	45	152
Nigeria	6	43.7	…	…	…	4	0.8	1.3	1.5	44	101
Rwanda	4	28.9	…	…	…	1.3	2.1	1.6	0.2	44	118
Senegal	6.2	41.3	20	30	15.6	4.4	1.4	2.1	…	56	78
Sierra Leone	7.4	62.9	…	…	…	2.5	1.6	2	…	41	165
Somalia	…	…	…	…	…	…	…	1.2	…	47	133
South Africa	3.7	57.8	51	35	29.4	1.8	1.5	3.2	4.6	45	54
Sudan	6	…	…	…	…	1.6	2.2	1.9	1	57	63
Swaziland	2.1	60.9	29	15	23.2	1.8	3	3.3	3.4	42	108
Tanzania	6.3	34.6	…	…	…	1.1	1.5	2.4	0.4	46	78
Togo	3	…	…	…	…	1.0	…	1.4	0.3	55	78
Uganda	5.7	43	12	24	22.8	1.5	2.5	2.2	0.1	49	80
Zambia	4.7	42.1	…	…	…	8.3	…	2.8	…	38	102
Zimbabwe	-4.2	50.1	…	…	…	2	3.4	2.8	0.6	37	79
World	…	**24.6**	…	…	**27.3**	…	**2.5**	**5.9**	…	**67**	**54**
Low & middle income	7.1	…	…	…	…	5.6	2	2.8	…	65	59
Sub-Saharan Africa	4.8	…	…	…	…	2.9	1.9	2.4	…	46	100
High income	…	26	…	28	28.9	…	2.6	6.7	…	79	6
Europe EMU	…	35.7	24	24	38.6	…	1.7	7.1	12.2	79	4

Source: World Bank: World Development Indicators 2005; http://devdata.worldbank.org/

Blank cells reflect unavailable data

[1] Total debt service is the sum of principal repayments and interest actually paid on total long-term debt (public and publicly guaranteed and private non-guaranteed), use of IMF credit, and interest on short-term debt.

poor health status in the region, which has been considerably exacerbated by the AIDS epidemic in the last decade or more.

Each health system is unique and it is, therefore, difficult to generalize about African health systems. Nevertheless, there are some common trends that can be identified and key issues affecting many African health systems that can be commented on.

From a historical perspective, the vast majority of African countries are heavily influenced by their colonial roots, which engendered health systems with a strong urban, hospital-centred bias. On achieving independence, many countries strove to provide fully tax-funded systems that tried to address some of the inequities in geographic distribution of health services. Particular attention was often paid to developing a network of primary care facilities across the country and to strengthening preventive interventions such as immunization of children.

Macroeconomic difficulties, with many African countries experiencing low or negative economic growth, posed a serious challenge to this approach. Government resources available for funding health services dwindled, spurred on by Structural Adjustment Programs (SAPs) imposed by the International Financial Institutions (IFIs), which required government expenditure reductions and the levying of user fees for health care as explicit loan conditionalities. Within this context, we have witnessed the systematic deterioration of government health services in Africa, verging on complete disintegration in some countries.

Unsurprisingly, the private health sector began to flourish where previously it had been minimal or non-existent (e.g., private health services were outlawed in some countries after independence, such as Tanzania). While this could be described as a 'natural' development, it was reinforced by very active promotion of greater commercialization of health services, again as a result of IFIs' directives. The clearest exposition of this IFI position is possibly the World Bank's 1993 World Development Report, which urged countries to create an 'enabling environment' for the private health sector and argued that governments should restrict themselves to funding an 'essential package' of services having substantial public good characteristics and limited additional services for the very poor.

The end result is that health services in African countries today comprise a confusing array of fragmented and disparate providers, with an increasing proportion being privately owned. In some countries, the not-for-profit private sector is quite substantial, mainly taking the form of mission health facilities that have provided hospital and clinic-based services in rural and other underserved areas for decades (Gilson *et al.* 1997). The goals of these not-for-profit providers are well aligned with public policy goals and the public-private mix discussion in the remainder of this chapter focuses on the private for-profit sector relative to the public sector. There has been limited growth of non-governmental organizations for some time now, not least of all because missions and other non-governmental organizations are partially dependent on government subventions, which were dramatically reduced during the era of Structural Adjustment Programs. The most rapid growth has been in the private for-profit sector, ranging from health professionals leaving the public sector to establish private practices or undertaking private practice while continuing to work in the public sector, to traditional healers and untrained providers such as informal drug sellers. This sector is largely unregulated, and its expansion has further contributed to the decline of public sector services as the key health care resource, namely health care workers, are enticed to the private sector (if not overseas) by higher earning potentials.

There is similar diversity in the funding of health care services, with resources being drawn from both public and private sources. Tax funding of health services is extremely limited in African countries. Over 60% of countries devote less than 10% of government budgets to the health sector (McIntyre *et al.* 2005), despite the commitment of African Heads of State in Abuja in 2001 to spend at least 15% on health care (OAU 2001). Many countries remain heavily dependent on donor funding for health care, with over a quarter of total health care funding coming from external sources in about a third of countries. One of the single largest sources of financing is that of out-of-pocket payments, which include user fees at public sector facilities and direct payments to private providers. These payments exceed 25% of total health care expenditure in more than three-quarters of sub-Saharan African countries. In 40% of sub-Saharan African countries, more than half of all health care expenditure is funded through out-of-pocket payments (McIntyre *et al.* 2005).

Figure 9.1 highlights the protective effect on households of government funding; in countries where there is a commitment to devoting a relatively large share of government resources to the health sector (often supported by high levels of donor funding), the burden of out-of-pocket payments is kept relatively low. In the figure, countries are ordered in terms of the percentage share of total health care expenditure attributable to out-of-pocket payments, from lowest to highest. The trend line shows that the percentage share of government expenditure devoted to health declines on average as out-of-pocket expenditure levels increase.

Figure 9.1 also indicates that many of the countries with the highest levels of out-of-pocket payments (of the order of 80–90% of total health care expenditure), and some of the lowest levels of government funding for health services (such as Sudan, Burundi, Côte d'Ivoire, Angola and Somalia) have experienced long-running civil conflicts. High levels of defence spending in these countries have undoubtedly contributed to the fact that 5% or less of government budgets are devoted to the health sector.

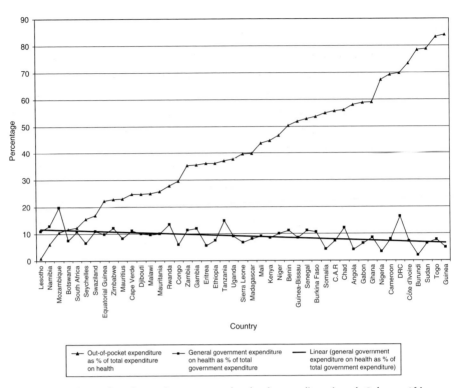

Figure 9.1   Comparison of out-of-pocket and government levels of expenditure in sub-Saharan African countries (McIntyre *et al.* 2005)

Another factor influencing the share of out-of-pocket payments in overall health care expenditure is the extent of coverage of health insurance (or pre-payment) schemes in a particular country. In general, health insurance is very limited in Africa. Private insurance of any magnitude is largely restricted to Southern Africa (including Botswana, Madagascar, South Africa, Swaziland and Zimbabwe) and Kenya in East Africa. In these countries, the major type of insurance is private voluntary coverage of formal sector employees. There has been a recent growth in community health insurance (or community-based pre-payment) schemes in some countries, particularly in Central and West Africa and more recently in East and to a limited extent Southern Africa, but this remains a small component of overall health care financing in terms of revenue share. Pre-payment via social security funding of any note is largely restricted to West Africa (Cape Verde, Côte d'Ivoire, Mali, Senegal and Togo), and is non-existent in most countries. However, a growing number of African countries are in the early stages of implementing, or exploring the potential for introducing, some form of mandatory health insurance (e.g., Tanzania, Ghana, Kenya, Uganda and South Africa).

Key concepts

The widely accepted definitions of equity in health care provision (or service benefits) of use of services according to need, and equity in health care financing of contributions according to ability to pay, are used in this analysis (Wagstaff and van Doorslaer 1993b). These definitions imply a strong element of cross-subsidy, from the healthy to the ill and from the wealthy to the poor. The degree of cross-subsidy is to some extent influenced by whether or not one chooses to focus on the horizontal or vertical equity component of the provision and financing definitions. In terms of provision, horizontal equity would focus particularly on ensuring that those in equal need have equal use of health services whereas a vertical equity approach would lead to disproportionate efforts to ensure that those with the greatest needs are able to use health services when needed. A vertical equity approach would appear appropriate in countries where there are large disparities in health status between different groups, as exists in many African countries (e.g., infant mortality rate in poorest and richest quintiles of 73 and 26 in Ghana, 119 and 63 in Benin, 104 and 51 in Cameroon, 96 and 40 in Kenya, 188 and 95 in Mozambique, 62 and 17 in South Africa) (UNDP 2005).

Similarly for financing, while horizontal equity is concerned with ensuring that those with equal ability to pay do in reality make equal health care financing contributions, vertical equity requires those with greater ability to pay to make appropriately higher contributions. The precise interpretation of 'appropriately higher' payments has been the subject of considerable debate. The World Health Organization (WHO) argued in its 2000 World Health Report that 'fair financing' required a proportional system, where everyone contributes the same percentage of their income towards health care funding, although the wealthy pay more in absolute monetary terms. The implication is that both progressive and regressive health care financing mechanisms would be regarded as inequitable or unfair. In contrast to the WHO approach, a strong case can be made for a progressive health care financing system in countries with high levels of income inequality, as exists throughout Africa (see Gini index in Table 9.1). For this reason, a progressive health care financing system is the preferred vertical equity definition in this analysis.

Having argued for paying particular attention to vertical equity in health care provision and financing, it is important to clarify that this is not equivalent to adopting a 'pro-poor' or poverty alleviation approach. Along with the IFI-led introduction of 'Poverty Reduction Strategies' in heavily-indebted poor countries (HIPC) and with initiatives such as the Millennium Development Goals, the dominant 'policy-speak' has been that of 'poverty reduction', 'poverty alleviation' or implementing 'pro-poor' strategies. Addressing the needs of the poorest in society, and protecting the poor from the potentially catastrophic economic consequences of ill health, is critical. However, efforts to ensure that policies are 'pro-poor' (which is frequently incorrectly conflated with equity) have translated into exercises in targeting limited public and donor resources for health care to the poorest, with little or no consideration of the overall health system. The end result is likely to be the entrenchment of fragmented health systems, where the poor are catered for under one set of arrangements and the rest of society pays for and uses entirely different services. In contrast, a vertical equity approach requires comprehensive and integrated consideration of the health system and actively promotes redistributive elements through cross-subsidies in the overall system. While vertical equity calls for preferential treatment of those with the greatest need and the least ability to pay, it does not do this by way of ignoring the rest of the population entirely, as is all too often the case in 'pro-poor' health policies.

Key characteristics of an equitable health system

Given the equity definitions outlined above, what would be the key characteristics of an equitable health system? From the health care provision perspective, there is growing evidence that countries with strong public sector health services are able to achieve high levels of health status relative to their level of economic development, and relatively small disparities in health status across socio-economic groups. Two countries that are widely regarded as particularly high achievers in this regard are Costa Rica and Sri Lanka. Costa Rica is a middle-income country with a gross domestic product (purchasing power parity) per capita of $9606, which is less than a third of the average for high-income countries of $29 898, yet has an infant mortality rate of 8 per 1000 live births and an average life expectancy of 78 years, which is very similar to that for high-income countries (infant mortality rate of 5 and life expectancy of 79 years). Sri Lanka's achievements are even more remarkable, given that its gross domestic product (purchasing power parity) per capita of $3778 is about 8 times less than that of high-income countries, yet it has an infant mortality rate of 13 per 1000 live births and an average life expectancy of 74 years (UNDP 2005).

Both countries have universal health systems in the sense that a single pre-payment health care financing mechanism is dominant (tax funding in Sri Lanka, and universal mandatory insurance combined with substantial tax funding to fully subsidize contributions for the poor in Costa Rica) and that the entire population are entitled to the same service benefits and use the same providers. In both countries, the government established a strong network of primary care facilities and hospitals at an early stage, which continue to be government-owned in Sri Lanka but which were transferred to the social security organization in the mid-1970s in Costa Rica. There are relatively few private for-profit providers in both countries, which are mainly confined to the primary care level.

In contrast, health systems with high levels of commercialization display considerable inequities in the use of services. A recent analysis of Demographic and Health Survey (DHS) data for 44 countries used the percentage of children who were treated by a private provider when they sought care for acute respiratory infection or diarrhoea as a measure of the level of commercialization within each country. A higher level of commercialization was significantly associated with lower levels of children receiving treatment at all, i.e., the higher the share of private provision in the health system, the lower the percentage of the population able to use health care when needed (Mackintosh and Koivusalo 2005). While it is difficult to establish causality, as noted by the authors, '... cross-country evidence carries *no* comfort for those promoting commercialization as a generally beneficial process', (p. 13).

The commercialization of health services, as an explicit policy intervention, was based on ideological imperatives and not on any evidence of superior performance in the private sector. The argument underlying the policy of commercialization was that government involvement in economic and social affairs should be restricted to the bare minimum, as 'the market' provided the best way of meeting the economic and social (including health) needs of any society (World Bank 1993). Recent empirical evidence indicates that while private for-profit providers are sometimes more efficient, in the sense that they may be able to provide certain health services at lower cost to the company or organization than government providers, the cost to individuals (or to government in the case of contracted-out services) is generally considerably higher once the profit margin is included than direct public provision (Broomberg *et al.* 1997; Liu *et al.* 2004; Mills *et al.* 2004).

There are also concerns about certain aspects of private for-profit health sector provision, particularly in relation to the quality and safety of informal providers' care, which is the predominant component of the private for-profit health sector in many African countries (Mackintosh 2003). There is extensive evidence that informal providers sell inappropriate drug dosages (e.g., selling only a few tablets according to the customer's cash budget). This has contributed dramatically to increased drug resistance, particularly with respect to antimalarials and antibiotics (Le Grand *et al.* 1999; Marsh *et al.* 1999).

From an equity perspective, there are a number of concerns about the existence of a large private for-profit health care sector. Most importantly, use of these services is distributed across the population not on the basis of need but that of ability to pay. In addition, there are countless examples of the adverse impact of private provision on public sector services, on which the majority of the population in African countries is dependent, particularly with respect to the drain of scarce health professional resources from the public services. For these reasons, and to ensure safety and quality of care, there is general agreement that the activities of private providers should be regulated. However, given extremely limited enforcement capacity, the private health sector in Africa is largely unregulated.

In relation to health care financing, analyses from both high-income countries (van Doorslaer and Wagstaff 1993; Wagstaff *et al.* 1999), and high-income, middle-income and low-income countries in Asia (O'Donnell *et al.* 2005) demonstrate that general tax revenue is usually the most progressive health care financing mechanism. However, this depends on the type of taxes levied (direct income taxes, indirect taxes such as VAT, etc.) and the relative contribution of each tax to overall government revenue. Mandatory health insurance (i.e., where certain individuals and groups are required by law to contribute to a health insurance scheme) in high-income countries can be either regressive or progressive, depending on how contribution rates are structured and whether or not there is a maximum contribution rate. The Asian study indicated that mandatory insurance is usually progressive in low-income and middle-income countries, largely because mandatory insurance in these countries only covers those in formal sector employment, who are the highest-income individuals. In high-income countries, private voluntary insurance is regressive, and more so than mandatory insurance, while in low-income and middle-income countries it tends to be progressive (as it is again restricted to the highest income earners), but less so than mandatory insurance.

Out-of-pocket payments are widely recognized as the most regressive way of funding health services. This is partly related to the fact that those with the lowest income levels tend to bear the greatest burden of ill health and thus bear the greatest financing burden as payment is directly linked to use of health services. Out-of-pocket payments, in systems where a relatively large share of health care financing is attributable to this source, will always be regressive unless the majority of low-income people simply do not use health services when needed.

The relative progressivity of overall financing within a health system is clearly influenced by the mix of individual health care financing mechanisms and the relative progressivity of each. What is apparent is that health systems with a high degree of fragmentation in financing (i.e., a number of different financing mechanisms for different groups and fragmentation within mechanisms, such as many individual voluntary insurance schemes) have extremely limited cross-subsidies and thereby tend to be less progressive overall. Thus, from an equity perspective, fragmentation in health care financing should be minimized.

A key problem with health system equity analyses to date is that financing and service provision or benefit issues tend to be considered in relative isolation from each other. For example, the 'ECuity project' evaluated the relative progressivity of health care financing mechanisms (using the Kakwani Index methodology) and whether benefits from using health services are pro-rich or pro-poor (using concentration index methods) in a range of high-income countries (van Doorslaer and Wagstaff 1993; Wagstaff and van Doorslaer 1993a). However, the 'ECuity project' and other studies that have used the same methodology do not combine the financing and benefit sides in a comprehensive analysis of health system equity. The Asian 'EQUITAP study' notes in its evaluation of health care financing that although health insurance contributions are generally progressive in these countries, owing to insurance contributions being restricted to the highest income groups, it is also only these groups who benefit from these contributions (O'Donnell *et al.* 2005). This is a critical issue, and ideally, a comprehensive analysis of health system equity should combine the information on the magnitude of health care financing contributions and of health service benefits for each income group.

One way in which this can be achieved is by using the standard fiscal incidence methodology of combining the monetary value of tax contributions with the monetary value of tax-funded services to determine in which income groups contributions exceed benefits and in which groups benefits exceed contributions. This could be done for each health care financing mechanism and for the health system overall. Using the previously outlined vertical equity definitions, and given the fact that ill health and thus the relative need for health care is heavily concentrated amongst the low-income groups, the expectation is that contributions would exceed benefits by a considerable margin for the highest income groups while the lowest income groups would be substantial net beneficiaries. It can be argued that financing mechanisms in which this pattern is not evident *and* where there is no explicit mechanism for risk and income cross-subsidies between this mechanism and the rest of the health system does not enhance health system equity and should not be promoted. In addition, fragmentation between and within health care financing mechanisms should be reduced, as this also limits the extent of cross-subsidies.

This brief overview, drawn from international experience, suggests some key characteristics of equitable health systems. The evidence indicates that strong and accessible (available, affordable and acceptable) public health service provision is essential within an equitable health system. Further, there is neither a solid evidence base nor a rational reason for actively promoting the unfettered growth of the private for-profit health sector in African countries. Some form of pre-payment mechanism for financing health care (tax or insurance) is the only basis for an equitable health system, and the larger the population covered (e.g., by health insurance), the greater the potential for cross-subsidies. The experience of countries such as Costa Rica and Sri Lanka strongly suggests that achieving good health status among citizens despite limited economic resources is enhanced by universal pre-payment coverage and entitlement to the same service benefits provided through an integrated network of providers.

A comparison of the nature of existing health systems in Africa with these broad characteristics makes the magnitude of the challenge confronting African countries immediately evident. Strong public sector services are critical from an equity perspective, yet the public sector in African countries has been systematically neglected and its services have deteriorated dramatically over the past few decades. In addition, there is evidence that higher-income groups benefit more from the public sector health services that do exist than poorer groups (Castro-Leal et al. 1999). Private for-profit providers are a pervasive and firmly entrenched part of health systems in African countries, but are largely unregulated. Pre-payment in the form of general tax revenue or large-scale health insurance should be the major form of health care financing, yet tax funding and health insurance are very limited with out-of-pocket payments predominating in most African countries. In essence, a complete reversal of the public-private mix in health care provision and financing is required to promote equity. The question of how African health systems can be transformed, and particularly the potential role of health care financing mechanisms in this transformation process, is the focus of the remainder of this chapter.

Transforming the public-private mix: the role of financing

From the preceding discussion, it is clear that in pursuing equitable health systems, African countries should focus particularly on increased general tax funding for health services or mandatory health insurance. It is assumed that donor funding can be directed towards supporting whichever domestic funding mechanisms predominate. In addition to seeking to limit fragmentation between different financing mechanisms through focusing on those which best achieve universal coverage, fragmentation on the provision side should also be reduced in order to limit differences in the type, range and quality of services to which different population groups have access. The key issue in this regard is addressing the public-private mix in the health system. As indicated previously, regulation of the private sector in African countries has not been very effective, largely owing to limited enforcement capacity, so other ways must be sought to influence the behaviour of the private for-profit sector in line with public health goals.

There are two major reasons why it may be important to consider a role for mandatory insurance, and not rely solely on general tax funding, in the African context. First, tax funding for health services is very constrained and second, an entirely tax-funded system is unlikely to be able to substantially influence the behaviour of the private for-profit sector. These two issues are considered in the following sections, which focus on tax funding and mandatory insurance, respectively.

General tax funding

The first issue to consider is: what is the potential for substantial increases in general tax funding of health services in African countries? Table 9.1 provides an overview of the key macroeconomic and fiscal indicators for sub-Saharan African countries. With one or two notable exceptions (e.g., Zimbabwe), African countries have been experiencing higher economic (gross domestic product) growth rates in recent years than they have in decades. However, these growth rates are still relatively low by global standards; only six African countries had an average annual gross domestic product growth exceeding the average for all low-income and middle-income countries. Despite these improved economic growth rates, this is from a very low base, with the average gross domestic product per capita being an average of (purchasing power parity) $1856 for sub-Saharan African countries compared with an average of (purchasing power parity) $2168 in low-income countries, (purchasing power parity) $6104 in middle-income countries and (purchasing power parity) $29 898 in high-income countries (UNDP 2005). The Gini index also indicates that there are relatively high levels of inequalities in the distribution of income within the majority of African countries. These factors constrain the amount of tax revenue that can be generated.

Table 9.1 also provides insights into the distribution of government revenue between two of the main categories of taxes: direct taxes on income, profits and capital gains (i.e., personal and company income taxes) and indirect taxes on goods and services (e.g., value added tax – VAT, or general sales tax – GST). In most cases, taxes on goods and services contribute more to government revenue than personal and company income taxes. Given the relatively low levels of formal sector employment and large informal sectors in most African countries, combined with poor tax collection capacity, this distribution of tax revenue is perhaps to be expected. However, there are serious equity concerns about a heavy reliance on VAT or GST and other indirect taxes, which are far less progressive than personal and company income taxes (O'Donnell *et al.* 2005) and, outside of the lowest-income countries, are generally regressive (van Doorslaer and Wagstaff 1993).

The tax revenue generation capacity of a country clearly limits government expenditure levels; only six of the African countries for which data are available have a deficit budget. Government expenditure in most African countries is of the order of 10–20% of gross domestic product and all (with the exception of Lesotho and Madagascar) are well below the European level of 39%.

Given the heavy debt burden in Africa, debt servicing as a percentage of national income is, in many cases, substantially higher than government spending on other individual sectors (e.g., education or health). Of the government resources that remain after debt servicing commitments, it is a matter of concern that in about half of African countries for which there are data, military expenditure exceeds government spending on health (see Table 9.1). As indicated in Figure 9.1, the health sector's share of total government spending is 10% or less in the vast majority of countries. This is well below the Abuja commitment that 15% should be devoted to health services.

These indicators suggest that there is limited fiscal space for increased government expenditure on health services. There are two main mechanisms by which additional government resources could be directed towards the health sector, namely increasing government revenue and allocating a higher percentage of total government expenditure to health care.

In relation to increased government revenue, although it has long been assumed that it is not really feasible for African countries to increase their tax revenue significantly, this may not necessarily be the case. While tax rates in Africa are similar to other parts of the world (with the highest marginal tax rate being between 20–40% in most cases) and there is limited scope for rate increases, tax collection could be dramatically improved. However, this requires improved overall governance, a serious challenge in the African context, which would encourage greater tax compliance. Some have argued for the introduction of a wider range of wealth taxes (e.g., taxes on financial transaction flows, luxury airline travel, currency exchanges) (Bond 2006). Another way of increasing tax revenue is to abolish tax deductibility of private voluntary health insurance contributions given that these subsidies are highly inequitable. For example, in South Africa, more government revenue is devoted to these tax deduction subsidies and civil servants' private health insurance contributions per beneficiary than is spent in per capita terms on the 86% of the population dependent on public sector health care. Abolishing these deductions could result in large tax revenue increases, but only in the few African countries that have these insurance schemes. Revenue available for increased government spending could also be increased through external grants. The main drawback of this funding source is its unpredictability, as such grants can be withheld with little or no notice (McIntyre *et al.* 2005). Given the extent of existing debt (exceeding 100% of gross domestic product in some African countries), further loans would be undesirable.

While increased revenue should certainly be pursued, the major potential mechanism for improved funding of public sector health services is to increase the health sector's share of total government expenditure. There is certainly scope for reduced military spending in some African countries, but this requires an end to the ongoing civil conflicts that plague the continent and again is related to dramatic changes in governance. The one area that may offer greater potential is that of debt relief, and indeed total debt cancellation. Debt relief efforts under the heavily-indebted poor countries (HIPC) initiative have, in many instances, been wholly inadequate. Recent G8 'debt cancellation' initiatives appear to be similarly inadequate; the G8 debt relief will be provided over 40 years, translating into relatively small annual reductions in the debt burden, and conditions are linked to this debt relief (McIntyre *et al.* 2005). A wider range of more substantive efforts to reduce the debt burden on African governments is required to enable governments to devote more of their limited tax funding to the provision of health and other social services.

Would these efforts to improve tax funding for health services impact on the public-private mix and promote an equitable health system to any great extent? Unfortunately, the answer is likely to be no. Increased tax funding could lead to quite dramatic improvements in public sector health services, such as through increased staff numbers, improved routine availability of essential drugs and improved geographic access to health facilities (by either building more clinics, expanding mobile clinic services or introducing 'close to client' services). This will result in a greater proportion of the population using public sector health services and more protection against incurring out-of-pocket expenditure. However, given the enormous fiscal space constraints, these efforts are unlikely to transform the public health sector into the provider of choice for the vast majority of the population. Thus, it will not necessarily impact markedly on private sector provision.

Regulatory efforts to control the worst excesses of the private for-profit health sector could be enhanced, but given the track record to date, this may not be particularly effective. It is more likely that the private sector will not receive much policy consideration (as is the current reality), and the emphasis placed on trying to ensure that limited government resources are effectively targeted to meeting the health care needs of the poorest and thereby improve the benefit incidence of government spending. The danger of this approach is that the adverse impacts of a continually expanding private sector, such as the loss of skilled health workers from the public sector, could continue unhindered. The disparities in resource availability between those using private providers and those served by the public health sector are likely to continue to grow, and the health system will move further away from, rather than closer to, equity. Equally importantly, this approach will leave the financial resources located in the private health sector untouched. Thus, it will have relatively limited impact on improving cross-subsidies in the overall health system.

Mandatory health insurance

There are three main categories of health insurance in Africa, namely private voluntary insurance, community-based pre-payment or insurance, and mandatory (often called social or national) health insurance. Private voluntary health insurance covers a minority elite (usually the highest-income formal sector employees) and entrenches stark differences in the type and quantity of health services to which different groups have access. Another problem is that the private insurance market tends to be very fragmented, with many competing schemes in a single country, which severely limits risk pooling. Community-based health insurance (CBHI) schemes exist within localized communities, most frequently in rural areas, where members (usually those outside the formal employment sector) make small payments (often on an annual basis after the harvest time) to the scheme, which then covers their user fee charges at health facilities. While these schemes provide some financial protection against unexpected health care costs for their members, they tend to cover a very small proportion of the population and there is almost never a mechanism for pooling risk across the many different schemes within a country. There is also overwhelming evidence that the poorest and most vulnerable groups, for whom even relatively small contributions are unaffordable, are excluded from these schemes. Given the limitations of private voluntary and community-based insurance schemes, they are not considered further here (save in relation to where they may form part of a mandatory health insurance system).

Mandatory insurance, sometimes called social health insurance (SHI) (where only certain groups are required to become members and benefit from insurance cover) or national health insurance (NHI) (which is universal in that everyone receives coverage benefits irrespective of whether they have contributed or not), is an option that is receiving considerable attention in a number of African countries. This interest was heightened when the 2005 World Health Assembly passed a resolution encouraging member states to pursue social and other forms of health insurance (World Health Organization 2005).

Most African countries are exploring or pursuing the social health insurance option, which brings with it many of the same problems associated with private voluntary health insurance. In particular, it only covers the high-income and middle-income population and entrenches a two-tier health system. In addition, as civil servants tend to be the single largest group of formal sector employees in African countries, they are often the first group to be covered by mandatory health insurance. Limited government funds are used to purchase mandatory insurance cover for this group, further reducing government resources available for providing services for those dependent on publicly-funded services. Social health insurance does have one very significant advantage over private voluntary health insurance; it usually consists of a single risk pool (i.e., even if it comprises several smaller funds as intermediaries, there is a risk-equalization mechanism). In this way, it promotes cross-subsidies, but this is limited to the insured population.

One country that has decided to adopt a more universal approach to mandatory health insurance is Ghana. The basis of the national health insurance system will be district-wide 'Mutual Health Insurance Schemes' (MHIS) (Government of Ghana 2003). The contributions of formal sector employees will be collected through payroll-deducted contributions to the Social Security and National Insurance Trust (SSNIT) Fund. Those outside the formal sector are expected to make direct contributions to their district MHIS. Significant tax funding will be provided to the National Health Insurance Fund (NHIF). The NHIF will allocate funds to each district MHIS, in order to transfer the contributions of formal sector workers secured from the SSNIT payroll contributions, partially subsidize contributions for low-income households, fully subsidize contributions for the indigent and serve a risk equalization and reinsurance function. There is a relatively comprehensive benefit package and services can be sought at any provider accredited by the system (almost exclusively public and mission or non-governmental organization providers).

A key advantage of the Ghanaian approach is that there is the political intention to achieve, from the outset, universal coverage in an integrated health system in the shortest possible period, and that there are explicit mechanisms to include those both inside and outside the formal sector (McIntyre *et al.* 2005). The government does recognize that coverage will have to be extended gradually and the aim is to achieve enrolment levels of about 60% of residents in Ghana within 10 years of starting mandatory health insurance (Ministerial Task Team 2002). Experience from other low-income and middle-income countries has shown that it is very difficult to move to a universal health insurance system once a social health insurance scheme has become entrenched. Beneficiaries of social schemes strongly resist moving to a national scheme, because of concerns about contribution increases (to cross-subsidize membership for low-income groups not covered by the social scheme) and fears of declining benefits. The Ghanaian approach holds promise that this can be avoided.

While very few other African countries have an integrated financing system, as is being introduced in Ghana, a few have an integrated general tax and donor funded system with no user fees, yet there are still considerable out-of-pocket payments to private providers; an example is Uganda, which removed all user fees at public health facilities in 2001. Others, such as South Africa, are trying to reduce fragmentation in health care financing by establishing a risk-equalization mechanism between individual voluntary health insurance schemes, as a basis for moving towards a social health insurance, but are not considering a fully integrated financing system. The examples of countries that have sought (or are pursuing) integrated financing systems, whereby general tax and mandatory insurance contributions are used in combination to achieve universal coverage where all citizens have financial protection and are entitled to the same services, are found in other regions of the world and include Costa Rica in Latin America, Thailand in Asia, and Kyrgyzstan and Moldova in the former USSR.

As indicated previously, there are two questions about mandatory health insurance of particular relevance to the focus of this chapter. Can it offer any additional resource advantages for equitable health care financing in the African context over general tax revenue alone? Can it impact on the public-private mix in a way that promotes an equitable health system?

With respect to the first question, mandatory health insurance could potentially offer a number of advantages over general tax as the sole source of funding for public sector health services. As argued earlier, there is limited fiscal space for substantial, rapid increases in general tax funding for health care. Mandatory health insurance could supplement tax funds, and if structured appropriately, could do so in an equitable way. If a government is willing to introduce mandatory health insurance contributions for formal sector workers over and above existing taxation, this could generate additional revenue, although it would increase the cost of labour and hence have employment implications. More importantly, it could draw resources currently located in the private for-profit sector into an integrated financing system to benefit a greater proportion of the population. This particularly applies to countries having relatively large private voluntary health insurance schemes. For example, 47% of total health care expenditure in South Africa flows via private health insurance schemes, which cover less than 15% of the population. If the mandatory insurance does not allow 'opting out' (i.e., people are permitted to purchase cover via private insurance rather than contribute to the mandatory insurance system), these resources can be drawn into a mandatory insurance risk pool. In addition, as in the Ghanaian design, mandatory health insurance can provide a mechanism for drawing in resources from those working in the informal sector. In the African context, introducing mandatory insurance does not imply reduced tax funding; substantial tax funds are required to ensure a universal health system (e.g., by fully subsidizing contributions for the lowest-income groups to the mandatory insurance scheme). The key issue is that mandatory insurance contributions and general tax revenue should be integrated in some way to benefit the entire population.

In relation to impacting on the public-private mix, mandatory insurance can make a dramatic difference in the public-private health care *financing* mix, as described above. Mandatory insurance can also impact on the public-private health care *provision* mix. The additional resources that could be generated through this financing mechanism could be directed towards rebuilding the public sector with the goal of it becoming the provider of choice for the majority of the population. This could be achieved if mandatory insurance revenue were treated as a dedicated tax, combined with existing tax resources for health services and directed to public facilities. Alternatively, if funding flows via reimbursement of providers for services used by insurance members, the benefit package could specify use of public sector facilities (and non-government organization facilities where appropriate), or allow choice of provider but only cover the equivalent of full cost-recovery fees in public facilities (i.e., if a private for-profit facility is used, the member has to cover any difference in cost). This would also direct a substantial amount of mandatory insurance revenue to public facilities. Given that the link between mandatory health insurance contributions and service benefits is more 'visible' than is the case with general tax, the mandatory insurance option is more likely to encourage the widest range of income groups possible to use public health services. This limits the potential for 'the better-off to segregate themselves institutionally' (Mackintosh 2001 p. 187) and can foster social solidarity.

Active purchasing of services and careful management of reimbursement mechanisms by the mandatory insurance scheme can also serve to ensure that all providers, public or private, deliver services in line with public health goals. Through 'holding the purse-strings', whereby the vast majority of funds available for health services are channelled in an integrated way, there is effective control over the use of the funds and considerable influence can be exerted on health care providers – 'paying the piper and calling the tune'. For example, where there is universal mandatory insurance cover, the insurance scheme has monopsonistic purchasing power. Providers can only claim from the scheme if they have been accredited (mainly to ensure quality, safety and appropriate range of services) and are willing to serve any insurance member who seeks care from them *and* if they charge fees that are specified by the scheme. It can thereby also promote efficiency, resulting in more services for more people with the available resources.

Most importantly, an integrated financing system with a clearly specified benefit package to which all citizens are entitled, combined with active purchasing, can promote overall health system cross-subsidies. Not only does it promote contributions according to ability to pay (equitable financing incidence), there is also a far greater likelihood that health service use will be distributed according to need under such a system (equitable benefit incidence).

Conclusions

African countries face enormous challenges in moving towards equitable health systems. Health care financing and provision is very fragmented with limited mechanisms for promoting cross-subsidies in income or risk across citizens. The effects are seen in the high levels of infant mortality and low life expectancy documented in Table 9.1. However, hope of reversing this situation is provided by the very encouraging examples of low-income and middle-income countries in other parts of the world that have achieved excellent levels of health status despite constrained economic resources. Key elements of their success have been universal coverage of the population with either mandatory health insurance of general tax funded services, where the entire population is entitled to the same service benefits and use the same providers, which are either owned by government or the social security organization. These systems have both equitable financing incidence, where higher-income groups contribute considerably more of their income to health care funding than lower-income groups, and equitable benefit incidence, where service use is closely linked with need for, or capacity to benefit from, health care.

While similar health systems' structures in the African context cannot be achieved overnight, it is possible to embark on a process of gradually reducing fragmentation in health care financing and thereby promoting cross-subsidies. This requires a move away from the reliance on out-of-pocket payments and enhancement of pre-payment mechanisms, such as tax funding and health insurance. Where voluntary insurance schemes (either commercial insurance for higher income formal sector workers or community-based insurance) exist, efforts should be made to link these small risk pools, such as through risk-equalization mechanisms, preferably within the context of a move to mandatory insurance. Where mandatory insurance already exists but only covers a minority elite, universal coverage in the shortest possible time should be actively pursued by putting in place mechanisms to include informal sector workers and the poor. Whether or not mandatory health insurance is adopted, general tax funding for the health sector must be expanded, primarily through increasing the health sector's share of total government expenditure, which can be greatly facilitated through enhanced debt relief and cancellation initiatives.

In relation to provision, reducing fragmentation and differentials in the type, range and quality of care between the public and private sectors should be the aim. Probably one of the biggest challenges facing African countries is to rebuild public sector services as the foundation of transformed health systems. This requires a substantial injection of financial resources and specific strategies for improving the retention and morale of health workers. While regulation of the private for-profit health sector has been singularly unsuccessful to date, a universal mandatory insurance system with active purchasing and carefully managed provider reimbursement mechanisms in the context of monopsonistic purchasing power can dramatically impact on provider behaviour. International experience suggests that 'holding the purse-strings' through an integrated pre-payment financing mechanism may be the most effective way of redressing the inequitable public–private mix in African health systems.

REFERENCES

Bond, P. (2006) *The Dispossession of African Wealth at the Cost of African Health.* Harare: Regional Network for Equity in Health in Southern Africa (EQUINET). www.equinetafrica.org/bibl/docs/DISbondTRADE.pdf.

Broomberg, J., Masobe, P. and Mills, A. (1997) To purchase or to provide? The relative efficiency of contracting out versus direct public provision of hospital services in South Africa. In Bennett, S., McPake, B. and Mills, A., eds., *Private Health Providers in Developing Countries: Serving the Public Interest?* London: Zed Books.

Castro-Leal, F., Dayton, J., Demery, L. and Mehra, K. (1999) Public social spending in Africa: do the poor benefit? *World Bank Research Observer.* **14**: 49–72.

Gilson, L., Adusei, J., Arhin, D. *et al.* (1997) Should African governments contract out clinical health services to church providers? In Bennett, S., McPake, B. and Mills, A., eds., *Private Health Providers in Developing Countries: Serving the Public Interest?* London: Zed Books.

Government of Ghana (2003) *National Health Insurance Act (Act 650).* Accra: Government of Ghana.

Le Grand, A., Hogerzeil, H. and Haaijer-Ruskamp, F. (1999) Intervention research on rational use of drugs: a review. *Health Policy and Planning.* **14**: 89–102.

Liu, X., Hotchkiss, D., Bose, S., Bitran, R. and Giedion, U. (2004) *Contracting for Primary Health Services: Evidence on its Effects and a Framework for Evaluation.* Bethesda: PHR Plus, Abt Associates.

Mackintosh, M. (2001) Do health care systems contribute to inequalities? In Leon, D. and Walt, G., eds., *Poverty, Inequality and Health: an International Perspective.* Oxford: Oxford University Press.

Mackintosh, M. (2003) *Health Care Commercialisation and the Embedding of Inequality.* RUIG/UNRISD Health Project paper. Geneva: UNRISD.

Mackintosh, M. and Koivusalo, M. (2005) Health systems and commercialization: in search of good sense. In Mackintosh, M. and Koivusalo, M., eds., *Commercialization of Health Care: Global and Local Dynamics and Policy Responses.* Basingstoke: Palgrave MacMillan.

Marsh, V., Mutemi, W., Muturi, J. *et al.* (1999) Changing home treatment of childhood fevers by training shop keepers in rural Kenya. *Tropical Medicine and International Health.* **4**: 383–389.

McIntyre, D., Gilson, L. and Mutyambizi, V. (2005) *Promoting Equitable Health Care Financing in the African Context: Current Challenges and Future Prospects.* Harare: Regional Network for Equity in Health in Southern Africa (EQUINET). www.equinetafrica.org/bibl/docs/McIfin092005.pdf.

Mills, A., Palmer, N., Gilson, L. *et al.* (2004) The performance of different models of primary care provision in Southern Africa. *Social Science and Medicine.* **59**: 931–943.

Ministerial Task Team (2002) *Policy Framework for Establishment of Health Insurance in Ghana.* Accra: Ministry of Health.

OAU (2001) *Abuja Declaration on HIV/AIDS, Tuberculosis and Other Related Infectious Diseases.* Organisation of African Unity.

O'Donnell, O., van Doorslaer, E., Rannan-Eliya, R. P. *et al.* (2005) *Who Pays for Health Care in Asia?* Colombo: Institute of Policy Studies. EQUITAP Project working paper No 1. www.equitap.org.

UNDP (2005) *Human Development Report 2005.* New York: United Nations Development Programme.

van Doorslaer, E. and Wagstaff, A. (1993) Equity in the finance of health care: methods and findings. In van Doorslaer, E., Wagstaff, A. and Rutten, F., eds., *Equity in the Finance and Delivery of Health Care: an International Perspective.* New York: Oxford University Press.

Wagstaff, A. and van Doorslaer, E. (1993a) Equity in the delivery of health care: methods and findings. In van Doorslaer, E., Wagstaff, A. and Rutten, F., eds., *Equity in the Finance and Delivery of Health Care: an International Perspective.* New York: Oxford University Press.

Wagstaff, A. and van Doorslaer, E. (1993b) Equity in the finance and delivery of health care: concepts and definitions. In van Doorslaer, E., Wagstaff, A. and Rutten, F., eds., *Equity in the Finance and Delivery of Health Care: an International Perspective.* New York: Oxford University Press.

Wagstaff, A., van Doorslaer, E., van der Burg, H. *et al.* (1999) Equity in the finance of health care: some further international comparisons. *Journal of Health Economics.* **18**: 263–290.

World Bank (1993) *World Development Report 1993: Investing in Health.* New York: Oxford University Press.

World Health Organization (2005) *Sustainable Health Financing, Universal Coverage and Social Health Insurance: World Health Assembly Resolution WHA58.33.* Geneva: World Health Organization.

Lessons from individual countries

10

Equity in health financing, resource allocation and health service utilization in Brazil: past, present and future

Silvia Marta Porto, Claudia Travassos, Maria Alicia Domínguez Ugá and Isabela Soares Santos

Summary

This chapter analyzes equity in the Brazilian health system from three perspectives: in its financing; in the geographical distribution of financial resources; and in health services utilization. The first section deals with the burden of health service financing across income deciles, by type of expenditure. The second section presents a comparison of the distribution of expenditure as established by the Ministry of Health in 2002 with an estimation by the authors of resource allocation based on need. This is followed in the final section by a review of some studies on inequalities across different socio-economic groups in health care services utilization in Brazil.

Although there remain substantial social inequalities with respect to access to and utilization of health services in Brazil, the relevant data indicate improvements in access to health services and reductions in social inequalities between 1998 and 2003. There has also been an improvement in the equity of resource allocation from the central government to the states and municipalities. While the financing of public health services out of taxation is almost proportional, this represents a rather low percentage of the overall health spend. This results in large out-of-pocket expenditures, particularly for the poor, which is clearly regressive, and at the same time reduces the ability of the state to implement redistributive policies.

Introduction

The current model of the Brazilian health system was introduced under the new Constitution of 1988 which, inspired by the idea of a national health system, created the *Sistema Único de Saúde – the SUS*, the principles of which are universality, comprehensiveness and free access to health care.

The Economics of Health Equity, ed. Di McIntyre and Gavin Mooney. Published by Cambridge University Press. © Cambridge University Press 2007.

Article 196 of the Constitution of 1988 states:

Health is the right of all; it is the duty of the state to promote, protect and recover health through social and economic policies, by reducing the risk of diseases and other hazards, and through universal and egalitarian access to actions and services aimed at these ends.

Before 1988, there was a system of social insurance, which provided cover only to those workers who were formally employed, retired people and their families. The poor were covered by state or municipal systems (mostly composed of primary care services) while the wealthier used private services. After 1988, with the creation of the SUS, every Brazilian citizen became formally entitled to free health care.

In addition to the fact that coverage became universal, another important element of the reform was the decentralization of responsibilities for health care to local governments. Those health care functions that operate at the federal level are mostly related to the formulation of national policies: the regulation and financing of the system; evaluation of health system performance; and the co-ordination of the Health Information System. The state and municipal levels of government are also responsible for financing the system and executing health policies, as well as for monitoring providers.

At the time that the new Constitution was promulgated, there was a large private hospital sector (with 65% of total hospitals being private). There were also substantial private health insurance and managed care organizations. These cover approximately 40 million people out of a total population of 188 million in 2006.

What this means in practice is that the Brazilian health system consists of two subsectors. The principal subsector is the public system (SUS), based on a national health system model. The other is the voluntary private sector, which comprises both private health insurance and private providers and which operates alongside the public sector. Thus, all Brazilians are covered by SUS but some also have coverage through private insurance.

Equity in utilization depends largely on the availability of health care services, human resources and health technology. Additionally, the geographical distribution of population and services, together with organizational and financial barriers have an impact on equity in utilization. With respect to financial barriers, the distribution of the burden of financing (mainly of private expenditures, especially out-of-pocket expenditures) affects equity in utilization, in that it penalizes disproportionally the poor more than the rich. It is also the case that a fair geographical distribution of financial resources, which is based on needs, is a necessary (although not sufficient) condition for achieving equity in health care utilization.

This chapter analyzes equity in the Brazilian health system on three fronts: its financing; the geographical distribution of financial resources; and health services utilization. It is based on different studies, each one focusing in turn on one of these issues. The first study analyzes for 2002 the burden of health service financing across income deciles, by type of expenditure. The second study presents the geographical distribution of financial resources, comparing the distribution arising from the strategy adopted by the Ministry of Health in 2002 with an estimate made of resource allocation based on need. The last one presents a review of some studies on social inequalities in health care services utilization in Brazil. The main reason for writing the chapter is to explore some important issues on each of these three fronts; these issues are relevant to public policy in the pursuit of greater equity in health care in Brazil. Together they represent the best way of moving forward to improve equity in health care in Brazil.

Equity in health financing

This section, based on Ugá and Santos (2006), analyzes the financing of the Brazilian health system from the perspective of vertical equity, identifying the effects of health payments on different income classes or, in other words, the impact of health financing on income distribution.

Methodology

In pursuing this analysis, we adopted the methodology developed by Wagstaff and van Doorslaer (van Doorslaer *et al.* 1999; Wagstaff 2001), which allows the identification of the impact of health payments on income distribution. It incorporates elements introduced by Kakwani (1976; 1977) to analyze the degree of progressivity (or regressivity) in tax systems and applies them to health system financing (including private expenditure and the taxes that finance the health system).

The model generates a progressivity index, K, which corresponds to twice the area between the curve of the tax payment distribution and the Lorenz curve. In the specific situation of health care, the Kakwani index (K) is measured as the difference between the Payments Concentration index and the Gini index. This provides an indicator in the range -1 to $+1$. A positive result for K means that the tax or payments structure is progressive; a negative value of K corresponds to a regressive system (Kakwani 1976; 1977).

Following Wagstaff (2001), we define equitable health sector financing as a system based on progressivity, that is, those with higher incomes pay a higher proportion of their incomes in tax. The extent of equity in health sector financing is to be judged by the degree of progressivity of the system.

As mentioned above, the Brazilian health system consists of two sectors. the public system (SUS) and the voluntary private sector. As a result, the analysis of health sector financing has to consider three expenditure flows:

- Those by the three levels of Government (central, states and municipalities) for the supply of public health care in public facilities and those contracted or outsourced by the national health system (SUS);
- Families' out-of-pocket expenditure directly on health services but also on private health insurance;
- Expenditure by companies providing medical and hospital coverage for their employees. (Companies also contribute to the finance of the SUS by paying taxes such as Corporate Income Tax (IRPJ), Social Contribution on Net Profit (CSLL), and Tax for Social Security Financing (COFINS). These, however, are included under the first heading above.)

Given the lack of information on health expenditure flows by companies, this study did not include them in the analysis. This is unfortunate. However these represent only about 18% of total health expenditure in Brazil. These payments are, of course, made to private health plans by companies to their workers and as such are not neutral in terms of distributional concerns, since, through them, some people have what amounts to 'double coverage' in the Brazilian health system. However, this issue could not be treated through the methodology adopted.

To analyze the impact of health sector financing on Brazil's income distribution, it was necessary to establish the sources of financing for both the SUS and private expenditure, and the distribution of this financing across different income levels.

Data sources and treatment

The distribution of the burden of public and private financing of the Brazilian health system was estimated on the basis of data from the National Family Budget Survey (POF) of the Brazilian Institute of Geography and Statistics, or National Census Bureau – IBGE (IBGE 2005a). This provides information about the income and expenditure of Brazilian families. The Family Budget Survey was conducted in 2002–2003 and includes all socio-economic strata of the resident Brazilian population, using 2002 as the reference year.

With respect to the tax structure, the data used were those from the estimated tax burden for 2001 (Afonso *et al.* 2002). Estimates for the financing of the SUS in 2002 were based on data from the Institute for Applied Economic Research (IPEA/MPOG) and the Information System for the Public Budget in Health (Brazil, Ministério da Saúde, www.datasus.gov.br).

Estimates were made of the distribution of the tax burden for the share of taxes and social contributions for the financing of the SUS, across income deciles.

The year 2002 was used as the reference period for the public health sector's financing structure and for the tax rates for indirect taxes.

The share of taxes financing the SUS included indirect taxes (COFINS, IPI, ICMS and ISS, levied respectively on invoicing, industrial output, circulation of merchandise, and services) and direct taxes (CPMF, IRPF, IPTU and IPVA, levied respectively on financial transactions, income, urban property, and automotive vehicles). These account for 70% of the public financing of the health system.

Family expenditure and income were adjusted by two weightings. One is the weighting of each family, used in the sample for the population. The other is an equalization factor to calculate per capita values. It is important to correct, on the one hand, for the difference between the number of persons in each family, which is usually bigger among poorer families and, on the other hand, for the difference in the numbers of possible contributors to the family income. To adjust for these problems, Wagstaff and van Doorslaer calculated a medium factor using data from European families that equalizes the family expenditure and income by the exponential 0.75, as proposed by Wagstaff at www.worldbank.org/poverty/health/wbact/. We opted to use this in the Brazilian analyses to make it possible to compare our analyses with others.

Results and analysis

Brazilian society is marked by very substantial income inequality: the Gini co-efficient is 0.57, indicating an enormous income concentration. The wealthiest 10% of the population receives 46.1% of total income, while the poorest 20% receive only 2.9%. The poorest half of the population have only 13.7% of income.

Expenditure on Brazil's health system absorbs 9.7% of family income. As can be seen in Figure 10.1 and Table 10.1, the burden of the financing of the sector and the share of each type of expenditure on health vary considerably across income deciles.

Thus, in the lowest (by family income) decile of the population, health expenditures absorb 10.6% of income, while in the highest decile this drops to 9.1%. Worthy of note is the out-of-pocket expenditure among the poorest families: this expense, which is, in part, for catastrophic care, where in essence there is little or no choice involved, represents 6.8% of family income in the lowest decile but accounts for only 3.1% of income in the highest decile.

Health insurance expenditures only become substantial in the three wealthiest income deciles, where people have the financial capacity to purchase plans and are also mostly in formal employment, which at the same time gives them access to the group plans provided by companies.

Data on the concentration of health sector financing in Brazil are presented in Table 10.1. These show both income and health expenditure by sector.

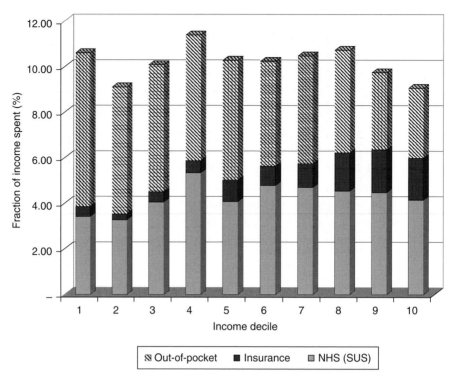

Figure 10.1 Fraction of income spent on health by income decile. Brazil, 2002 (IBGE 2005a)

The distribution of private expenditure in health is clearly regressive: while the poor spend proportionally more of their income on health, the wealthiest, with 46.1% of the national income, contribute only 42.2% to private health expenditure. This regressivity is yet more apparent at the very top of the income range, where the wealthiest 5% of the population spend proportionally much less on private health care.

For out-of-pocket expenditures, the regressivity is even greater. The lowest decile, with 1.00% of income, has 1.76% of out-of-pocket expenditure; the wealthiest decile, with 46.10%, only contributes 37.05% of this expenditure. For each of the deciles by income from the lowest to the eighth, the share in expenditure is disproportionaly more than income. This confirms more generally the regressivity of out-of-pocket expenditure. It also points to an explanation of such spending in terms of the need to acquire health goods and services rather than of the families' capacity to pay for them. Particularly noteworthy is the extremely high degree of regressivity in spending on medicines. The poorest decile, with only 1.00% of the income, bears 2.59% of the burden of this expense, while the wealthiest decile, with 46.10% of income, has only 27.84% of the spending on medicines. This is reflected in a Kakwani index for out-of-pocket financing of − 0.108.

Table 10.1. Distribution of the weight of health sector financing on per capita family income by type of expenditure, according to income decile. Brazil, 2002

	Income	SUS		Health insurance		Out-of-pocket		Total private		Total financing	
	%	%	Weight in income	%	Weight in income	%	Weight in income	%	Weight in income	%	Weight in income
1	1.00	0.78	3.42	0.28	0.43	1.76	6.76	1.33	7.19	1.09	10.61
2	1.92	1.45	3.28	0.32	0.25	2.79	5.58	2.08	5.83	1.80	9.11
3	2.74	2.56	4.06	0.78	0.44	3.99	5.59	3.07	6.02	2.84	10.08
4	3.56	4.39	5.34	1.22	0.53	5.14	5.52	4.01	6.05	4.18	11.39
5	4.53	4.26	4.08	2.77	0.94	6.21	5.26	5.23	6.20	4.79	10.28
6	5.80	6.40	4.78	3.15	0.83	7.00	4.62	5.89	5.46	6.12	10.24
7	7.59	8.23	4.70	5.09	1.03	9.38	4.74	8.16	5.77	8.19	10.48
8	10.43	10.93	4.54	11.42	1.68	12.26	4.50	12.02	6.19	11.53	10.73
9	16.34	16.89	4.48	19.94	1.88	14.44	3.39	16.01	5.26	16.41	9.75
10	46.10	44.11	4.15	55.03	1.84	37.05	3.08	42.20	4.92	43.05	9.07
TOTAL	100.00	100.00	100.00	100.00	100.00	100.00		100.00		100.00	

Source: IBGE (2005a) MOH/SIOPS (www.datasus.gov.br/siops) and National Health Agency for Private Health Insurance (ANS/MOH) (2004 www.ans.gov.br) data from DIOPS for fiscal year 2003. Includes financing by individuals and companies.

With respect to payments on health plans and insurance, these are apparently (but only apparently) progressive: the percentage share of the lowest seven deciles in this expenditure is far less than proportional to the individuals' income. The Kakwani index is positive: 0.133. However, this seeming progressivity is in reality a function of the fact that the low expenditure by lower-income groups is a result of their exclusion from the private insurance system because of their lack of access to health plans in the formal labour market and, more generally, their low income. Clearly when excluded they do not pay but then they do not get the benefits either. The low percentages of expenditure on health plans in the poorest income deciles thus reflect Brazil's maldistribution of income.

In the financing of the public system (SUS), through payment of taxes, the lower-income deciles contribute less than proportionally to their income. The lowest decile, with 1.0% of income, contributes only 0.8% of the payments; while the second lowest, with 1.9% of income, pays 1.4% of the taxes and the third, with 2.7% of income, pays 2.6% of the tax payments. This might imply that the tax structure is progressive. However, the highest decile, with 46.1% of income, contributes only 44.1% of the total tax; across the fourth to the ninth decile, the income-to-payments ratio is very close to proportional. One can thus argue that the financing of the SUS as a whole is progressive in relation to the treatment of the poorest three deciles, regressive in relation to the wealthiest decile, and proportional for the population strata from the fourth through to the ninth deciles. These last correspond to the lower-income and lower-middle-income populations.

This pattern is reflected in the Kakwani index for public financing (–0.008), which corresponds to being nearly proportional. This is the result of progressive direct taxes, such as income tax ($K=0.333$) and vehicle tax ($K=0.120$), together with heavily regressive indirect taxes, like the ICMS or value-added tax on goods ($K=-0.759$), ISS or services tax ($K=-0.081$), and the Contribution to Social Security Financing, which is levied on companies' revenues ($K=-0.058$).

Kakwani index for financing the Brazilian health system

The K value for health system financing is slightly regressive overall but close to proportional (-0.012). The potential for being progressive is countered by the weight of out-of-pocket expenditure (which is heavily regressive, with $K=-0.108$) in the weighted sum of K for financing the system as a whole.

Two basic conditions must be considered in any interpretation of the results presented in this section. The first relates to the huge income concentration in Brazilian society, as expressed by the Brazilian Gini index of 0.57. The second arises from the nature of the composition of Brazilian health expenditure. Although there is a national health system, defined constitutionally as having universal and comprehensive access, the structure of health expenditure in Brazil is quite different from that of national health systems in many other countries with respect to the state's participation in health sector financing. In Brazil, the public sector's contribution to national health spending is only 44%, about the same as that of the United States.

As indicated the Kakwani index for financing the SUS (-0.008) corresponds to a nearly proportional system. In a society as unequal as Brazil, to have proportional financing of the SUS cannot, however, be regarded as a major success from the perspective of social justice. Public expenditure as a proportion of the overall health spend is low. This results in out-of-pocket expenditures that are regressive being a relatively large proportion of the total. It also means that the ability of the state to implement redistributive policies is reduced.

Equity in the geographical allocation of resources

The 1988 Constitution and the Health Act spelt out the principles on which the SUS is based. Among these are universal access, full health care coverage, equality in health care, and political and administrative decentralization. Although there has been progress on these fronts since 1988, as will be shown, Brazil is still far from fully accomplishing these objectives.

Related to the composition of public health financing, the current Brazilian legislation lays out the extent of the contributions to health care expenditure in the budgets of federal government, as well as in those of the states and municipalities. For the federal (central) level, in any particular year the financial contributions are set out in the budget in the previous year, with adjustments being made which are in line with variations in gross domestic product. For the states and municipalities, the percentages of their total budgets to be spent on health care is laid down. These are respectively 12% and 15% for the states and municipalities. Overall, this means that that federal funding amounts to about 51% of the total public health care spend while the states and municipalities contribute respectively 23% and 26% (Ugá and Santos 2006).

Initially, in 1991, the resource allocation system from the federal level to states and municipalities was based in essence on reimbursement for what outpatient and inpatient services were provided. Inpatient care with the SUS was remunerated through a prospective payment system. On the other hand, outpatient care was remunerated on a fee-for-service basis, the fees being weighted according to the type of outpatient care category.

This resource allocation model was thus based solely on the existing supply of services. These were concentrated in those geographical areas where the population was in the higher socio-economic groups and had better health. As a result, rather than ameliorating existing differences, this approach to resource allocation only served to make the situation yet more inequitable (Porto and Ugá 1992 p. 189), as it overlooked criteria that might have resulted in offsetting or narrowing existing inequalities (Médici 1991 p. 51; Rezende 1992 p. 12).

That allocation approach prevailed until 1998, when major changes were introduced to the resource distribution framework from the federal level down to other jurisdictional spheres (states and municipalities).

Some key innovations that were effectively implemented and are still operating include:

(a) The establishment of per capita payments for each geographical area to cover primary care. These payments replaced a system that had been based simply on the supply of services. It is to be noted, however, that these per capita payments varied from R\$8 to R\$18 (1 dollar = 1.16 real, average exchange rate in 1998). The minimum value (R\$8) was arbitrarily determined without any kind of clear rationale, while the upper values were based on levels of expenditures historically. This resulted in higher figures being applicable in the more developed regions. Therefore, although this system did result in improvements in the financial situation of several small municipalities that previously had received less than R\$8 per capita, inequalities still persisted.

(b) The creation of financial incentives for the development of special primary care programmes, such as family health teams within the 'Family Health Program' (described in detail later) and to expand the coverage of these programmes.

(c) Caps on expenditure were introduced for higher levels of complexity of care. These caps, however, merely reflected the practice of paying for services previously provided. As such they failed to bring about any substantial change to the financing arrangements.

Despite the fact that differences in allocations per capita have been reduced as a result of these actions, significant inequalities remain. To attempt to provide a better basis for dealing with these inequities, an alternative method for allocating resources based on need criteria, as explained below, has been previously formulated by SMP and others (Porto *et al.* 2002).

Procedures for resource allocation according to population needs

A review of the proposals submitted and of existing experiences shows that when equitable resource allocation models are designed to take levels of health needs into consideration, the most common approach is to treat recurrent expenditures separately from capital investments, the latter usually being determined on the basis of strategic planning.

A key issue in the various methodological approaches is the acknowledgement that equitable resource allocation must include a proxy for need to help determine the relative inequalities between the health and socio-economic status of target populations in the different geographical areas. Obviously, any proposed approach must take as a starting point the target populations involved. However, since a simple per capita allocation does not take into account other potentially relevant differences between target populations, such as sex and age variables, any proposal aiming to be based on health needs must take into account the fact that these vary in line with various demographic and other characteristics. Another common feature of such proposals is that there is a need to consider differences in the average costs of different types of treatment that are required by different population subgroups.

In short, resource allocation formulae are reached through gradual adjustments of the target population, taking into account their demographic profile, inequalities between the cost of health care types required by each population segment, and inequalities between health needs. Beyond that, approaches differ in the way in which they then calculate need. It should be noted that there are both simpler and more sophisticated approaches to determining and measuring relative needs, but none of them captures fully each and every aspect of the complexity of health needs in target populations.[1]

In health care resource allocation, the UK is the country with the most experience and their approach has served as a benchmark to other countries initiating plans for geographical allocation of resources based on the principle of equal resources for equal needs. Since the 1970s, the UK has adopted an allocation approach (Resource Allocation Working Party, or RAWP) in which health care resources are allocated according to population size adjusted for three factors: sex and age differences, service utilization needs, and regional variations in health care cost (Department of Health and Social Security, UK 1976).

The core issue is and always has been in these formulae how to get a proxy for relative health care needs beyond those pertaining to sex and age. The earliest RAWP guidelines (in England but followed later for the rest of the UK) utilized mortality rates broken down by cause and standardized by sex and age. The adoption of a formula on these bases in the United Kingdom resulted in a more equitable allocation of resources. However, the methodology was widely criticized because it lacked empirical evidence to support the assumption that those standard mortality rates were an adequate proxy for health care needs (Rice and Smith 1999 p. 36).

---

[1] A summary of experiences in 19 countries can be found in Rice and Smith (1999).

In the 1990s, Carr-Hill *et al.* (1994) developed a new methodological approach, based on the use of inpatient care, to estimate the potential demand for services generated by health care need, adjusted by the distribution of the supply of services. The central objective of their proposal is to estimate health need through a model of health services utilization, controlling for the supply variations that are not justified by need.

The research report *Methodology for Equitable Resource Allocation* (Porto *et al.* 2002) details the method proposed by Carr-Hill *et al.* (1994) and discusses its applicability to the Brazilian situation. The method was judged not to be suitable for Brazil. This is principally because, as compared with the UK, even when adjusted for the distribution of supply, in Brazil several indicators of needs were inversely related to health services utilization. For example, in the areas which had the worst living conditions (higher infant mortality and higher illiteracy rate), the model estimated a lower volume of health services utilization than in areas with better life conditions. These results suggest that, in addition to supply differences, there are other access barriers at work in Brazil.

An alternative approach to estimating health care needs for the Brazilian environment

Given the limitations concerning the application to Brazil of the UK models mentioned above, both RAWP and the Carr-Hill approach (see Porto *et al.* 2002), an alternative measure was developed to estimate needs, initially on the basis of the following twelve epidemiological and socio-economic variables:

(a) Illiteracy rate;
(b) Number of persons per household;
(c) Rate of child deaths of undetermined origin;
(d) Rate of child deaths due to diarrhoea or malnutrition;
(e) Child mortality rate;
(f) Mortality rate, ages 65 and over;
(g) Ratio of rural population;
(h) Mortality rate, ages 1 to 64;
(i) Mortality rate due to cardiovascular disease;
(j) Mortality rate due to neoplasm;
(k) Mortality rate due to infectious or parasitic diseases;
(l) Rate of teenage mothers.

Those social indicators for which there exists sufficient scientific evidence about their positive association with health needs were prioritized. It is to be noted that certain variables, known to be related to health care needs, e.g., the percentage of households with basic sanitation facilities (sewage, water and garbage collection), were not used here because the statistics from the 2000 census were not available at the time of this study.

This need indicator was obtained using multivariate statistical analysis (principal components analysis), which consists of representing the original multivariate space by a smaller number of factors known as 'principal components'. These fewer factors, developed through linear combinations of the original variables, are not correlated with each other (are orthogonal), and are estimated mathematically to maximize the overall original variance.

Further simulations with only three variables (infant mortality, illiteracy rate and the proportion of households without a sewerage system) gave as good results as those using all twelve variables, owing to the high correlation between several of the original twelve variables. If the Ministry of Health did elect to adopt this methodology, using only three variables would also facilitate the introduction of the process, as managers can more easily understand it.

The states with the lowest relative needs were São Paulo, Santa Catarina, Rio Grande do Sul and the Federal District. These are all among the richest states in Brazil. In contrast, all Northeastern states, the poorest ones, displayed the highest relative needs (Figure 10.2).

Table 10.2 compares the allocations made by the Ministry of Health in 2002 to finance inpatient and outpatient health care, and those estimated on the basis of the methodology developed (as above) for the Brazilian environment.

Note that using this new formula the group of states in the Northern and Northeastern regions which, taken together, represent those with the worst socio-economic and sanitation conditions, would receive average increases of 20.7% and 28.1%, respectively, as compared with the per capita allocations currently made by the Ministry of Health. Clearly, to achieve this within the existing budget allocation would entail a reduction in resources to the other regions. Alternatively, to allocate according to this new formula without there being any decrease in any state would require an increase in the health service budget in the order of 6.4% (Porto *et al.* 2002).

The same table presents the percentage estimated difference for 1999. As indicated, the inequalities estimated for 2002 are smaller as compared with the differences computed for 1999 for the Northern, Southern and Midwest regions. They remain, however, virtually unchanged for the Northeastern and Southeastern regions.

Additionally, it should be recalled that to achieve greater interregional equity, the allocation of financial resources to cover recurrent health care costs must be backed by investment programmes to support the supply of services between the regions. Otherwise, the states with a shortage of capital facilities might receive more resources than they could, in practice, use. At the same time, states with more complex health care systems might have their health care quality compromised if their budgets were revised downward by a new interregional reallocation of resources.

Figure 10.2 Geographical distribution of relative need. Brazil, 1999

Between 1999 and 2002, as shown in Table 10.2, there was a reduction in the difference (in percentage terms) between the allocation estimated by the formula and the actual allocation by the Ministry of Health in the Northern and Southern regions. There was also an increase in this difference in the Midwest region. Particularly in the Northern region, the new system of resource allocation for primary care together with financial incentives to implement the 'Family Health Program', discussed above, may explain these changes. Certainly since 2002, this Family Health Program is continually being spread wider and wider across more and more municipalities in the country.

The needs-based methodology presented here has not yet been implemented by the Ministry of Health. Some states, however, such as Minas Gerais have

Table 10.2. Ministry of Health inpatient and outpatient expenditures compared with allocations based on the needs-based formula, by Region, Brazil 1999–2002

Regions	Actual per capita (R$)	2002		
		Per capita esti-mated per need (R$)	% difference	% age diff in 1999
Northern region	72.3	87.2	20.7	34.1
Northeastern region	84.2	107.9	28.1	27.9
Southeastern region	98.0	83.1	−15.2	−15.1
Southern region	89.9	82.2	−8.5	−14.4
Midwest region	85.1	81.1	−4.7	0.8

Source: Porto *et al.* (2002).

implemented a formula based on need for the allocation of resources for primary care between municipalities.

Finally, a more equitable distribution of financial resources between geographical areas is a necessary (but not sufficient) condition for achieving equality of opportunity for health care access, as proposed in the Brazilian Constitution. The following section analyzes equity in health services utilization, which clearly relates to the subject of this and of the previous sections.

Equity in health services utilization

Generally speaking, it can be postulated that the most relevant factor in determining the utilization of health service facilities should be need. Yet, in Brazil, those with the greatest need, who are the people in low socio-economic status (SES) groups, have the lowest probability of using those services (Figure 10.3). Individuals with higher incomes and higher schooling rates, who are covered by private health plans, and are living in urban areas and in the more-developed regions of the country are those who use health services the most. However, in relation to the mix of services, by comparison with the rich, poorer individuals tend to seek more curative services, while the rich make greater use of health services for routine tests and prevention.

The rate of physician consultation per 100 inhabitants was 62.9% in 2003 (Figure 10.4). This figure is low as compared with the findings for the adult populations in OECD countries (van Doorslaer *et al.* 2006), which showed an average of between 70% and 80%. Countries like Greece (63%) and Mexico (21%) had the lowest rates. In Brazil, the rate of physician consultation for those in the highest family income group – 78.3% – is close to those in more-developed

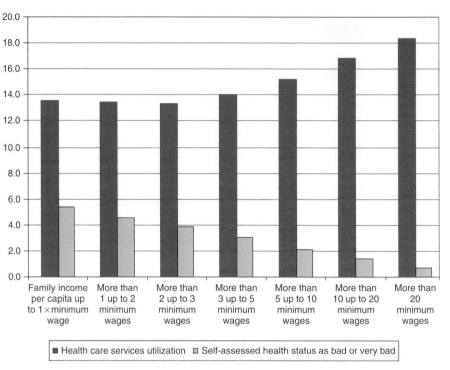

Figure 10.3   Health care service utilization rate (two weeks before interview) and self-assessed health status by family income bracket. Brazil, 2003 (IBGE 2005b)

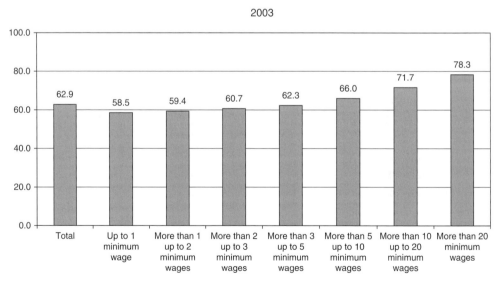

Figure 10.4   Physician consultation rate in the year prior to the interview per 100 inhabitants by family income groups. Brazil, 2003 (IBGE 2005b)

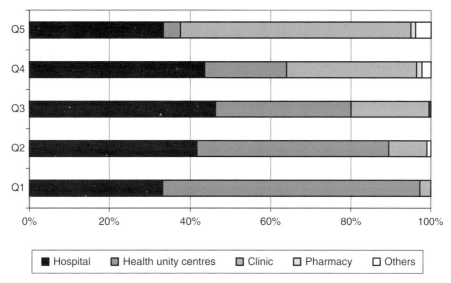

Figure 10.5   Proportional health service use rate, standardized for age and sex, by quintile of family income per capita, by type of establishment (Southeast Region, 1996–7), Brazil (IBGE 2005b)

countries. At the bottom end, however, the rate falls to 58.5%. These Brazilian rates are not adjusted for health needs, so that, given the very high morbidity rate among the lower-income groups, these differences in utilization adjusted by need between rich and poor are really very marked indeed.

The pattern of utilization per type of service is also different between social groups for equal need. Individuals in the lower family income per capita quintiles most often use health centres, emergency services and inpatient services. In Figure 10.5, the pattern of utilization per type of services across quintiles of family income per capita is presented for the Southeast region. On the other hand, they make less use of private physicians and specialized medical services than people in the upper quintiles (Almeida *et al.* 2000). Inequalities are large for specialist care, such as dental care. In 1998, amongst those with an income up to the equivalent of the legal minimum wage, 35.6% had never been seen by a dentist, while this proportion was only 4.1% among those with family incomes equal to or greater than 20 times the legal minimum wage (IBGE 2005b).

Factors affecting inequalities in utilization

In Brazil in 2003 a quarter of the population was covered by some type of private health insurance (IBGE 2005b). Such individuals are more likely to use health services than those not covered. Such coverage is greater in the more affluent regions, in urban areas and for higher income groups. In 1996–7 the difference in health care utilization in general between people covered by private insurance and those not, adjusted by need, was 70% greater for the former (Travassos *et al.* 2000). One study has shown that, other things being equal, private health insurance increases the chance of people on low incomes being admitted to hospital (Castro *et al.* 2002).

Place of residence matters

On utilization of health services, place of residence is another important explanatory factor. Travassos *et al.* (2006) have shown that regional inequalities in the utilization of health services are consistent with the development pattern of the regions, while inequalities in utilization between income groups (i.e., social intraregional inequalities) are unconnected to regional development levels. The importance of the place of residence is also tied to individual income. In the more affluent neighbourhoods of the city of Rio de Janeiro the income of elderly people does not affect their ability to use health services, while in the poorer districts, income does have a bearing on this. Furthermore, the poorer residents of wealthier neighbourhoods utilize relatively more services than the poorer residents of poorer areas (Pinheiro and Travassos 1999). More services and social networks in wealthier neighbourhoods are possible explanations for these differences.

The SUS pays for about 12 million hospital admissions per year. About 80% of these are within 60 km of the municipality where the patient lives. For children under 5 years old, this proportion is a little bigger (83.5%). The probability of inpatient admission is more evenly distributed across health regions for the most frequent procedures (which account for 60% of all admissions) than for complex and costly procedures such as coronary artery bypass graft (CABG) surgery. For the latter, the relative probability for those living in the less-developed regions (North, Northeast and Middle West) is much smaller than for those living in the most-developed ones (South and Southeast), see Figure 10.6 (Oliveira 2005).

Education affects income inequalities in utilization of services

A study by Mendonza-Sassi *et al.* (2003) in the state of Rio Grande do Sul, Brazil, has shown that there is a correlation between education and income, which in turn affects health service utilization. Each additional year of schooling increases use among the poorer and reduces it among the more affluent. The authors suggest that among the underserved groups access can be improved if they are provided with information about the services available and how to gain access to the health system. Policies directed at increasing the level of education will thus have an impact on health care service utilization.

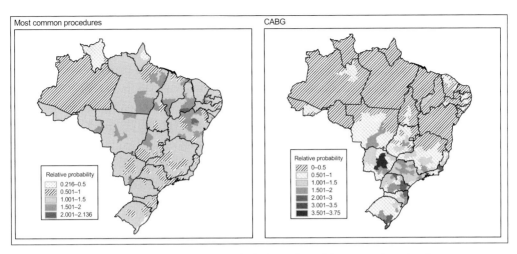

Figure 10.6   Relative probability of inpatient admission adjusted by age and sex for the most common procedures and for coronary artery bypass graft (CABG) surgery by health regions. Brazil, 2000[2]

Recent trends in inequalities in health care service utilization in Brazil

Although substantial social inequalities remain in the utilization of health services in Brazil, data from the 2003 National Household Survey (PNAD) indicate that these have been reduced since 1998 (IBGE 2005b).

- Income inequalities in utilization were somewhat reduced; and there has been a marked increase in the rate of physician visits in both urban and rural areas;
  - A higher proportion of individuals of both sexes used services in all age and income groups. In general, there was a growth rate of 15.0%. Increases were slightly greater (18.6%) for the lower income groups;
- Public health centres played a major role in these changes, with a growth in utilization over this period of 25.8%. This is likely to be due to the Family Health Program established in 1994, which involves a strategy directed towards changing the SUS health care model. It is based around multiprofessional health teams based in primary health care units. Each team takes care of a set number of families in a geographical area. The programme is orientated towards health promotion, preventive care and curative care of the most common health problems. In 2003 it covered 35.7% of the Brazilian population. This had increased to 44.4% in 2005, which represents 78.6 million people (http://dtr2004.saude.gov.br/dab/abnumeros.php#historico).

---

[2] The relative probability is calculated by dividing the number of inpatient admissions by the expected number of admissions estimated for each region on the basis of the national rate, adjusted by age and sex. Values less than 1 indicate admission probabilities lower than the national average, those greater than 1 admission probabilities above the national average. The maps use a colour key to highlight this difference.

- Reductions in financial barriers: services paid by the SUS were also instrumental in these changes;
  - In 2003, the SUS paid for 57.2% of all medical care and 66.7% of all inpatient care in the country. It was the only source of payment for health care delivery that grew between 1998 and 2003. Over this period, the growth rate in the participation of the SUS in the payment of all medical care delivered in the country was 16.0%. The share of out-of-pocket payments remained quite stable, 15.8% in 1998 and 14.8% in 2003. These calculations are not adjusted for price changes over the period.
- The size of the private health insurance market did not change with coverage remaining at 25.0% and its share of the payment of services delivered remained constant at 26.0%.

As a more specific example of the effect of health care in reducing inequalities in health in Brazil, the case of the AIDS programme is noteworthy. In this programme, universal access to effective treatment was sought with a view to reducing inequalities in mortality across different social classes. Since 1996, AIDS patients in Brazil have been eligible for unlimited, zero-priced access to antiretroviral medicines. Over this period, there was a decrease in incidence and the social distribution of HIV has changed. The AIDS epidemic began among people with high socio-economic status, but progressed steadily to lower socio-economic status groups, including women (Fonseca *et al.* 2003). A recent study (Antunes *et al.* 2005) showed that, at the ecological level, despite socio-economic status differences in incidence, reductions in mortality were not correlated with socio-economic status.

Conclusions

In the wake of democracy returning to Brazil and the inauguration of the SUS in the wake of the new constitution of 1988, with its principles of equity, integrality and universality of health care access, the country has had an excellent opportunity to achieve more equitable policies in health care. In practice, there have been a number of advances in equity. Although substantial social inequalities remain with respect to access to and utilization of health services in Brazil, the relevant data indicate that there were improvements in access to health services and reductions in social inequalities between 1998 and 2003. There has also been an improvement in the equity of resource allocation from the central government to the states and municipalities, and this has been reinforced by an effective decentralization process from the federal level to the states and municipalities in the health system.

However, inequalities in health care in Brazil remain very great. A major shortcoming is the unfair health financing system. Despite the fact that health financing in the SUS is almost proportional, compared with other countries public expenditure remains a rather small proportion of total health spending. Out-of-pocket spending is proportionally high, especially in the lowest income deciles. At the same time this situation reduces the ability of the state both to redistribute public resources across geographical areas and to increase the supply of services of good quality to everyone.

The data presented in this chapter indicate that the key to reducing inequalities in health care in Brazil is for there to be a substantial increase in public expenditure in health care. This would be best and most equitably achieved through the introduction of more progressive taxation. It is also necessary to move towards a more equitable allocation of public resources geographically with emphasis on investing capital resources in those areas less well served by both public and private sectors. Further the geographical differences in the ability to finance the delivery of services, as well as epidemiological differences which determine differences in relative needs, should also be considered, to promote more equitable utilization.

Since the end of the 1990s the main strategy adopted to increase access to health services has been the 'Family Health Program', which involves a re-organization of primary health care and its expansion and introduces a 'gatekeeper' role in the health system. It is still unclear, however, whether this strategy will be able to transform the existing pattern of inequities in health care utilization. Major challenges involve gaining the support of the population for this strategy (which implies providing services responsive to people's preferences and needs) and expanding the supply at the higher levels of care sufficiently to meet the demand generated by this programme.

The health policy adopted since the initiation of the SUS has had, as we have seen, an important redistributive impact. It is also to be noted that the new sources of finance for the SUS which were created after the new Constitution, such as taxes over net benefits and over financial transactions, are clearly more progressive than those existing before 1988. Nevertheless, they have not been sufficient to bring about substantial change in the extent of public expenditure in total health expenses. Because of the magnitude of the existing inequities in Brazilian society, this sectoral policy is inevitably limited in its ability to promote, on its own, an effective reduction in inequities in the utilization of health services. As discussed before, improvements in education in the population would have a positive impact in reducing socio-economic inequalities in health care.

These socio-economic differences are exacerbated by the fragmentation of the health system, with the existence of both the SUS and private health insurance. The latter is an important element in generating inequalities in access. Although stable, owing to the fact that there have been few changes in the market for private insurance in the last decade, this sector retains considerable strength as a result of the size of the population covered and the volume of financial resources that it mobilizes.

These issues can only be addressed more fully if the Brazilian people are more prepared to incorporate the values of equality and solidarity into their society and, in turn, their health care system. Unfortunately, such a move is in sharp contrast to the individualistic values that predominate in Brazilian society today. Without endorsement by the Brazilian people and Brazilian governments of equality and solidarity, it will still be possible to make some inroads into the existing inequities in health and health care. However, the key to success in equity in health in the future in Brazil rests first and foremost in these broad issues of principle revolving around equality and solidarity on the one hand and individualism on the other.

REFERENCES

Afonso, J. R., Silveira, R. F. and Araújo, E. (2002) Carga tributária global: estimativa para 2001. *Informe-se.* **40**: 8. www.bndes.gov.br/conhecimento/informesf/inf_40.pdf.

Almeida, C., Travassos, C., Porto, S. and Labra, M. E. (2000) Health sector reform in Brazil: a case study of inequity. *Journal of Health Services.* **30**: 129–162.

Antunes, J. L. F., Waldman, E. A. and Borrell, C. (2005) Is it possible to reduce AIDS deaths without reinforcing socioeconomic inequalities in health? *International Journal of Epidemiology.* **34**: 586–592.

Carr-Hill, R., Hardman, G., Martin, S. *et al.* (1994) *A Formula for Distributing NHS Revenues Based on Small Area Use of Hospital Beds.* York: University of York.

Castro, M. S. C., Travassos, C. and Carvalho, M. S. (2002) Fatores Associados às Internações Hospitalares no Brasil. *Ciência e Saúde Coletiva.* **7**(4): 795–811.

Department of Health and Social Security, UK (1976) *Sharing Resources for Health in England.* Report of the Resource Allocation Working Party. London: HMSO.

Fonseca, M. G. P., Travassos, C., Bastos, F. I., Silva, N. V. and Szwarcwald, C. L. (2003) Distribuição social da AIDS no Brasil, segundo participação no mercado de trabalho, ocupação e status sócio-econômico dos casos de 1987 a 1998. *Cadernos de Saúde Pública.* **19**(5): 1351–1363.

Instituto Brasileiro de Geografia e Estatística (IBGE) (2005a) *Pesquisa de Orçamentos Familiares, 2002–2003.* Rio de Janeiro: IBGE.

Instituto Brasileiro de Geografia e Estatística (IBGE) (2005b) *Acesso e Utilização de Serviços de Saúde: 2003.* Rio de Janeiro: IBGE.

Kakwani, N. (1976) Measurement of tax progressivity: an international comparison. *The Economic Journal.* **87**: 71–80.

Kakwani, N. (1977) Applications on Lorenz curves in economic analysis. *Econometrica.* **48**(3): 719–727.

Médici, A. C. (1991) A perspectiva do financiamento à saúde no governo Collor de Mello. *OPAS Série Economia e Financiamento.* **2**.

Mendonza-Sassi, R., Béria, J. U. and Barros, A. J. (2003) Outpatient health service utilization and associated factors: a population-based study. *Revista de Saúde Pública*. **37**: 372–378.

Oliveira, E. X. G. (2005). *A Multiplicidade do Único – Territórios do SUS*. Doctoral thesis Rio de Janeiro: Escola Nacional de Saúde Pública, Fundação Oswaldo Cruz.

Pinheiro, R. S. and Travassos, C. (1999) Estudo da desigualdade na utilização de serviços de saúde por idosos em três regiões da cidade do Rio de Janeiro. *Cadernos de Saúde Pública*. **15**(3): 487–496.

Porto, S. M. and Ugá, M. A. (1992) Avanços e percalços do financiamento do Setor Saúde no Brasil. In Gallo, E. *et al.*, eds, *Planejamento Criativo: Novos Desafios Teóricos em Políticas de Saúde*, Rio de Janeiro: Relume-Dumará.

Porto, S. M., Vianna, S. M, Ugá, M. A. D *et al.* (2002) *Metodologia de Alocação Equitativa de Recursos*. Relatório final de projeto. Rio de Janeiro: ENSP/FIOCRUZ.

Rezende, F. (1992) O financiamento da saúde no marco das propostas de reforma do Estado e do sistema tributário brasileiro. *Série Economia e Financiamento*. **3**. Brasília: Organização Pan-Americana da Saúde.

Rice, N. and Smith, P. (1999) *Approaches to Capitation and Risk Adjustment in Health Care: an International Survey*. Occasional Paper. Centre for Health Economics, University of York.

Travassos, C., Viacava, F., Fernandes, C. and Almeida, C. (2000) Desigualdades geográficas e sociais na utilização de serviços de saúde no Brasil. *Ciência e Saúde Coletiva*. **5**(1): 133–149.

Travassos, C., Oliveira, E. X. G. and Viacava, F. (2006) Desigualdades geográficas e sociais no acesso aos serviços de saúde no Brasil: 1998 e 2003. *Ciência e Saúde Coletiva*. **11**(4): 975–986.

Ugá, M. A. D. and Santos, I. S. S. (2006) Uma análise da progressividade do financiamento do Sistema Único de Saúde (SUS). *Cadernos de Saúde Pública*. **22**(8): 1597–1610.

van Doorslaer, E., Wagstaff, A., van der Burg, H. *et al.* (1999) The redistributive effect of health care in twelve OECD countries. *Journal of Health Economics*. **18**(3): 291–313.

van Doorslaer, E., Masseria, C., Koolman, X. *et al.* (2006) Inequalities in access to medical care by income in developed countries. *Canadian Medical Association Journal*. **174**: 177–183.

Wagstaff, A. (2001) *Measuring Equity in Health Care Financing: Reflection on and Alternatives to the WHO's Fairness of Financing Index*. World Bank: Development Research Group and Human Development Network.

11

Improving health-related information systems to monitor equity in health: lessons from Thailand

Viroj Tangcharoensathien, Supon Limwattananon and Phusit Prakongsai

Summary[1]

In 2001, Thailand achieved universal access to health care. This has had a significant impact on the reduction in direct household payments for health care and promoted an equitable health care system. Empirical evidence from health information systems has revealed that there is now more equitable health care use across economic strata, the pro-poor nature of health care subsidies, especially for district health services provided by the Ministry of Public Health (MOPH), and a further reduction in the incidence of catastrophic and poverty impacts of health care expenditure. This is in line with the results of opinion surveys of public health administrators nationwide. The country-initiated National Health Accounts (NHA), compiled since 1994, are the backbone of resource tracking according to health care functions. In addition to the time-series NHA, monitoring and evaluation of equity in health care financial contributions is possible because of the long-standing, nationally representative household surveys conducted by the National Statistical Office (NSO), namely the Socio-Economic Survey (SES) and Health and Welfare Survey (HWS). Based on trust and mutual recognition and interests, a genuine partnership to improve the policy utility and equity monitoring capability of these two national databases has been fostered between the main user (MOPH) and data producer (NSO). Other large-scale regular surveys, conducted by health research institutes and various departments in the MOPH, contain quantitative data on health service use, payments for health care services, illnesses and health conditions, and general and specific health behaviour. Other

[1] The authors are grateful for the National Statistical Office (NSO) of Thailand for its genuine collaboration with all data users, especially the International Health Policy Program (IHPP) of Thailand and the Ministry of Public Health (MOPH). Particular thanks go to the Thailand Research Fund (TRF), Health Systems Research Institute (HSRI) and MOPH for their institutional grant and financial support for a Senior Research Scholar in Health Systems and Policy Research.

The Economics of Health Equity, ed. Di McIntyre and Gavin Mooney. Published by Cambridge University Press. © Cambridge University Press 2007.

major data sources include disease surveillance and registry systems, and information on health care use in administrative data and routine reports, which all suffer from a lack of data on the social determinants of health. The time-series NSO national data sets have ample parameters for monitoring health equity and are a real national asset in Thailand for evidence-based, equity-related policy formulation and evaluation.

Introduction

Empirical evidence over the past several decades in both developed and developing countries has consistently shown inequalities in health among different socio-economic groups and by sex, race, geographical areas, and other social circumstances (Whitehead and Diderichsen 1997; Evans *et al.* 2001; Wagstaff 2001; World Bank 2005). Health disparities linked to social advantage rather than to inherent biological differences are generally considered to be inequitable or unjust, and can be avoidable (Whitehead 1992). Addressing such inequalities is the main objective of global health development efforts, starting from the Alma Ata Conference on primary health care in 1978 (World Health Organization 1978), followed by several initiatives of WHO and the World Bank, the Global Health Equity Initiative during 1995–2000, and finally the Millennium Development Goals initiated by the United Nations in 2000 (United Nations 2005), which has explicit statements on sex equity, especially in education. Despite the considerable increase in global concerns over health inequalities, most national health information systems lack the key information needed to assess and monitor health inequities at national and subnational levels. Without reliable and representative data for monitoring and assessing such inequalities, policy instruments towards improving health equity are unlikely to be effective.

Thailand, a lower-middle-income country, has been moving towards improving health equity for nearly three decades (Wibulpolprasert 2002). A national policy on providing free medical care targeting low-income households was first implemented in 1975, followed by '*Health for All by the Year 2000*' in 1979, in association with the Alma Ata Declaration. There was a continuous extension of public health insurance schemes, including covering borderline poor households through a publicly subsidized voluntary health insurance scheme, covering formal sector employees through a social health insurance scheme, which gradually covered employees from larger to smaller private enterprises, and, recently, a policy on universal coverage (UC) of health insurance which was implemented nationwide in 2001 (Tangcharoensathien *et al.* 2004; Towse *et al.* 2004). A tax-funded health insurance scheme or 'the universal coverage scheme' was introduced for approximately 45 million people, about 75% of the total population who were not beneficiaries of the Civil Servant Medical Benefit Scheme (CSMBS) or Social Security Scheme (SSS), and included those who were uninsured or beneficiaries of the Low Income and the Voluntary Health Card schemes.

The new scheme employs a capitation model and diagnostic-related groups (DRG) with a global budget to pay health care providers for outpatient and inpatient services, respectively. A minimal co-payment of 30 Baht (US $0.75) per ambulatory visit or hospital admission was introduced in 2001, but abolished in 2006. Primary care facilities at the district level have been promoted as the main contractor for health service delivery. The benefit package of the universal coverage scheme is very comprehensive covering ambulatory care, hospitalization, health promotion and disease prevention, as well as a wide range of high-cost care. However, some expensive health services, such as renal replacement therapy for end-stage renal disease patients, have been excluded from the benefit package because of their high costs and long-term financial burden on the government health budget.

Prior to the achievement of universal coverage, health care financing was dominated by out-of-pocket payments, the most regressive source of finance, fragmented insurance schemes with a large variation in benefit package and level of public subsidies, in favour of CSMBS and against the Low Income Scheme. Evidence from several studies indicates that health care financing in Thailand from 1986 to 1996 was regressive (Pannarunothai 2000), with the poorest decile of households spending a higher percentage of their income on health care than the richest decile (Pannarunothai 2000; Wibulpolprasert 2002). Apart from the high level of household out-of-pocket payments, evidence also showed that a high percentage of the population was uninsured and that there was inequitable access to health services, especially for the poor and disadvantaged groups (Nitayarumphong 1998; Foundation for Thai Consumers 1999). With this evidence on inequity in health care finance and health service utilization, the universal coverage policy launched by the new government in 2001 was widely welcomed by the public.

A two-pronged approach has been adopted by successive governments since the 1980s with, on the one hand, a piecemeal targeting approach of insurance coverage extension to the formal and informal sectors and, on the other hand, the extension of public health infrastructure. It took almost two decades to achieve a full extension of public health infrastructure in all districts. In a typical district with a population of 50 000, there is a district hospital with 30–60 beds, staffed by 3–5 physicians, 2–3 pharmacists, one dentist, some 20 professional nurses and other paraprofessionals, providing comprehensive curative, preventive and health promotion services. At subdistrict level, which typically covers a population of 5000, a health centre staffed by 3–5 health workers provides comprehensive health promotion, prevention and basic curative services.

As all public health and medicine graduates are trained at publicly funded medical colleges, students are heavily subsidized by the government. In return, a mandatory rural service by new graduates, notably at district hospitals, was enforced. This plays a significant role in the functioning of district hospitals. The programme started with medical graduates in 1972 and remains in place now; it was later extended to enforce rural service by other groups including nurses, dentists and pharmacists, and all other paramedical personnel. It should be noted that the extension of public health infrastructure to rural areas and mandatory rural service by all graduates were explicit pro-poor government health policies.

The success and failure of these strategies and government policies in improving health equity have been assessed through the development of the country's health information and monitoring systems. This chapter reviews experiences in employing and improving health-related information systems to monitor health disparities in Thailand and draws lessons from the health systems development strategies introduced during the past decades. Experiences in using health information to assess changes in equity in health care finance, health service use and government health subsidies before and after universal coverage are described. Furthermore, the current status of the information system with respect to monitoring health inequalities, as well as strengths and weaknesses of each database, are analyzed in greater detail. Finally, lessons learnt and policy recommendations for other developing countries are presented.

Evidence of health equity achievements in Thailand[2]

The International Society for Equity in Health (ISEqH) has defined the term 'equity in health' as '*the absence of systematic and potentially remediable differences in one or more aspects of health across population groups defined socially, geographically, or demographically*' (ISEqH 2001). By this definition, health inequity can be determined through measurement of the variation in certain domains of health systems with respect to differences in population characteristics. A determinant called 'an equity stratifier' (Nolen *et al.* 2005) categorizes health domains into six dimensions: financing; coverage and availability; utilization; quality or responsiveness; health status; and health risk behaviour.

For the inequity determinants, the population groups can be divided according to (a) geographic; (b) demographic; (c) social and (d) economic characteristics.

---

[2] Much of this empirical evidence has been generated from previous analyses of two major nationally representative household surveys in Thailand, namely the 2001 and 2003 Health and Welfare Survey (HWS); and the 2000, 2002 and 2004 Socio-Economic Surveys (SES) under the European Commission funded EQUITAP Project. The final part of this section was elaborated from findings in research on monitoring and evaluation of equity in health, funded by the World Bank's ASEM Trust Fund in 2006.

	Health financing	Coverage/ availability	Healthcare utilization	Quality and respon- siveness	Health status	Health risk
Geographic Province Urban vs. rural						
Demographic Sex Age group						
Social Education Occupation						
Economic Wealth Income Consumption						

Figure 11.1 Matrix of health equity dimensions

This 6×4 conceptual matrix[3] of health equity requires data from the health information system (HIS) to be filled in for every cell (Figure 11.1).

We need empirical evidence to demonstrate whether or not Thailand has achieved its equity goals for the health system, especially after implementation of the universal coverage policy for five years. To date, the available health information system has provided relatively rich data to give a clear picture on how equitable the Thai health system is. Findings from research on these issues are presented in the following subsections.

Applying National Health Accounts and the household socio-economic survey for monitoring equity in health care finance

As in other developing countries, the Thai health care system has been financed from a mixture of sources, namely general taxes, social insurance contributions, private insurance premiums and direct out-of-pocket payments. The proportion of different financing sources evolved slowly in view of the country's socio-economic and health financing development. For example, a voluntary publicly subsidized insurance scheme (the Health Card Project) and Social Health Insurance were implemented in 1982 and 1990 respectively. Before the economic crisis in 1997, household out-of-pocket payments were the major source of health care finance, but their percentage share has decreased since 1997, while

---

[3] Six dimensions of the health system and four dimensions of the determinants of inequity.

the proportion of public health financing sources has gradually increased (Tangcharoensathien *et al.* 2005a). Apart from the reduction in household purchasing power, former government policies on the expansion of health insurance coverage to targeted populations and implementation of the universal coverage policy in 2001 contributed considerably to the reduction in household out-of-pocket payments. The increase in government health spending on the Civil Servant Medical Benefit Scheme and Social Health Insurance is the main factor for the increase in public health financing sources after 1997.

'National Health Accounts' (NHA) is a resource tracking tool describing the flow of the country's health financing and expenditure. It shows how much was spent by which sources (government, donors, households) for different types of services, such as preventive, health promotion and curative services. The NHA in Thailand, which was locally initiated in 1994, is a strong foundation for monitoring changes in health care financing relating to government policies on health sector reforms. The Health Systems Research Institute (HSRI) commissioned a group of researchers to produce the first NHA of Thailand in 1994, owing concerns over the validity of health expenditure estimates in the overall National Accounts.

After that, HSRI supported the second phase of the NHA development during 1996–1998. The third phase of institutionalization of NHA was transferred to the International Health Policy Program (IHPP) of Thailand in which the 1994 to 2001 NHA was subsequently revised and updated. Problems of accurate aggregated and disaggregated data on household health care expenditure, and limitations in the breakdown of health financing sources and health care providers, were experienced during the early phase of NHA (Tangcharoensathien *et al.* 1999). This led to the application of the OECD System of Health Accounts whereby three-dimensional matrices were produced. The three-dimensional matrix depicts flows of expenditure from financing agents to health care functions, and from the agents to health care providers.

Thailand is one of the developing countries where direct payments from households play an important role in financing health care. The share of out-of-pocket payments (OOP) to the total health expenditure in 2000 was approximately 33% (Figure 11.2). The major health care financing source is public funding, especially from tax revenue (56%) and the mandatory contributory Social Health Insurance Scheme among formal private sector employees (5%). Private voluntary insurance schemes contribute 6% of total health expenditure. In Figure 11.2, countries or territories close to the diagonal line, e.g., Sri Lanka, the Punjab of India and the Kyrgyz Republic, are almost totally funded from general government revenue and out-of-pocket payments, whereas in Japan and Taiwan, Social Health Insurance plays a significant role, owing to very large formal sector employment.

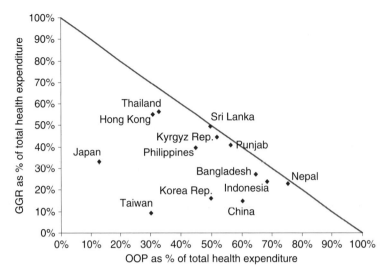

Figure 11.2   Share of out-of-pocket payments (OOP) and general government revenue (GGR) in total health care expenditure in the Asia-Pacific region (O'Donnell *et al.* 2005)

An analysis of financing incidence using data on household consumption expenditure in the SES indicates that the better-off population contributed more to health care financing, compared with the worse-off. The concentration indices (CI)[4] of health care financing in 2002 (after universal coverage) were very positive across all major funding sources: 0.9057 and 0.5776 for direct and indirect taxes, which covered 50.2% of total health expenditures (O'Donnell *et al.* 2005). This resulted in a concentration index of 0.6996 for general taxation and 0.5929 for total health care financing. The way Thailand finances its health care system was the most progressive among 13 countries and territories in the Asia-Pacific region.[5]

The study of equity in health care financing contributions in Thailand is based on two major foundations, the NHA and nationally representative household surveys, particularly the Socio-Economic Surveys (SES) conducted by the National Statistical Office (NSO). A genuine partnership has been fostered between information users, especially the Ministry of Public Health as the major stakeholder, and the information producer, the National Statistical Office, to improve the

[4] The concentration index (CI), an index of the distribution of payments, ranges from −1 to 1. A positive (negative) value indicates that the rich (poor) contribute a larger share than the poor (rich), while a value of zero indicates that everyone pays the same, irrespective of ability to pay.

[5] In the EQUITAP project, countries and territories include Bangladesh, the People's Republic of China, Hong Kong SAR, India (Punjab), Indonesia, Japan, Korea Republic, the Kyrgyz Republic, Philippines, Nepal, Sri Lanka, Taiwan ROC and Thailand.

national household survey questionnaires that facilitate the analyses and monitoring systems on equity in health.

A biennial household survey, the Socio-Economic Survey, is an important data source for monitoring changes in equity in health care finance before and after universal coverage.[6] The Socio-Economic Survey provides a comprehensive account of household income and expenditure, including that related to health care. Household income and expenditure per capita were employed as a measure of allotting households into different socio-economic status categories. Information about tax payments, household expenditure for ambulatory health care visits in the last month and hospitalization in the last year, payments for private health insurance premiums, Social Health Insurance contributions and other consumption expenditure (which are liable for consumption tax) can be computed as different types of household payments for health care, namely direct tax, out-of-pocket payments, private insurance premiums, social insurance contributions and indirect tax payments, respectively.

In addition, ownership of assets, durables and housing characteristics facilitate the development of an asset (or wealth) index, and stratification of households according to wealth quintiles or deciles. The national representative and regularity of the Socio-Economic Survey, being conducted every two years, allows for the development of a longitudinal monitoring system on changes in health care finance and household financial burdens for health care.

Lessons learned since the implementation of the universal coverage policy have been enormous. Apart from the Socio-Economic Survey, data from the Health and Welfare Survey (HWS), and the monthly input and output reports of government health facilities are other major data sources that generate evidence on and knowledge about changes in health service use and government health subsidies. Examples of equity achievements in the Thai health care system after implementation of the universal coverage policy are detailed next.

Using the Health and Welfare Survey to monitor equity in health service use and the public subsidy to health care

To monitor changes in equity in health service use and the distribution of government health subsidies, data were drawn from two main sources: a national household survey, the Health and Welfare Survey (HWS), and unit costs of government health services. The former, conducted by the National Statistical Office, is the national household survey on utilization profiles of the sampled household members, both for ambulatory services during the last month and hospitalization

---

[6] Since 2005, the Socio-Economic Survey became an annual survey conducted by the National Statistical Office. This allows more regular and up-to-date monitoring of equity in health.

during the last year. A single question on estimated monthly household income and a set of questions on household assets can be used as a tool to categorize households into different socio-economic groups, for rich and poor comparisons. Analysis of the public subsidy is achieved by using the monthly input and output report for facilities under the Ministry of Public Health to estimate unit costs of public health facilities. Owing to differences in the quality of health services provided by public health facilities to beneficiaries of different health insurance schemes, unit subsidies of government health services for users from different schemes are also important for computing benefit incidence.

An analysis of the distribution of health service use across different socio-economic groups revealed the pro-poor nature of the Thai health care system before and after universal coverage, especially in the public sector. In 2004, ambulatory service use was favoured by the poor[7], as households in the first income quintile (the poorest) had the highest proportions of all ambulatory visits at district (DH) and provincial hospitals (PH), while the richest quintile accounted for only 7.3% and 17.6% of all outpatient visits at the same health facilities, respectively (see Table 11.1) (Limwattananon *et al.* 2005). In terms of government health subsidies, the CI and Kakwani index (KI)[8] for ambulatory care at district hospitals were −0.2921 and −0.8367, respectively, and those for provincial hospitals were −0.1496 and −0.6888. This benefit incidence analysis indicated the pro-poor nature of the government health subsidies for ambulatory care after universal coverage, and confirms that these subsidies reduce health and social inequality.

For in-patient (IP) care in the public sector, poor households had the lion's share of health service use and government subsidy. In 2001 and 2004, the poorest household quintile accounted for 30.3% and 26.9% of hospitalization in district hospitals, whereas 8.1% and 8.7% were attributable to the richest household quintile in the same years (see Table 11.2). The pro-poor nature of hospital admissions and government health subsidies at the district hospital level was consistent with the findings of ambulatory care. During the same years, 20.6% and 20.3% of the in-patient services at provincial hospitals were used by the poorest quintile, whereas the richest quintile accounted for 17.5% and 16.9%. The extent of pro-poor hospitalization and public subsidies at the district hospital level (concentration index in 2001 and 2004 = −0.3041 and −0.2589 for utilization, respectively

---

[7] Data available in HWS before 2004 were not complete. There was no information on the number of ambulatory visits to health care facilities per survey respondent. Thus, we cannot calculate the amount of individual utilization and determine the utilization distribution across population subgroups.

[8] The Kakwani index (*KI*), which is equal to the concentration index less the Gini index, is used to establish whether the subsidy is inequality-reducing relative to the original distribution of income. A negative Kakwani index indicates that the subsidy on health reduces the inequality of income.

Table 11.1. Distribution of public health care utilization and subsidy for outpatient care, after universal coverage (2004)

	District hospital	Provincial hospital
Utilization		
Quintile 1 (poorest)	31.2%	25.4%
Quintile 2	25.7%	19.3%
Quintile 3	20.1%	21.8%
Quintile 4	15.8%	15.9%
Quintile 5 (richest)	7.3%	17.6%
Concentration index	−0.2843	−0.1477
Standard error	0.0210	0.0293
Kakwani index	−0.8286	−0.6868
Standard error	0.0224	0.0308
Public subsidy		
Quintile 1 (poorest)	31.9%	25.8%
Quintile 2	25.8%	19.2%
Quintile 3	20.3%	21.7%
Quintile 4	14.6%	15.3%
Quintile 5 (richest)	7.4%	18.0%
Concentration index	−0.2921	−0.1496
Standard error	0.0212	0.0302
Kakwani index	−0.8367	−0.6888
Standard error	0.0225	0.0318

Source: National Statistical Office (2004).

and −0.3130 and −0.2666 for government health subsidy, respectively) were much greater than at the provincial hospital level (concentration index = −0.0729 and −0.1149 for utilization and −0.1104 and −0.1221 for subsidy).

It is noteworthy that the progressive pattern of health service use and public subsidy, in favour of the poor, was demonstrated in health facilities at the district level. The District Health System (DHS) is a major strategy for achieving health equity in the Thai health care system. Developing countries can learn from Thailand about how a pro-poor public subsidy can be achieved. To foster pro-poor health financing, policy makers need to allocate adequate resources strategically to levels of health facilities that are better accessed, especially by the poor (Pearson 2002). In the Thai health system context, the District Health System is the most crucial strategic hub for providing comprehensive and integrated health services covering curative care, disease prevention and health promotion.

Table 11.2. Distribution of public health care utilization and subsidy for inpatient care (2001 and 2004)

	District hospital		Provincial hospital	
	2001	2004	2001	2004
Utilization				
Quintile 1 (poorest)	30.3%	26.9%	20.6%	20.3%
Quintile 2	26.6%	25.0%	17.8%	18.8%
Quintile 3	18.9%	23.3%	19.9%	21.3%
Quintile 4	16.0%	16.1%	24.1%	22.7%
Quintile 5 (richest)	8.1%	8.7%	17.5%	16.9%
Concentration index	−0.3041	−0.2589	−0.0729	−0.1149
Standard error	0.0154	0.0196	0.0110	0.0187
Kakwani index	−0.8329	−0.8046	−0.5948	−0.6551
Standard error	0.0159	0.0209	0.0115	0.0201
Public subsidy				
Quintile 1 (poorest)	31.2%	27.4%	22.1%	20.9%
Quintile 2	26.6%	25.5%	19.4%	18.6%
Quintile 3	18.7%	22.7%	20.4%	21.8%
Quintile 4	15.5%	16.0%	22.5%	22.0%
Quintile 5 (richest)	7.9%	8.4%	15.6%	16.6%
Concentration index	−0.3130	−0.2666	−0.1104	−0.1221
Standard error	0.0162	0.0201	0.0117	0.0193
Kakwani index	−0.8421	−0.8125	−0.6334	−0.6626
Standard error	0.0167	0.0214	0.0122	0.0207

Source: National Statistical Office (2001; 2004).

Chronic illness and health-related quality of life

Using self-reported chronic diseases as a proxy for population health status, a study on disparities in health status among different socio-economic groups of Thais shows a lower health status in the poorer quintiles. Approximately 20% of the poorest quintile reported themselves having at least one chronic condition, such as hypertension, diabetes or asthma (Figure 11.3). The richer quintiles reported a lower prevalence of chronic diseases, ranging between 14.0% and 14.5%.

Corresponding with the chronic disease condition, households in the poorer quintiles tended to report a relatively lower score for their health-related quality of life than those in the richer categories (Figure 11.4). Households whose quality of life was perceived as perfect (100% full score) accounted for 41.3% of the lowest income quintile and 61.8% in the highest quintile.

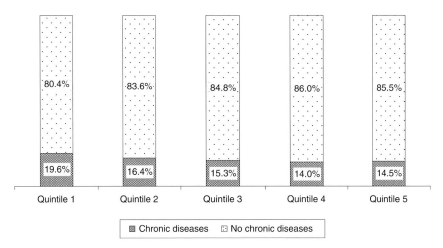

Figure 11.3   The prevalence of chronic disease by household income quintiles, 2003 (National Statistical Office 2003)

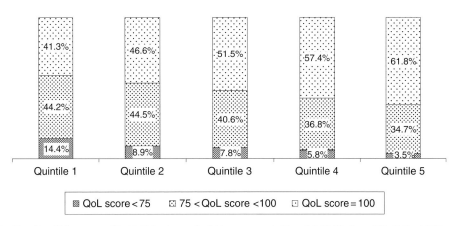

Figure 11.4   Quality of life scores (1–100) by household income quintiles, 2003 (National Statistical Office 2003)

Households in the poorest quintile also had a larger proportion of those reporting having poorer health status (27.9%), compared with the previous year, than their richer counterparts (12.7% of the richest quintile) (Figure 11.5). Those with an improvement in health status were found more frequently in the richer quintiles than in the poorer categories.

The Thai experience of including self-reported health status in the Health and Welfare Survey questionnaire indicates that it is possible to use national household surveys for monitoring equity improvements in the health status of the

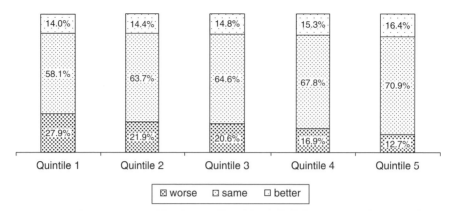

Figure 11.5 Overall health status compared to previous year by household income quintiles, 2003 (National Statistical Office 2003)

population. This seems to be more affordable and feasible in developing countries than a health examination survey, which is time-consuming and requires considerable resources, including laboratory facilities. Despite containing some errors or biases, a longitudinal assessment of self-reported health status among different income quintiles can reflect, to some extent, the success or failure of government health policies in redressing health inequalities.

Stakeholders' views on the priority health equity issues

Apart from empirical evidence, given that ideologies underpin whether or not there is a commitment to providing equitable access to health services regardless of individual's income and other social circumstances, it is necessary to assess the perspectives of stakeholders, especially health policy makers. After implementation of the universal coverage policy, it was necessary to explore remaining health inequalities and their determinants in the Thai health care system, and the feasibility of resolving these equity problems.

Two recent questionnaire-based surveys of Thai health policy makers' perspectives on health equity revealed those health inequity issues that had high urgency and impact scores. The first survey solicited the views of senior administrators in central authorities of the Ministry of Public Health (MOPH) on the priority of equity in health in eight dimensions. These were (a) out-of-pocket (OOP) health payments, (b) public subsidy, (c) health insurance coverage, (d) resource allocation, (e) health care utilization, (f) health care responsiveness, (g) health status, and (h) health risk. The respondents were asked to score each dimension using a Likert-type five-point scale based on two criteria: (a) the urgency of remedying the inequity problems and (b) the potential impact of each problem

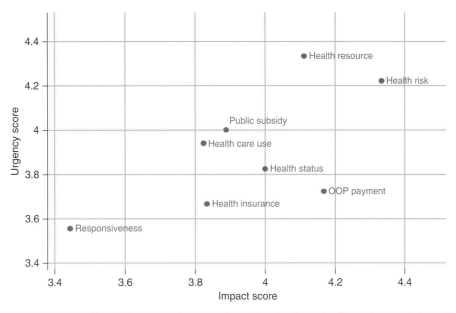

Figure 11.6   Average scores of health impact and urgency for addressing inequity dimensions: opinions of central Ministry of Public Health administrators

on population health, where 1 meant 'least urgent or impact' and 5 meant 'most urgent or impact', respectively.

Results reveal that the MOPH administrators viewed inequity in the allocation of health resources and in health risk behaviour as the highest priority issues, whereas health care responsiveness was given the lowest priority rating (Tangcharoensathien *et al.* 2005b). All eight equity dimensions were rated above the average possible score range for the combined priority criteria (3.0 = medium urgency and impact), as demonstrated in the scatter plots in Figure 11.6. The two dimensions that were given very high priority, resource allocation and health risk, have average scores of 4.33 (standard deviation (SD) = 0.69) and 4.22 (SD = 0.73) for the urgency, and of 4.11 (SD = 0.68) and 4.33 (SD = 0.69) for the impact on population health respectively. At the other extreme, health care responsiveness was given the least priority according to both criteria with the lowest average score of 3.56 (SD = 0.70) for urgency and of 3.44 (SD = 0.78) for impact.

The second survey investigated the perspectives on the key inequity determinants of senior officers at provincial health offices (PHO) of all 75 provinces throughout the country, who are programme implementers at local levels (Tangcharoensathien *et al.* 2006b). The criteria for rating include the degree of importance of such determinants in explaining inequity and the feasibility of solving such a problem, where 1 meant 'least important or feasible' and 5 meant 'most important or feasible', respectively.

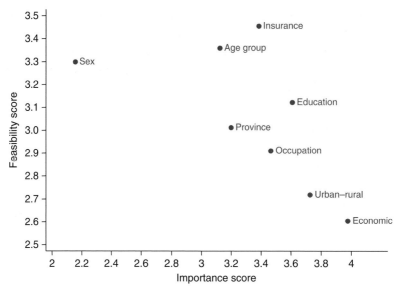

Figure 11.7   Average scores of importance and feasibility for addressing inequity determinants: opinions of provincial health officers

The distribution of the average scores for all eight inequity determinants is illustrated in Figure 11.7 as a scatter plot between the importance scores (on the horizontal axis) and the feasibility scores (on the vertical axis). The senior provincial health officers viewed inequity in the distribution of health care personnel and health facilities as being associated mostly with geographic determinants. Demographic differences played a minor role in explaining most domains of health inequity, except the health risk issue. Economic disparities and urban–rural differences were perceived as the most important determinants of inequities and were unlikely to be resolved. Inequity due to health insurance coverage by the three major schemes (CSMBS, SSS and universal coverage) was perceived as the most important and most feasible issue to be resolved, through harmonization across these three insurance schemes. Disparities across the three schemes were also perceived as the most important determinant of inequity in public subsidies for health care.

All determinants of inequity in health, except sex (average = 2.16, SD = 1.05), have their average scores above 3.0 on the importance scale. Economic status has the highest importance score of 3.98 (SD = 0.98), on average. Urban–rural and educational differences were rated the second and third most important issues with average scores of 3.73 (SD = 1.03) and 3.61 (SD = 1.07), respectively.

Results from the provincial health office survey were consistent with the survey of Ministry of Public Health top-level executives (n = 45) conducted in 2004 (Tangcharoensathien et al. 2005b). These health executives regarded adequate financing, quality health services, universal access to care and improved access by the poor as priority health policies to boost equity. To achieve equity goals, a policy of universalism that enables all, including the poor, to access basic health services is needed. Most respondents perceived the redistribution of health resources as less easily achievable.

Perceptions about equity achievements, before and after the introduction of universal health care coverage

According to recent empirical evidence on equity achievements in health care across different socio-economic groups, the provincial health office administrators were asked what dimensions of equity were achieved most after the implementation of universal coverage (Tangcharoensathien *et al.* 2006b). Rating of perceived equity between the pre-UC and post-UC periods was undertaken (1 = least equity, 5 = most equity).

Improvements with respect to health care use and out-of-pocket health payments are two dimensions that provincial health office respondents viewed as the greatest equity achievement of the universal coverage policy. Approximately one-third (35.8%) of the respondents rated utilization of health care as having a low degree of equity (score = 1–2) before universal coverage and a medium-to-high degree (score 3–5) after universal coverage, whereas only 2.1% viewed the impact as having been in the opposite direction (from medium-to-high equity during pre-UC to low equity post-UC). For out-of-pocket payments, 37.6% perceived the pre-UC to post-UC change from low to medium-to-high degrees of equity, whereas 5.4% saw the reverse change from medium-to-high to low equity.

Both dimensions of health service use and out-of-pocket payments also showed the greatest magnitude of equity score improvements from pre-UC to post-UC with means of 1.07 (SD = 0.89) and 1.02 (SD = 1.34), respectively (Table 11.3).

In contrast, an improvement in health care responsiveness was rated lowest by the provincial health office administrators; 17.0% and 12.8% of the respondents rated that there had been an equity improvement and that the status quo had been maintained, respectively. Based on changes in the pre-UC to post-UC scores, the magnitude of equity score changes in responsiveness is the lowest (mean = 0.29 and SD = 1.11) (see Table 11.3). This result is similar to a previous survey finding in 2001 of health professional viewpoints (*n* = 291) that the health system's responsiveness to people's expectations was moderate (Tantivess and Tangcharoensathien 2003). They recognized the existence of inequity in responsiveness across different subgroups of the Thai population. Social class and economic status were perceived as the most important underlying factors of inequity in health.

The perspectives of the provincial health officers who viewed health care use and out-of-pocket health payments as the greatest equity improvements are

Table 11.3. Change in equity scores: post-UC score minus pre-UC score

	Mean	SD	P value*
Out-of-pocket payments for health	1.02	1.34	<0.001
Public subsidy to health care	0.30	1.35	0.03
Health personnel allocation	0.37	1.04	<0.001
Health facility allocation	0.32	1.11	0.007
Health care utilization	1.07	0.89	<0.001
Health care responsiveness	0.29	1.11	0.014
Health status	0.34	0.93	<0.001
Health risk	0.53	1.04	<0.001

*paired t test.

consistent with empirical evidence from the pre-UC to post-UC national household surveys. These views on the importance of pro-poor health care use and greater public subsidies allocated to the poor, especially at the district health level, are supported by analyses of national household surveys (Limwattananon *et al.* 2005).

Information systems for health equity monitoring and evaluation

The magnitude and nature of equity in health can be monitored and evaluated through various measures of health and 'equity stratifiers' (Nolen *et al.* 2005). Health disparities can be documented by using information that fits into the 6×4 equity matrix of health system dimensions and equity stratifiers as depicted in Figure 11.1. To represent the general population, data from a large-scale observation are preferable, especially at the nationally or subnationally representative levels, and time-series or multiple cross-sectional survey data are preferable to a one-off survey, to generate inequity trends.

In Thailand, there are 33 large-scale databases serving as a foundation for health equity monitoring and the evaluation of health policies. A total of 22 institutions take primary responsibility for designing, collecting, maintaining and updating data sets on a regular basis, at intervals ranging from two to ten years, and disseminating results of data analyses to the public (Tangcharoensathien *et al.* 2006a).

These existing databases can be classified into three groups according to sources of data and methods of collection. The first group contains 19 databases, which are obtained directly from surveys of nationally representative or selective samples of the population or households. These databases can be divided into two subgroups according to host institutions. The first subgroup, comprising six data sets, are conducted and maintained by the National Statistical Office (NSO); and most of them are relatively long time-series data, which date back thirty to forty years. Typically, the National Statistical Office obtained household and individual data by using face-to-face interviews, based on interviewees' recall.

The second subgroup of the large-scale surveys of population and households comprises 13 databases owned by either academic or health research institutes (three databases), and mostly by various divisions or departments in the Ministry of Public Health (ten databases). These databases contain information on population health status and health behaviour in general relating to specific domains, for example, oral health, mental health, communicable diseases, physical exercise and nutrition. Data collection of the second subgroup of databases comprises various methods such as self-administered questionnaires, face-to-face interviews, physical examination and laboratory examination. The sampling frame ranges from the nationally representative scale to a selective population subgroup. Despite the richness of the data on health domains, major disadvantages of these data sets as compared with the National Statistical Office's HWS and SES are the absence of data on the socio-economic status of respondents, which are the major determinants of equity in health.

The second group of information is disease surveillance and registry systems; there are ten databases. All five surveillance databases are hosted by the Ministry of Public Health (e.g., Bureau of Epidemiology) and they are primarily population-based. The disease registries ($n = 5$) belong to various professional organizations, except the Cancer Registry of the National Cancer Institute. Coverage of these databases is limited to patients who have visited a health facility, not a population base. Lack of socio-economic data is a commonplace deficiency of facility-based data.

Apart from household surveys and disease surveillance and registries, information on health care use in administrative data and routine reports is also valuable for equity monitoring and evaluation. The National Health Security Office (NHSO), an organization responsible for the universal coverage scheme, requires contracted provider networks to submit aggregate information for ambulatory care and individual transaction information for admission services, in order to pay contracting facilities on capitation and case-mix bases, respectively. This information can be grouped into routine statistics and administrative reports, which are contained in four databases. Three databases are owned by different departments of the Ministry of Public Health and one by the Central Office for Health Information (CHI) – a government-contracted national clearing house for administrative claims data for all three public health insurance schemes. These data come from secondary sources that were originally designed mainly for administrative purposes, and not for research and equity monitoring and evaluation in particular.

Table 11.4. Number of surveys, surveillance records and registries, and administrative databases containing information on health dimension and inequity determinants

	Health financing	Coverage or availability	Health care utilization	Quality and responsiveness	Health status	Health risk
Geographic						
Province, urban vs. rural	3-0-2[1]	4-1-3	11-8-3	2-0-0	11-10-3	10-6-1
Demographic						
Sex, age group	3-0-2	4-0-2	12-8-2	2-0-0	12-9-2	11-5-0
Social						
Education, occupation	3-0-2	4-0-2	10-4-2	2-0-0	11-5-2	11-4-0
Economic						
Wealth, income, consumption	3-0-0	4-0-0	7-1-0	2-0-0	9-1-0	7-1-0

[1] First digit refers to the number of population and household surveys, second digit refers to surveillance or registries, and third digit refers to administrative databases, hence in this case, three surveys, no disease surveillance or registry, and two administrative databases.

Typically, the administrative data have already recorded day-to-day health care activities on a routine basis, hence, the minimal cost of data accumulation is the major advantage, compared with national household surveys or patient registries. Access to essential care as well as quality aspects of care can be monitored from these data sets. If the data from various databases over a long period of time are linked, the potential uses of these data are amplified.

To demonstrate the capacity of each of these 33 databases for monitoring and evaluation of health equity, Table 11.4 presents variations in the total number of databases in which variables are congruent with the dimension-determinant combination on the health equity assessment matrix. Details of the features in each type of database are explained in the sections to follow.

Population and household surveys

The three most common dimensions of health equity that can be monitored and evaluated through these large-scale survey databases are health status, health care utilization and health risk. The least available information on equity dimensions that is captured by the available surveys is quality of care and health systems' responsiveness. Only two databases contain variables on the responsiveness or satisfaction dimension and none contain the quality dimension. Five databases are available for the analysis of health care coverage and resource availability.

On the determinants of inequity, geographic location (urban–rural differentials) and demographic parameters are the most common variables available in these databases. In contrast, economic characteristics of the population are the least common variables collected in the survey databases.

In Thailand, the Health and Welfare Survey (HWS) and Socio-Economic Survey (SES) are among the oldest information systems. Like the purposes of internationally well-recognized databases, such as USAID's Demographic and Health Survey (DHS) and UNICEF's Multiple Indicator Cluster Surveys (MICS), the Health and Welfare Survey has been designed to capture data on self-reported illnesses of nationally representative households. The nature and frequency of illnesses are followed by the quantification of corresponding service utilization disaggregated into levels of health care and types of health facilities. Utilization of health services (including self-medication and treatment by traditional medicine) that did not require hospitalization is recalled within a two-week period, whereas frequency of hospital admission is based on one-year recall.

For the monitoring and evaluation of health care financing, the Socio-Economic Survey focuses on household expenditures associated with regular consumption of health care and all other goods and services. Household direct payment for health care when compared with total consumption expenditures (as an indicator of living standard) can signal if households are vulnerable to the risk of catastrophic health care payments or impoverishment. Availability of data on equity determinants, including geographic, demographic, social and economic variables, in these databases allows for a comprehensive analysis of health inequity across population subgroups. Whereas the Health and Welfare Survey measures household living standards using both cash and in-kind incomes, the Socio-Economic Survey incorporates an additional set of questions on asset ownership. As the Socio-Economic Survey also contains data on household pre-payment for health, including taxes and insurance premiums, it can be used for analyzing financing incidence. A merger between the Health and Welfare Survey and the Socio-Economic Survey in 2006 provides an opportunity to quantify and differentiate illness and health care use across the population according to different socio-economic status, classified by household consumption expenses rather than income.

Disease surveillance and registries

Owing to the purposive design of disease registries to measure detailed characteristics of diseases, treatments provided and outcomes, this type of database contains information mostly on the measured health status, health services provided and outcomes. All disease surveillance and registry databases available have variables related to reported morbidity and its variation by geographic distribution.

The Weekly Epidemiological Surveillance Report (WESR), with its regular publication, very long time-series (since the 1980s) and wide distribution, is the only disease surveillance database that is useful for policy purposes. Unfortunately, most surveillance systems and registries do not include information on the economic status of patients.

As previously mentioned, the sampling frame in this type of database, especially the registries, is not population-based or nationally representative. Selection bias is a major limitation of this database type.

Another major drawback of this type of database is the source of information, which is usually obtained only from the patients. There is no denominator (i.e., total population at risk) to calculate incidence or prevalence rates. The design of disease registries is to provide clinical risk and treatment information, and outcome and survival probabilities, rather than to facilitate equity monitoring.

Administrative data and routine reports

In Thailand, health care use, births and deaths are the most common parameters available in administrative data and routine reports. Out-of-pocket payments for health care, utilization of services according to insurance entitlement, and types of morbidity are available in electronic databases. Variables on health care quality and responsiveness and risk behaviours are not available in any of this type of database.

A major drawback of these databases is the source of data that contain only facility-based information. As with the disease registries, the data obtained suffer from selection bias. Only patients who visit a facility have been included in the administrative reports and the profiles of non-users are unavailable. For health status parameters, the incidence and prevalence rates of morbidity and mortality generated from the reports tend to be lower than the actual situation. For example, reported morbidity is subject to geographical and cultural accessibility and affordability of services to the population. Mortality as the health status outcome includes only death in hospitals or at discharge. In addition, inadequate coverage of data for non-MOPH public hospitals and private facilities is another limitation of administrative data sets, which leads to underestimates of all parameters related to health equity.

Conclusion and recommendations

An extensive review of health equity achievement in Thailand indicates favourable results, in which health care financing has been progressive, namely the rich pay more than the poor after implementation of the universal coverage policy. The concentration indices of direct and indirect taxes in 2002 were 0.9057 and 0.5776, respectively, which result in the concentration indices of general tax and total health care finance being 0.6996 and 0.5929, respectively. The availability of information from nationally representative household surveys enables the analyses of changes in health equity before and after implementation of the universal coverage policy.

The impact of the commitment to human rights and universalism, in which free health care has been provided to all citizens since 2002, and the distribution of benefits from the government health budget after universal coverage, has been demonstrated by studies on equity in health service use and benefit incidence in Thailand. The findings indicate that the use and public subsidy for ambulatory care were very pro-poor, and somewhat less so for inpatient services. This analysis highlights the need for well-designed national household surveys on health service use and for data on the value of the unit government subsidy, in order to measure equity in health service use and the distribution of government health subsidies. Furthermore, socio-economic parameters in household surveys are necessary for categorizing households or individuals into different socio-economic groups.

The pro-poor nature of utilization and benefit incidence in Thailand is largely due to the well functioning and decent quality of health services provided by the district health system, including health centres and district hospitals. District-level facilities provide comprehensive geographical coverage, in which a health centre with three to five paraprofessionals covers three to five thousand people. A typical district hospital covers approximately 50 000 people and is staffed by three to five general practitioners and other types of health personnel. These serve as close-to-client services, providing a comprehensive range of public health interventions and clinical services, with strong referral backups. Other developing countries can learn from the Thai experiences of district health services, with the key policy message being to foster the functioning of the district health services, supported by adequate staffing and financing.

While it is important that the relevant provisions in the Constitution and Patient Rights Declarations are endorsed by professional groups, the political commitment and health systems' capacity to implement pro-poor and pro-equity policies are crucial to translating this concept into practice.

The existence of 33 well-functioning large-scale databases provides a solid platform for monitoring and evaluating equity in the Thai health care system. Our observation, and work experiences with many partners over 20 agencies who generate these data sets, indicate strong commitment to improve and update survey questionnaires to capture the six key health dimensions and five inequity determinants. This documentary review found both diversity and commonality of the equity-related information included in the databases.

The National Statistical Office databases have the greatest capacity to contribute essential information to the analysis of health equity. Information obtained from the two national household surveys (the Health and Welfare and Socio-Economic Surveys) is very comprehensive, in the light of their coverage of a number of health dimensions, ranging from health care use and payments to health status and risks. In addition, variations in these health dimensions can be analyzed across subgroups with respect to social determinants of inequity, such as geographic, demographic, social and economic characteristics of the population. The major weakness of the National Statistical Office databases is a lack of information on some aspects of equity in health, such as infant, child and maternal mortality across socio-economic stratifications. However, this potentially major problem has been solved by the close collaboration between the National Statistical Office and the International Heath Policy Program of the Ministry of Public Health to insert a comprehensive set of social determinants in a national household survey on birth, death and migration of the population, the Survey on Population Change (SPC). By the end of 2007, the National Statistical Office should be able to produce details of differentials in these health status measures.

Non-NSO health surveys, disease surveillance and registries, and routine administrative databases often lack the socio-economic parameters necessary for the analysis of health disparities driven by non-health and other social barriers. However, there is a possibility of including relevant socio-economic variables in the next round of these health surveys.

Several databases contain overlapping data elements. Among the most common are health risk behaviour, perceived health status and the use of disease-screening services. Further actions to improve overall data quality should include the standardization of definitions, length of recall period and measurement techniques, and harmonization of the data collection across these databases.

Experiences from the historical development of partnership with the National Statistical Office are worthy of attention. Since 1994, involvement of the National Statistical Office as a crucial partner in developing the National Health Accounts has led to improvements in the Socio-Economic Status questionnaire so as to capture household expenditure on health more accurately, and the introduction of a post-enumeration survey to verify the magnitude of household under-reporting of expenditure, which serves as a correcting factor in the National Health Accounts estimates of household health spending. Subsequently, the major achievements were the improvement of the Health and Welfare Survey questionnaire to include household income and asset ownership data (to stratify households into income and asset quintiles), and increasing the frequency of the Health and Welfare Survey from once every five years to an annual survey for five consecutive years after the universal coverage implementation (2003–2007) to permit more frequent equity monitoring.

A final experience, the insertion of income and ownership of assets into the ten-yearly Survey of Population Changes in 2005–2006 (an inter-census survey) provides, for the first time ever in Thai history, information on health status distribution in terms of infant, under-five and maternal mortality across poor and rich quintiles, low and highly educated mothers and urban–rural differentials.

A key lesson from the Thai experience reveals that there is a need to build up an institutional partnership between the statistics constituency who generate information, and the health constituency who use information for their policy making and equity monitoring. A genuine partnership between the National Statistical Office and the Ministry of Public Health through consistent dialogue, mutual recognition and, most importantly, trust is the 'social asset' that fosters and strengthens health equity monitoring capacity in Thailand. Other countries can draw from the experience of how Thailand has developed such rich data for health equity monitoring.

REFERENCES

Evans, T., Whitehead, M., Diderichsen, F., Bhuiya, A. and Worth, M. (2001) *Challenging Inequities in Health: From Ethics to Action*. New York: Oxford University Press.

Foundation for Thai Consumers (1999) *Fifteen Case Studies Suffering from Hospital Treatments in Thailand*. Nonthaburi: Health Systems Research Institute.

International Society for Equity in Health (ISEqH) (2001) *Working Definitions*. www.iseqh.org/workdef_en.htm.

Limwattananon, S., Tangcharoensathien, V. and Prakongsai, P. (2005) *Equity in Financing Health Care: Impact of Universal Access to Health Care in Thailand*. EQUITAP project: working paper No 16. www.equitap.org/publications/wps/Equitap WP16.pdf.

National Statistical Office (2001) *Health and Welfare Survey 2001*. Thailand: National Health Statistical Office, Office of the Prime Minister.

National Statistical Office (2003) *Health and Welfare Survey 2003*. Thailand: National Health Statistical Office, Ministry of Information and Communication Technology.

National Statistical Office (2004) *Health and Welfare Survey 2004*. Thailand: National Health Statistical Office, Ministry of Information and Communication Technology.

Nitayarumphong, S. (1998) Universal coverage of health care: challenges for the developing countries. In Nitayarumphong, S. and Mills, A., eds, *Achieving Universal Coverage of Health Care*. Nonthaburi: Office of Health Care Reform, Ministry of Public Health.

Nolen, L. B., Braveman, P., Dachs, J. N. W. *et al.* (2005) Strengthening health information systems to address health equity challenges. *Bulletin of the World Health Organization*. **83**:597–603.

O'Donnell, O., van Doorslaer, E., Rannan-Eliya, R. P. *et al.* (2005) *Who Pays for Health Care in Asia?* EQUITAP project: working paper No 1. www.equitap.org/publications/wps/EquitapWP1.pdf.

Pannarunothai, S. (2000) *Equity in the Thai Health Care System*. Nonthaburi: Health Systems Research Institute.

Pearson, M. (2002) *Benefit Incidence Analysis: How Can it Contribute to Our Understanding of Health Systems Performance?* London: DFID.

Sen, A. (2002) Why health equity? *Health Economics.* **11**:659–666.

Tangcharoensathien, V., Laixuthai, A., Vasavit, J. *et al.* (1999) National Health Accounts development: lessons from Thailand. *Health Policy and Planning.* **14**:342–353.

Tangcharoensathien, V., Wibulpolprasert, S. and Nitayarumphong, S. (2004) Knowledge-based changes to health systems: the Thai experience in policy development. *Bulletin of the World Health Organization.* **82**:750–756.

Tangcharoensathien, V., Vasavid, C., Patcharanarumol, W. *et al.* (2005a) *National Health Account in Thailand 1994–2001.* Nonthaburi: International Health Policy Program.

Tangcharoensathien, V., Tisayaticom, K., Prakongsai, P. *et al.* (2005b). Equity in the Thai health system: experiences of high executive administrators in the Ministry of Public Health, Thailand. *Journal of Health Science.* **14**(3):436–452.

Tangcharoensathien, V., Limwattananon, S., Pannarunothai, S. *et al.* (2006a) *Reviews of Existing Databases for Monitoring and Evaluation of Equity in Health in Thailand.* Nonthaburi: ASEM Trust Fund, work package No 3.

Tangcharoensathien, V., Limwattananon, S., Tisayaticom, K. *et al.* (2006b) *Perspectives of Thai Stakeholders on Equity in Health.* Nonthaburi: ASEM Trust Fund, work package No 5.

Tantivess, S. and Tangcharoensathien, V. (2003) Thai health systems responsiveness: viewpoints of health workers. *Journal of Health Science.* **12**:56–67.

Towse, A., Mills, A. and Tangcharoensathien, V. (2004) Learning from Thailand's health reforms. *British Medical Journal.* **328**:103–105.

United Nations (2005) *UN Millennium Development Goals.* www.un.org/millenniumgoals/.

Wagstaff, A. (2001) *Poverty and Health.* In CMH Working Paper series: Paper no. WG1:5. Washington DC: The World Bank.

Whitehead, M. (1992) The concepts and principles of equity and health. *International Journal of Health Services.* **22**:429–445.

Whitehead, M. and Diderichsen, F. (1997) International evidence on social inequalities in health. In *Health Inequalities. Decennial Supplement.* London: Stationery Office. (National statistics series DS No 15) pp. 45–69.

Wibulpolprasert, S. (2002) *Thailand Health Profile 1999–2000.* Nonthaburi: Bureau of Policy and Strategies, Ministry of Public Health.

World Bank (2005) *World Development Report 2006: Equity and Development.* Washington DC: The World Bank. p. 324.

World Health Organization (1978) *Declaration of Alma-Ata.* The International Conference on Primary Health Care. Alma-Ata: The World Health Organization.

Section 6

Future action

12

Where now with equity?

Di McIntyre and Gavin Mooney

Introduction

Both equity in health and equity in health care matter. Yet it is clear that recently in many countries policy has been rather neglectful of both of them. It is also the case that health economics has not contributed to equity policy as it might have. This book has drawn attention to these issues, globally and in some nation states, Brazil and Thailand in particular.

The authors in this book have sought to explain why equity has been failing and also why health economics has not made more of a contribution to equity policy. Yet more importantly, each in his or her own way has indicated how things might proceed better in future.

In this concluding chapter it is not the intent to summarize the contents of this book but rather to highlight what we as editors see as the key issues for improving health equity in the future. In particular, we present some concrete ideas on what health economists could be doing or doing better to promote equity in health and health systems. We have identified seven key messages.

Neo-liberalism is bad for our health and our health systems

Given that the extent and nature of economic development can have a dramatic impact on health status, health economists need to get more involved than they have in the past in macroeconomic policy debates. We not only have a right, but an obligation to engage in such debates. Global trends in economic development and the increasing divide between North and South clearly merit health economics analyses. Some of the works of Amartya Sen (2000) and Vicente Navarro (2002) highlight the fact that it is not simply a matter of faster economic growth that will overcome the ills of disease, poverty and inequality on the world stage. How resources are used, how economies are structured, how cultures are maintained or not, and how health care systems are organized and financed are all critical.

The Economics of Health Equity, ed. Di McIntyre and Gavin Mooney. Published by Cambridge University Press. © Cambridge University Press 2007.

Health economists need to do three things. *First*, we must highlight the evidence on how neo-liberal policies adversely impact on health and on health systems. A classic example is provided by Navarro in his analysis of changes in income and health in Brazil during the period of the 'economic miracle' from 1968 to 1981. While there was very substantial economic growth in the wake of neo-liberal advocacy from the World Bank and the IMF, Navarro (2002 p. 462) spotted that, nonetheless and surprisingly, infant mortality rates rose during this same period from 70 to 92 per 1000 live births.

A closer look at what was happening to incomes, and in particular income distribution, revealed to Navarro that the extra resources from economic growth were very much skewed to the rich. 'For the top 5% of the Brazilian population, the percentage of national consumption increased from 20% . . . to 48%; for the bottom 50% . . . consumption declined from 20% to 12%.' There lies the explanation of the rise in infant mortality rates.

It is worthy of note that Navarro tells this story in the context of his critique of Sen's work on development in which he (Navarro) argues that what is missing from Sen's analysis is the question of power and class. We return to this issue below.

It is clear to anyone who examines the relevant ideology and the relevant figures on income and health distribution that result from implementing neo-liberal policies, that neo-liberalism breeds inequality within countries and almost certainly across countries. It is also possible that, as it operates in the global economy today, it can act to prevent some countries from lifting themselves out of poverty.

If we look at the World Trade Organization (WTO) sponsored Doha agreement (Hertel and Winters 2006), for example, which has been heralded as the road to reduce poverty in the developing world, it becomes clear that, even if it were to be implemented in full, the impact on incomes in poor countries would be, at best, mixed. Some countries may on average be better-off; for some, those at the bottom of the income distribution will be worse-off; while in other instances it seems that in some poor countries almost everyone will be worse-off. Yet the bleating of the developed world about the adverse impact on their standards of living (which would be minimal) will almost certainly mean that any implementation of the Doha agreement will be a much watered down version of the original plan and intent.

Whether implemented in full or in part, from the literature it seems that the impact on health has not been calculated, although, given the estimates on incomes, we can be rather sure that it will not be good, if positive at all. Here is a major area for work by health economists that we have largely neglected in the past.

There is also a need for health economists to extend the work started by Navarro (see, for example, Navarro 2002) and Coburn and Coburn (Chapter 2) to examine the more macroscopic effects of neo-liberalism on population health in individual countries but also globally. This is very much a question of the exercise of power within a class system and the disempowerment of so many in neo-liberal societies. When people's autonomy is thus threatened, loss of self-esteem and self-respect can negatively affect their health status; for large sections of the population to be thus disadvantaged in terms of the exercise of power can have serious effects on population health as a whole and on health equity. When efforts are made through redistribution not just of income but of health care and education to give whole disadvantaged classes back some political power and autonomy, as in Venezuela currently under Chavez (Muntaner *et al.* 2006) then the opportunities to reduce social inequalities are very real with both direct and indirect effects on health equity.

More research is required to gain a better understanding of those mechanisms at work within neo-liberalism that impact adversely on population health and its equitable distribution. Can all the problems here be laid at the door of the individualism and lack of sense of community and social solidarity that neo-liberalism breeds? What can be done, if anything, to ameliorate the adverse effects on health of neo-liberalism? How important to population health is the move in so many countries to lower taxation, reduce public spending, create less progressive tax systems and be less concerned about income distribution? Should not health impact assessments be routinely conducted of proposed changes in taxation policies?

There is a range of questions here for which health economics analyses need to be organized. Some are at a nation state level, others international, others still globally.

Second, health economists need to contribute more to research on the social determinants of health. For example, there is a need to gather more detailed evidence on the pathways to ill health and the interrelationship between ill health and poverty and between ill health and inequality. Analyses are required of how neo-liberal economic structures and policies contribute to the social determinants of ill health and ways of seeing how what appears to be a vicious cycle can be broken.

To date, health economics has focused almost exclusively on health systems' economics. This has also been the focus with respect to equity. Equity in health as opposed to equity in health care has been neglected. Funding of health care and the impact of different funding systems on both incomes and health has been fairly well researched by health economists, but largely in the context of high-income countries. Which social determinants of health it is best to invest in to improve population health and health equity is an area of research that needs much more work. There are clearly efforts being made by economists to analyze interventions in housing, education, the environment, road safety, and so on, but there is little economic work on the health impact of such interventions.

Perhaps in looking to more and better analyses of the impact on equity of the social determinants of health there is a need to prioritize where research is best conducted. Given the importance of poverty and inequality as such determinants, and the key nature of these as issues in social equity more generally, these are, in our view, where to concentrate attention, at least in the short to medium term. The sorts of studies that are needed here involve examining the impact on population health and health equity of changes in levels of poverty in individual countries and shifts in inequalities. While the social epidemiologists have worked at length and in depth on these issues, apart from a few (such as Angus Deaton 2004), there is all too little work by economists and even less by health economists (but there is some – see, for example, the work of Bob Evans (Evans and Stoddart 1994).

Third, turning to the hegemony of neo-liberalism, at this more ideological level there are a number of areas where health economists might be doing more. By and large we tend not to get into debates about the ideologies or even the philosophies underlying our work. Most of us work almost exclusively as technicians and at the more microscopic end of the scale; as technicians, that is probably fair enough. When it comes to more macroscopic or even global issues, especially with respect to equity, it is almost impossible and certainly not desirable to continue to ignore issues of ideology (and philosophy). There is thus a need for health economists to become more concerned about what is best described as the political economy of health and health care. This involves not only a shift in terms of ways of thinking about health and health care but also a shift of the focus. Macroscopic and global issues need more attention.

Related to this, there is a need to draw more attention to the very existence of the hegemony of neo-liberalism and its impact on health and health services. This hegemony also builds an ethos that 'good government is small government,' which can undermine social institutions that might otherwise support social justice not only in health but in society more generally. Public health care, which is more supportive of equity than private health care, is also threatened in a world where the dominance of neo-liberalism can lead to a general thinking that commercialization of health care is a good thing.

There is thus an educative role for health economists to play in highlighting the problems for health globally, internationally and nationally of the hegemony of neo-liberalism. There is an analytical role in addressing some of the issues involved and an evaluative role in assessing the impact of neo-liberalism on different populations' health, before putting forward different ways of dealing with these problems. What are the alternatives to neo-liberalism? What lessons can we learn from other existing economic structures such as those in Cuba or Kerala or Costa Rica?

It is clear that, in shifting the focus, health economists should be collaborating more with development economists in breaking down this hegemony. Given that so many of the issues here relate to the social determinants of health rather than health care per se, it is immediately apparent that many of the problems in health are present in somewhat similar forms in other sectors such as education. The questions faced by development economists about rates of development, reducing poverty and inequality, the impacts on income and its distribution of different tariff and trade policies, agricultural and industrial development are all ones that inevitably affect levels of income and inequality. There is much then for health economists to learn from teaming up with their colleagues in development economics.

Equitable development is good for our health and our health systems

If not neo-liberalism, then what? Health economists must explore ways of contributing to debates about the choice of options for equitable development paths, where health can be placed centre stage. This endeavour should draw on evidence about the social determinants of health. In particular, the focus here has to be on what kinds of economic structures that foster development can contribute to a virtuous cycle of health and economic growth. How can such development best be organized and funded? How can the fruits of such development best be distributed not only across different groupings in the community but across different goods and services? Where does health care 'fit' in the priorities for development as compared with education, housing, the environment, transport and foreign trade? There also needs to be a recognition that 'one size does not fit all' and that different stages of development and different cultures will have differing priorities. In some and perhaps many instances, investment in the maintenance and fostering of cultures will be a major priority. In some countries it will be necessary to look at the complex relationships that can exist between health, culture and economic systems, first to understand these linkages better but thereafter to see how and where investment in this three-way linkage process can be used to further population health in general but health equity more specifically.

A key issue here is the urgent need for research into success stories such as Costa Rica, Cuba, Kerala and Sri Lanka. These appear outwardly rather different societies. Are there some common features? How have they achieved such good health status in the context of relatively low levels of economic development? Why are health and health equity in Scandinavia generally better than in comparable countries?

While these are often referred to as success stories, it is noteworthy that there has been very little detailed consideration of how these 'successes' have been achieved, with the notable exception of the work of Drèze and Sen (1989). They noted that

Costa Rica, Cuba, Sri Lanka and the Indian state of Kerala all adopted a development approach that they termed 'support-led security'. The foundation of this approach was not to wait for economic growth to 'trickle down' to promote social development and reduce inequalities. Instead, all of these countries prioritized public funding and provision of a range of social services, with a particular emphasis on education and health, which were provided free of charge to the population. Sri Lanka is seen as a particularly important example of the 'support-led security' development path, not only because it embarked on this strategy at an early stage in its history (in fact before the end of colonialism) but also because it did so at a lower level of national income than any other countries adopting such an approach. The 'support-led security' approach warrants far greater attention as an equitable development strategy, including by health economists. We should also be considering whether, given cultural differences internationally, any learning about such successes are transferable to other countries or regions of the world, as Bagchi (Chapter 3) discusses in the context of Cuba.

What we know so little about is the impact of not only the social determinants of health but what might be termed the key social determinants of a society: the culture and the economic system. We can be confident that these can have a significant effect on population health and its distribution. They will also influence the nature of the health care system in so far as different countries' systems are often a product of their culture and the structure of their economy. Research by health economists to investigate and measure these effects is needed.

There are likely to be lessons that emerge here for a number of different actors. Certainly health economics analyses on this front could help to inform policy at the World Bank, the IMF and the WHO. These organizations seem less well informed than they might be about alternatives to neo-liberalism and, while one might want to argue that there is an ideological block in their looking further or deeper, if health economists could show that there are alternatives that can result in better population health and greater equity, then these global organizations could no longer claim ignorance and hide behind the notion that there is no alternative to neo-liberalism and the current ideological underpinnings of globalization. The question of debt relief highlighted by McIntyre (Chapter 9) brings into sharp focus the links between poverty and ill health for many countries and at the same time the seeming indifference of the developed world to such matters. Health economists cannot be expected to organize a more compassionate world but our analyses can assist in demonstrating how the current lack of compassion in developed countries and in the global organizations supposedly representing the governments of the world are failing to provide the debt relief and other humanitarian policies that could have such a beneficial effect on the health of so many in the developing world. As Coburn and Coburn (Chapter 2) suggest, what is perhaps needed here is to bring the voices of the world community rather than of governments to bear on health and health care policy. Again, while this is not strictly a task for health economists, tapping into such ideas and the values that might emerge from pursuing them is something that health economists could promote through appropriate analyses and studies.

Donor organizations are another set of actors who would benefit from some health economics literacy on equity policy and especially in recognizing the problems for the maintenance and protection of local culture if some alien economic structure is foisted on a society, be it neo-liberalism or whatever. The need to respect local values and local culture is imperative for all sorts of reasons. In the context of this book, there is a requirement to support the positives in the social determinants of health. This is crucial for both population health and its distribution. Donors might want to think very hard about accepting the need for more systems support rather than continuing to invest, as currently all too often is the case, in disease-specific programmes. Listening to the informed voices of the local society about the deployment and use of resources for the improvement of health systems is likely to bring about not only greater efficiency in resource use (both the donors' and the local resources) but also greater equity in how the resources are used. There is then the prospect of adding to the self-esteem of the local population by empowering them in decision-making. That, in itself, is likely to prove good for their health and in turn for health equity.

So much of this equitable development is about building social cohesion and self-esteem. It is also about recognizing (as discussed below) that poverty and health are inextricably linked. As McIntyre (Chapter 9) highlights, out-of-pocket expenses are in many countries very inequitable with the poor having to pay relatively large proportions of their incomes to meet the bills, particularly for medicines, when members of the family are sick. One of the best ways of promoting equity in both incomes and health is, thus, to reduce these out-of-pocket expenses. This is an area where the work of health economists has been critical. Most of the evidence about the impoverishing effects of out-of-pocket payments has been gathered by health economists, which has been so overwhelming that even the World Bank, the arch supporter of user-fee policies, has been forced to reconsider its position. However, by appropriate health economics analyses we can do more, particularly in persuading more donor organizations of the merits of direct subsidies to the health systems of recipient countries.

Health care service organizations would also benefit from having better information from health economists about how to finance and deliver health services more equitably. There can be a willingness on the part of such organizations to try to do better in terms of equity but also a lack of knowledge as to 'what works'. There is a clear duty on the part of health economists to assist such 'equity-willing-but-information-lacking' policy makers to see more clearly how they can be more equity orientated not just in desire but in practice.

Given the importance of providers, especially doctors, in the decision-making processes over resource allocation in most health services, these represent another audience for health economists' advice on delivering equitable care. There are equity issues at the 'coal face' in who gets treated and how quickly. It is more, however, at the level of the clinicians as resource managers that their knowledge of the processes of resource allocation becomes pertinent. Equipping clinical staff with some basic knowledge of the health economics of equity can be useful in the general fight for and over scarce resources in health care. Fighting for 'my' patients and more resources for them can, of course, be ethically justified by individual clinicians but there also needs to be an acceptance of some basic health economics ideas such as opportunity cost, and some agreement that the social goal of equity is one to which most health care systems might legitimately aspire. The difficulty is that while there are clinical champions for individual patients and sometimes champions or pressure groups for patients with diabetes or multiple sclerosis or cancer, there are few champions for equity. Health economics analyses can provide ammunition to help those who are prepared to take on this role of championing equity.

This listing of those groups or people who would benefit from the greater understanding of equity issues in both financing and delivery would be incomplete without recognition of the need for providing relevant health economics information on equity to communities and citizens served by these health services. There is some tentative evidence that citizens may be more equity focused than health service organizations (Mooney and Blackwell 2004) and if this were to be substantiated then it may well be that communities could become first the drivers and in turn the guardians of equitable health care. Health economists need to be more active in eliciting community preferences for the principles (such as equity) that citizens wish to underpin their health services and then encouraging communities to engage with their health services in the pursuit of equity. They can also use their influence to try to ensure that politicians, bureaucrats and providers are prepared to listen to the voices of the community. The difficulty here is that distribution of property rights over decision-making on health care resource allocation is highly political. There are many vested interests involved, especially those of the medical profession. Giving power to the people will not be well received in some existing health care decision-making quarters.

Tackling the worst excesses of globalization

While there are some positive aspects to globalization, such as increased potential for global public action (see Chapter 2), there is a rapidly growing literature on the adverse impacts of globalization on health and health systems, as well as on economies more generally. However, very little has been written on potential strategies for addressing these adverse consequences of globalization. We suggest that one way forward is to focus on the worst excesses of globalization and that there are three key areas that quite directly impact on health and health systems, which should receive priority attention. These are the inequitable net flow of financial resources between low-income and middle-income countries (LMICs) and high-income countries, the inequitable net flow of human resources between these groups of countries and issues relating to pharmaceutical products arising from World Trade Organization agreements.

Currently, there is a net outflow of financial resources from many low-income and middle-income countries, particularly in Africa and to some extent Asia, to high-income countries. This is the result of the removal of exchange controls and unfair terms of trade; 'the cumulative loss from declining terms of trade cost non-oil-exporting African countries 119% of their total gross domestic product,' (Bond 2006 p. 4). Vandana Shiva (2004) states: 'We [in developing countries] are biodiversity rich but every year . . . $60 billion worth of wealth transfer is taking place because the control over the products is in the hands of the North. Monopolies of patents are in their hands. Monopolies on trade are in their hands.' Private financial outflows from, for example, African residents to banks and tax havens in high-income countries are significant and now exceed $10 billion per year, yet foreign direct investment is limited. Tax fraud, transfer pricing and other methods of financial extraction by multinational corporations also exact a heavy toll on the economies of low-income and middle-income countries. Of particular concern from a health system perspective is the resource outflows from poorer countries to high-income countries in the form of debt servicing and debt repayments, with African countries' debt repayments being three times the inflow of loans. At the same time, aid inflows to African countries declined by 40% in the 1990s (Bond 2006). Health economists could well devote more energy to addressing questions such as how these 'wealth transfers' translate into increased income inequalities and in turn inequities in health across the globe.

Combined, these net outflows of financial resources limit the potential for economic growth in low-income and middle-income countries and their ability to meet the health and other social needs of their citizens. Recent debt relief initiatives have done little to change the pattern and extent of these flows and high-income countries have become serial offenders in failing to meet their aid commitments. The net outflows of wealth from LMICs need to be seen within the context of colonialism, systematic extraction of the mineral and other natural wealth of LMICs and the fact that much of the debt that has accumulated in Africa and other LMICs was granted to corrupt and illegitimate regimes. There is, then, clearly a powerful case for restitution, or repayment for benefits gained and the righting of ethical wrongs, by reversing the flow of financial resources.

Complete and unconditional debt cancellation would be a first step in this direction. Not only will this enable low-income and middle-income countries to devote a greater share of their limited government resources to health and other social services, it will also ease the stranglehold that international financial institutions have on domestic macroeconomic and fiscal policy in many low-income and middle-income countries. This could open the way for countries to adopt equitable economic development policies rather than the neo-liberal policies that predominate at present. Debt cancellation should be accompanied by increased 'aid' grants from high-income countries, which should not take the form of these resources being spent in the 'donor' country (e.g., purchasing vehicles and equipment or hiring consultants from the grantor country).

A similar argument on the need for restitution in relation to the net outflow of health sector human resources from low-income and middle-income countries to high-income countries was put forward in the chapter by Mackintosh. She calls for financial compensation by high-income country governments, not out of charity but as a duty, to LMICs of origin of health workers. These financial resources can then be used for funding health services in these countries, including improving the conditions of service of health workers remaining in the country, which may serve somewhat to stem the flow of health worker out-migration. Mackintosh (Chapter 8) also proposes that these financial transfers should occur within the context of 'exchanges and support between health professionals and health institutions' in the poorer country of origin and the high-income recipient country of health workers.

Along with financial and human resources, pharmaceutical products are a key health system resource that is adversely affected by globalization. The Agreement on Trade-Related aspects of Intellectual Property rights (TRIPS) of the World Trade Organization (WTO) is particularly important in relation to medicines. The TRIPS Agreement effectively gives multinational pharmaceutical corporations (which undertake most of the research and development of new drugs) a 20-year monopoly on the production and sale of new drugs. It is noteworthy that the TRIPS Agreement was effectively drafted by a self-appointed Intellectual Property Committee consisting of *Bristol Myers*, DuPont, General Electric, Hewlett Packard, IBM, *Johnson and Johnson*, *Merck*, Monsanto (a producer of genetically modified seeds), *Pfizer*, Rockwell and Time-Warner (with multinational pharmaceutical companies indicated in italics).

All WTO member countries were required to become TRIPS compliant through amending their patents legislation by 2005. There was particularly vociferous debate when India amended its legislation to comply with the TRIPS Agreement in early 2005, largely owing to concerns about the implications for other LMICs who are dependent on generic medicines produced in India. India is the world's leading supplier of generic medicines, with two-thirds of its generic exports going to developing countries. With respect to the AIDS epidemic facing many low-income and middle-income countries, Indian production of generic antiretroviral (ARV) medicines has reduced the price of these medicines by as much as 98% (from as much as $10 000–$15 000 to about $140 per year of treatment with a first-line combination therapy). About half of all patients on antiretroviral drugs in LMICs use generic medicines produced in India.

Enormous pressure has been exerted, primarily by the US government on behalf of the American Pharmaceutical Manufacturers Association, on some LMIC governments to adopt so-called 'TRIPS-plus' patent legislation. This would prevent these countries from using entirely legitimate mechanisms, such as compulsory licensing and parallel importation, to limit the potential impact of TRIPS, (Kumaranayake and Lake 2002). TRIPS and efforts to impose 'TRIPS-plus' legislative amendments have played an important role in keeping the price of medicines unacceptably high in LMICs (Bagchi 2005). Multinational pharmaceutical manufacturers have also used strategies such as 'ever-greening', whereby they apply for patents for existing or slightly modified pharmaceutical products for treating a different disease to that for which it was initially developed, to delay repeatedly the generic production of their medicine and maintain monopoly level prices. The argument that patents are necessary to allow multinationals to recoup their research and development costs should be considered in the light of these costs only being between 10% and 16% of these companies' turnover and considerably less than the value of their profits (Angell 2004).

Health economists have played a very little role in addressing these issues and contributing to improved affordability of pharmaceutical products in low-income and middle-income countries. There is an urgent need for a new 'pharmaco-economics paradigm'. The current breed of pharmaco-economists are employed by the pharmaceutical industry or so-called 'independent' consultancy groups with the express aim of undertaking economic evaluations to prove that a new product is 'cost-effective' and thereby encourage health professionals to prescribe it and health care funders to reimburse patients for its use.

A new breed of pharmaco-economists should be tracking the effects of the World Trade Organization's activities, particularly in relation to TRIPS-related issues, on access to affordable medicines and on health and its distribution. They should also be gathering information on the cost structures and profitability of multinational pharmaceutical companies, and developing the theoretical and empirical base for strategies such as price regulation and differential pricing across countries according to the level of economic development. There is also the need for publicly accessible information on the price of medicines in different countries. This will allow low-income and middle-income countries to benchmark prices internationally, or at least to use this information in state tendering procedures or price negotiations with multinational pharmaceutical manufacturers. One of the advantages of improved global communication is that information on effective pharmaceutical price regulatory mechanisms can be shared (see example of South Africa, Box 12.1).

Box 12.1 Medicine pricing regulation in South Africa

Most countries that exercise control over the price of medicines do so by 'holding the purse-strings', that is the universal health insurance scheme establishes a price at which it will reimburse each medicine, with all medicines in the same therapeutic category being reimbursed at the level of the lowest-priced product. South Africa is an example of one of a growing number of countries that are introducing direct price controls through legislative means.

Key aspects of the South African legislation and accompanying regulations include:

- Introducing transparency into the pharmaceutical market so that everyone is aware of the manufacturer price, the wholesaler or distributor fee and the dispensing fee.
- The Act outlawed discounting and required manufacturers to sell at a 'single exit price' (i.e., sell at the same price to all purchasers). Previously, purchasers such as private hospitals and dispensing doctors were granted enormous discounts (sometimes up to 80% of the stated price) in order to ensure that particular products were included on the hospital formulary or dispensed by doctors. Small retail pharmacies, particularly in rural areas, paid the highest prices for medicines. The single exit price must be printed on the medicine packaging.
- Regulating the maximum fee for logistics service providers (wholesalers and distributors), retail pharmacists and dispensing doctors. Previously, large percentage mark-ups were placed on medicines all along the supply chain. The dispensing fee regulation moved retail pharmacists and dispensing doctors away from 'trading in medicines' to receiving a professional fee for the service they provide.
- Draft regulations released shortly before going to press will introduce international benchmarking of manufacturer prices. Countries which have strong regulation of the quality and price of medicines and accessible data on prices were selected as comparators. Each manufacturer of 'originator' or 'branded' products will be required to compare the price they charge for their product in South Africa with that charged in Australia, Canada, New Zealand and Spain and the price charged should be set at the lowest price (if the South African price is the lowest, it should remain at this level but if the price is lowest in one of the benchmark countries, the South African price must be reduced to that level). In the case of generic medicines, it is proposed that the price must be set at a level that is at least 40% below the price of the originator product.

There has been considerable and vociferous opposition to these regulations from the pharmaceutical sector. In the initial phase of regulations, pharmacists launched court

> **Box 12.1 (cont.)**
> action which ultimately was settled in the Constitutional Court. The Constitutional Court supported the efforts to regulate the price of medicines in South Africa but required the government to reconsider the level of the dispensing fee, and this has now been done. Pharmaceutical manufacturers are gearing up for a battle over the draft international benchmarking regulations. Such legal battles are not uncommon whenever the very high levels of profitability in the pharmaceutical sector are threatened, but experience has shown that these are most often won by the regulatory authority. Thus, there are mechanisms for ensuring affordable medicines in low-income and middle-income countries, although it takes considerable government commitment to challenge powerful pharmaceutical sector stakeholders successfully.

Health systems as a key redistributive mechanism

Public spending on social services is recognized as one of the key mechanisms for redistribution within a country. Given the degree of income inequality in many low-income and middle-income countries, the potential for the health sector to contribute to redistribution of resources and social benefits should be more actively pursued, and health economists have a major role to play in this regard.

To date, much of the attention has been focused on health care financing contributions, but this has, until very recently, only focused on high-income countries (Chapters 10 and 11 provide examples of recent work in two middle-income countries). Particular emphasis has been placed on assessing the relative progressivity of alternative health care financing mechanisms, although some research has directly evaluated how health care financing contributions alter the distribution of income by comparing income before and after health care financing contributions.

Health economists have made a significant contribution through these analyses as it is now indisputable that out-of-pocket payments for health care are the most regressive, or as a minimum the least progressive, mechanism for financing health care. These payments allow for no income redistribution whatsoever. However, health economists could have contributed much more actively to debates about out-of-pocket payments and should uniformly be calling for the careful removal of user fees for publicly provided health services (Gilson and McIntyre 2005) and for much less use of co-payments under health insurance systems. At the same time, the message from health economists should be equally unequivocal that pre-payment mechanisms in the form of tax or health insurance funding, particularly where this is universal, is the only basis for equitable health systems that promote redistribution.

Health economists have also, separately, evaluated the distribution of health service benefits, either through techniques such as concentration indices or evaluating the benefit incidence of public sector health care funding (as illustrated in Chapter 11). The latter analyses have been useful in highlighting the need for ensuring that the most socio-economically disadvantaged groups get a fairer share of the benefits of government health services. However, they ignore the distribution of private sector service benefits that massively compound health care inequities. No strong evidence exists on the purported benefits of commercialized health systems. Indeed, it is becoming increasingly clear that private health sector provision does not contribute to a redistributive health system. From this perspective, health economists should be contributing to identifying the most appropriate mechanisms for controlling the worst excesses of the private health sector through regulation or 'paying the piper and calling the tune' (as argued in Chapter 9).

Importantly, health economists have not explored in any detail the relationship between financing contributions and the distribution of health service benefits through integrated and comprehensive health care financing and benefit incidence analyses. This is a critical 'missing link' as it will provide the evidence needed (given the current emphasis on evidence-informed decision-making) to argue unambiguously for universal health systems. Fragmentation of health care financing and provision reduces the potential for cross-subsidies, between the wealthy and the poor and between the healthy and the sick, and therefore undermines the ability of health systems to redistribute income and social benefits. It is clearly necessary for policy makers to be able to understand better that fragmentation is a barrier to equitable health systems. In discussing the relative merits of public and private funding and provision, and more generally multiple sources of funding and disparate provision, the question of fragmentation and its adverse effects, especially on equity, need more attention from health economists in future. Even in the absence of 'hard empirical evidence', a conceptual exploration of the relationship between health care financing contributions and benefit distribution leads us to the conclusion that fragmentation between health care financing mechanisms should be minimized if one is to promote an equitable and redistributive health system. Certainly, Tangcharoensathien and colleagues (Chapter 11) have demonstrated that the integration of different funding mechanisms in the move to universal coverage in Thailand has promoted health system equity.

There is no doubt that those members of society who stand to lose in a redistributive health system, such as higher-income groups and private health care providers, will oppose efforts to change the status quo. However, as argued in Chapter 2, it is difficult to argue against health system equity as a positive good, and this makes the health sector a key arena for achieving redistributive gains.

The health system's redistributive contribution is also linked to the equitable allocation of tax and other health care funding. Between the 1970s and the 1980s, the Resource Allocation Working Party (RAWP) achieved considerable success in redistributing National Health Service resources between different geographic areas in England. As a result, RAWP-type resource allocation formulae have been widely adopted in other high-income and poorer countries, such as Ghana, Tanzania, Uganda and Zambia in Africa and Brazil (see Chapter 10), Chile and Colombia in Latin America.

Although these formulae-driven initiatives have assisted in breaking inertia in resource allocation decision-making processes and in securing additional resources for historically underfunded areas, as argued in Chapter 4, there are conceptual and methodological challenges in this approach that health economists should be addressing some four decades since the RAWP formula was developed. In particular, instead of using mortality indicators in a resource allocation formula (which assumes that if deaths in one area are twice as high as in another, twice the amount of money should be allocated for health care in the first area) societal views should be elicited on who should receive priority and the relative weighting of priority groups. Communities should also play a role in identifying how additional resources allocated to them should be used.

There is also a growing recognition that simply increasing the allocation of financial resources to an area that has been relatively underfunded given its health care claims will not automatically translate into improved services or health status. Communities have different capacities to absorb and benefit efficiently from additional funds. There is, then, an argument that part of these funds should be devoted to developing the management, economic, social and human (MESH) infrastructure in those communities deficient in their capacity to use funds efficiently, thereby promoting greater capacity to benefit (Mooney and Houston 2004).

Health systems as important social institutions

Health systems and the processes of funding, organization and delivering of health care are not only important in terms of their contribution to improvements in health status and their redistributive impacts. They can have a critical role as social institutions in their own right. This issue is one that health economists have tended to neglect. Quite why is not clear but the monopoly of consequentialism in most health economics analyses is probably a major part of the explanation. Issues surrounding processes, decision-making and institutional arrangements are not seen as being valued in themselves but only as instrumental. Again, neo-liberal societies tend not to see social institutions as being so important; their concerns are much more with individual welfare and not with social capital or social cohesion more generally.

Such social institutions, which include not only health care systems but education, the law, freedom of speech, the unions, etc., represent mechanisms for promoting social solidarity, nation building and cultural respect and can act as sites for progressive action and community involvement. They are a part of the social fabric, both pillars to support a more cohesive society but also the product of that more cohesive society.

The importance of social institutions is echoed by Stiglitz (2006). He writes (p. 150): 'The major responsibility for getting as much value as possible from their natural resources and using it well resides with the countries themselves. Their first priority should be to set up institutions that will reduce the scope for corruption and ensure that the money derived from oil and other natural resources is invested, and invested well. It may be desirable to have some hard and fast rules for that investment – a certain fraction devoted to expenditures on health, a certain fraction to education, a certain fraction to infrastructure.' What is not at all clear currently is what investing in the improvement of such social institutions (including, but not just, health care) might mean for population health and health equity. There is also a need to think through what the impact might be for economic evaluation of building the benefits of systems changes into such analyses. Methodologically, health economists would need to re-think economic evaluation and allow various aspects of process utility, including the utility associated with the systems of health care, into their analyses. With respect to equity some of this might be handled by social option values where the option of having access for all is valued by the community.

Again Navarro's work in this area provides a start, although that is primarily comparative across countries. What is now needed is to look at changes in these institutions in individual countries to try to assess what such changes might mean for population health and health equity. Such analyses may well create difficult challenges for health economists but if the population at large do value such institutions in their own right in addition to their outputs then this is a benefit that it behoves us as health economists to get to grips with.

Gilson's call (Chapter 7) for ethical institutions, especially here ethical health care systems, we see as crucial. As Gilson states, (p. 142) 'acceptability and trust barriers have an invidious influence over health care equity in all contexts' and 'tackling these barriers must be a central element of action to promote health care equity.' There are clearly different ways of doing this but after Gilson's identification of the need to address these barriers, the door is open for health economists to consider how most efficiently to lower them.

What is unfortunate is that the extent to which various multilateral organizations such as the WHO, the World Bank, the IMF and the WTO can be seen as global social institutions is very limited. They are not the people's but governments' institutions. While changing these organizations or gaining greater prominence for more genuinely people's organizations, such as the World Social Forum and the People's Health Movement, is not the task of health economists there is, nonetheless, a need to recognize the importance of health economists' adopting more of a political economy stance over some of these governance issues.

Equitable access as an achievable policy goal

Although equitable access is frequently a major health policy goal in high-income and poorer countries, it has received inadequate attention to date. Some health economists, along with medical sociologists and others, have made important contributions to conceptual debates around access but have not contributed much to translating this concept into applied evaluative techniques. Indeed, health economists have been guilty of incorrectly equating health care use with access in order to undertake empirical research, given that utilization is relatively easy to measure. At least part of the problem appears to be the predominance of quantitative techniques in the health economists' methodological toolkit and the discomfort when faced with evaluating an issue such as access, which clearly requires a combination of quantitative and qualitative research techniques.

Chapter 6 provides three innovations relative to previous contributions by health economists. First, it explores the concept of access with an explicit focus on identifying entry points for the empirical assessment of access. Second, it emphasizes that access is a relational concept in the sense that it involves interactions and interrelations between the potential user and the health care system. Third, it illustrates how access can be evaluated directly through an exploratory case study using Ghanaian data, albeit solely using quantitative data. This is but a first step. More debate is required among health economists about how to translate the concept of access into measurable terms. Further, there should be more empirical testing of the framework proposed for directly evaluating access. In particular, it is necessary to explore fully the relational aspects of access in order to identify underlying mismatches between individuals, households or communities and the health system. It is only by understanding these issues within a specific country context that access, as freedom to use health care and as an appropriate 'degree of fit' between individuals or households and the health system, can be realized.

The most neglected dimension of access is that of accessibility, sometimes referred to as cultural access, not least because its evaluation should rely heavily on qualitative techniques. The cultural dimension and the idea that equity and in turn access cannot, or at least should not, be defined the same everywhere are emphasized by Mooney (Chapter 4). Chapter 7 demonstrates how practical policy interventions can be identified by focusing directly on access issues as opposed to using health care utilization as a proxy. For example, Gilson identifies interventions such as the employment by the health system of members of disadvantaged groups, employing patient care advisors and developing peer support mechanisms as important interventions to address acceptability barriers faced by socially disadvantaged groups.

One thing of which we are increasingly confident but which seems not to be adequately reflected in health economists' analyses of access is that, on the potential user's side, access is in the eye of the beholder. It follows that health economists cannot get to grips with the measurement of access unless we take account of the views and preferences of potential health care users. Given the relational aspect emphasized by Thiede and colleagues, to argue that access is in the eye of the beholder does not mean that the whole focus of analysis of access should move solely to the 'demand' side. Clearly how the potential user perceives the barrier to use and its height is something that can be influenced by the health care system and individual health care professionals. In the final analysis, however, it is the potential user who decides, on the basis of perception, whether access is translated into use or not.

Remaining ever vigilant

Too often in health policy and even more so of late in health economics the question of equity has tended to fall off the agenda. This may be for all sorts of reasons: it is too hard to include it; it is better left for later or better treated separately (but it does not happen); it is overshadowed by concerns for efficiency; it is not additional to efficiency so if health economists deal with efficiency they will deal with equity; there is insufficient 'evidence' on it so, in this era of evidence-informed policy making, it is not feasible to address; it is not measurable as access so health economics analyses measure use (which means health economists move, and thereby miss, the target); it is ideologically unacceptable or, in a neo-liberal world, even redundant; there are no equity champions; the pursuit of equity is not in the interests of those currently exercising power in health care; or it is not anything that any of the existing power brokers want to pursue.

We must be vigilant. As Maynard (p. 96) so tellingly states: 'With libertarian wolves prowling ubiquitously in egalitarian sheep's clothing, it is essential to confront all reform proposals with scepticism.' As he goes on to say: 'All too often such efforts are poorly disguised attempts to redistribute resources from sometimes weakly performing collective health care systems to rich interest groups served by libertarian advocates.'

There is thus a need to ensure that equity remains high on the policy agenda and that national policy makers and international organizations such as the WHO and the World Bank are aware of the potential for equity improvements. Information and evidence to prompt policy action on equity is needed. As illustrated by Tangcharoensathien and colleagues (Chapter 11), the monitoring of the impact of policies on equity is necessary and improved information systems are required for adequate monitoring and evaluation. Attention particularly needs to be paid to monitoring the 'latest vogue' in neo-liberal policies. All changes in health care systems and in health care policy need as a minimum to have their equity dimension noted but they must also, preferably, be evaluated. Existing equity policy should be shown up for what it so often is: simply rhetoric, but then evidence must be presented to indicate what action might be taken to convert the rhetoric to reality. Backed by Mooney's compassion (Chapter 4) and Mackintosh's 'restitution' (Chapter 8), but not just for health care professionals, there is a prospect for a more equitable future for health and health care.

It may be that the best champions of equity are citizens – world citizens, or national or regional citizens and organizations. This would suggest that organizations such as the World Social Forum, as Coburn and Coburn (Chapter 2) suggest, and the People's Health Movement should be supported.

Equity goals are otherwise best achieved by continually drawing attention to existing inequities and to the fact that there is always the possibility of inequities growing rather than diminishing. Health economists can provide this sort of information to aid policy. We have an obligation to do so.

REFERENCES

Angell, M. (2004) The truth about the drug companies. *New York Review of Books.* **51**(12): 52–58.

Bagchi, A. (2005) *Perilous Passage: Mankind and the Global Ascendancy of Capital.* New York: Rowman and Littlefield.

Bond, P. (2006) *The Dispossession of African Wealth at the Cost of African Health.* EQUINET Discussion Paper No 30. Harare: Regional Network for Equity in Health in Southern Africa (EQUINET) and Southern African Centre for Economic Justice. www.equinetafrica.org/bib/DISbond Trade. pdf.

Deaton, A. (2004) Health in an age of globalization. In Collins, S. and Graham, C. eds, *Brookings Trade Forum.* Washington, DC: Brookings Institution Press. pp. 83–130.

Drèze, J. and Sen, A. (1989) *Hunger and Public Action.* Oxford: Clarendon.

Evans, R. G., and Stoddart, G. L. (1994) Producing health, consuming health care. In Evans, R. G., Barer, M. L. and Marmor,T. R., eds. *Why Are Some People Healthy and Others Not? The Determinants of Health of Populations.* New York: Aldine de Gruyter.

Gilson, L. and McIntyre, D. (2005) Removing user fees for primary care in Africa: the need for careful action. *British Medical Journal.* **331**: 762–765.

Hertel, T. W. and Winters, L. A. (2006) *Poverty and the WTO: Impacts of the Doha Development Agenda.* New York: Palgrave Macmillan.

Kumaranayake, L. and Lake, S. (2002) Regulation in the context of global health markets. In Lee, K., Buse, K. and Fustukian, S., eds, *Health Policy in a Globalising World*. Cambridge: Cambridge University Press.

Mooney, G. and Blackwell, S. (2004) Whose health service is it anyway? *Medical Journal of Australia*. **180**: 76–78.

Mooney, G. and Houston, S. (2004) An alternative approach to resource allocation: weighted capacity to benefit plus MESH infrastructure. *Applied Health Economics and Policy*. **3**(1): 29–33.

Muntaner C., Guerra Salazar, R. M., Benach, J. and Armada, F. (2006) Venezuela's barrio adentro: an alternative to neo liberalism in health care. *International Journal of Health Services*. **36**(4): 803–811.

Navarro, V. (2002) Development and quality of life: a critique of Amartya Sen's Development as Freedom. In Navarro V., ed, *The Political Economy of Social Inequalities*. New York: Baywood.

Sen, A. (2000) Economic progress and health. In Leon, D. A. and Walt, G., eds, *Poverty, Inequality and Health: an International Perspective*. Oxford: Oxford University Press, pp. 333–345.

Shiva, V. (2004) *The Role of Patents in the Rise of Globalization* www.inmotionmagazine.com/global/vshiva4_int.html#Anchor-16557.

Stiglitz, G. (2006) *Making Globalization Work*. New York: Horton.

Index